Therapeutic Communities for Offenders

The Wiley Series
in
Offender Rehabilitation

Edited by
Clive R. Hollin
Rampton Hospital, Nottinghamshire and
The University of Leicester, UK

and

Mary McMurran
East Midlands Centre for Forensic Mental Health
and The University of Leicester, UK

Therapeutic Commodities for Offenders
Edited by Eric Cullen, Lawrence Jones
and Roland Woodward

Addicted to Crime?
John E. Hodge, Mary McMurran and Clive R. Hollin

Young Offenders and Alcohol-Related Crime
Mary McMurran and Clive R. Hollin

What Works: Reducing Reoffending
Guidelines from Research and Practice
Edited by James McGuire

Therapeutic Communities for Offenders

Edited by

Eric Cullen
Director of Research & Development
HMP Grendon

Lawrence Jones
Therapy Manager
The Max Glatt Centre
HMP Wormwood Scrubs

Roland Woodward
Therapy Manager
Gartree Therapeutic Community
HMP Gartree

JOHN WILEY & SONS
Chichester · New York · Weinheim · Brisbane · Singapore · Toronto

Other Wiley Editorial Offices

John Wiley & Sons, Inc., 605 Third Avenue,
New York, NY 10158-0012, USA

VCH Verlagsgesellschaft,
Pappelallee 3, 0-69469 Weinheim,
Germany

Jacaranda Wiley Ltd, 33 Park Road, Milton,
Queensland 4064, Australia

John Wiley & Sons (Asia) Pte Ltd, 2 Clementi Loop #02-01,
Jin Xing Distripark, Singapore 129809

John Wiley & Sons (Canada) Ltd, 22 Worcester Road,
Rexdale, Ontario M9W 1L1, Canada

Library of Congress Cataloging-in-Publication Data

Therapeutic communities for offenders / edited by Eric Cullen,
    Lawrence Jones, Roland Woodward.
      p.   cm. — (The Wiley series in offender rehabilitation)
    Includes bibliographical references (p.   ) and index.
    ISBN 0-471-96545-6 (cloth : acid-free paper). — ISBN
    0-471-96980-X (paper : acid-free paper)
      1. Prisoners—Mental health services. 2. Therapeutic communities.
    3. Criminals—Rehabilitation. I. Cullen, Eric. II. Jones,
    Lawrence (Lawrence F.) III . Woodward, Roland. IV. Series.
    RC451.4.P68T4251996   616.85'8—dc20   96-30405
                                                           CIP

British Library Cataloguing in Publication Data

A catalogue record for this book is available from the British Library

ISBN 0-471-96545-6 (cased)
ISBN 0-471-96980-X (paper)

Typeset by Mathematical Composition Setters Ltd, Salisbury, UK
Printed and bound in Great Britain by Biddles Ltd, Guildford and Kings Lynn
This book is printed on acid-free paper responsibly manufactured from sustainable forestation,
for which at least two trees are planted for each one used for paper production.

Dedication

The editors would like to dedicate this book to all those therapeutic community members and staff who over the years have shared their lives with them. From this experience has come the knowledge and motivation to continue developing TCs for the future.

Contents

Part III: International Perspectives

Part IV: Staff Issues: Aptitude, Antipathy and Training

About the Editors

Eric Cullen Head of Department of Psychology, HM Prisons Grendon & Springhill, Grendon Underwood, Aylesbury, Bucks HP18 0TL, UK.

Eric Cullen has been a prison psychologist since 1974. He has worked with all offender groups, male and female, young offenders and adults. He has published work on therapeutic community treatment, anger-control and reducing self-injury. His doctorate research was on life sentence prisoners and regime stability. He was a member of a Home Office—Department of Health Task Force for treating personality disordered offenders and a Working Party on new Therapeutic Communities in the United Kingdom. He is now a consultant forensic psychologist.

Lawrence Jones Psychology Unit, HMP Wormwood Scrubs, PO Box 757, Du Cane Road, London W12 0AE., UK.

Lawrence Jones is a Chartered Forensic Psychologist currently working at HMP Wormwood Scrubs as Therapy Manager of The Max Glatt Centre, a therapeutic community in a prison setting. He has experience working with sex offenders, substance abusers and life sentence prisoners. He has published work on therapeutic communities and their evaluation. Prior to working for the Prison Service he worked in a therapeutic community for ex-offenders in the community.

Roland Woodward Therapy Manager, Gartree Therapeutic Community and Head of Psychology Department, HMP Gartree, Market Harborough, Leicestershire LE16 7RP, UK.

Roland Woodward is a Chartered Forensic Psychologist currently working in the Prison Service. He obtained degrees from the

Universities of London and Surrey and has carried out research with adolescent and adult offenders in a number of areas. He has opened and managed assessment units and most recently a Therapeutic Community for life sentence prisoners. Other areas of work include independent organizational consultancy, lecturing in consultancy and counselling skills. He has also worked as an independent trainer for several agencies.

Contributors

David J. Cooke   Director of Forensic Psychology, Community and Mental Health Services, Greater Glasgow NHS Trust, Douglas Inch Centre, 2 Woodside Terrace, Glasgow G3 7EY and Professor of Forensic Psychology, Glasgow Caledonian University, Glasgow, UK.

Bridget Dolan   Research Fellow in Forensic Psychiatry, Henderson Hospital, 2 Homelands Drive, Brighton Road, Sutton, Surrey SM2 5LT, UK.

Rudolph Egg   Professor, Center for Criminology, Adolfsallee 32, 65185 Wiesbaden, Weisbaden, Germany.

Peter Lewis   Director of Therapy, HMPs Grendon & Springhill, Aylesbury, Bucks HP18 0TL, UK.

Freidrich Lösel   Director, Institute of Psychology, University of Erlangen-Nurnberg, Bismarckstrasse 1, D-91054 Erlangen, Germany.

Tim Newell   Governor, HMPs Grendon & Springhill, Aylesbury, Bucks HP 18 0TL, UK.

Jeff Roberts   The Group Analytic Practice, 88 Montagu Mansions, London W1H 1LF, UK.

Roger Sapsford   Senior Lecturer, Social Sciences, The Open University, Walton Hall, Milton Keynes, MK7 6AA, UK.

Harry Wexler   Senior Principal Investigator for the Center for Therapeutic Community Research at the National Development & Research Institutes, Inc. 380 Glenneyre St., Laguna Beach, California 92651, USA.

Series Preface

Twenty years ago it is doubtful that any serious consideration would have been given to publishing a series of books on the topic of offender rehabilitation. While the notion of rehabilitation for offenders was widely accepted 30 years ago, the 1970s saw the collapse of what we might call the treatment ideal. As many other commentators have noted, the turning point can be pinpointed to the publication of an article titled 'What Works—Questions and Answers about Prison Reform', written by Robert Martinson and published in 1974. The essential message taken from this article was that, when it comes to the rehabilitation of offenders, what works is 'nothing works'. It would be stretching the case to say that Martinson single-handedly overturned the rehabilitative philosophy, but his message was obviously welcomed by a receptive audience. As writers such as Don Andrews have suggested there are many reasons why both the academic community and politicians and policy-makers were more than willing to subscribe to the 'nothing works philosophy. (Although the evidence suggests that the public at large did not buy completely the need to abandon rehabilitation.) Thus the 1970s and 1980s saw a return to hard sentencing, the predominance of punishment, and the handing out of just deserts to those who transgressed the law of the land. Throughout this period of rehabilitative nihilism a small group of academics and practitioners kept faith with the rehabilitative ideal, led perhaps by Paul Gendreau and Robert Ross, and slowly began to look for new ways to argue the case for rehabilitation. The turnabout, when it came, was dramatic. Through the development of a methodology for statistically reviewing large bodies of research, called 'meta-analysis', unequivocal evidence was produced that rehabilitative programmes did work. The view that 'nothing works' is simply wrong: rehabilitation programmes do have a positive effect in reducing recidivism. The effect is not always large, although sometimes it is; nor is it always present, although on average it is. However, it is there and that cannot be ignored. Since 1990, armed with these findings, there has been a remarkable resurgence of the rehabilitative ideal: practitioners have eagerly attended conferences, seminars, and training courses: researchers are working not to make the case for rehabilitation, but to improve and refine techniques for working with offenders.

This volume specifically addresses therapeutic communities for offenders. If we look at some of the most promising targets for intervention with offenders, as listed by Don Andrews in a previous book in this Series [Andrews, D.A. (1995). The psychology of criminal conduct and effective treatment. In J. McGuire (Ed). *What Works: Reducing Reoffending*. Chichester: Wiley], it is evident that these complex targets for change cannot adequately be addressed in a limited number of one-hour intervention sessions. Changing anti-social attitudes, increasing self-control, and improving problem-solving, social, and life skills need the prolonged attention afforded by therapeutic communities, both within formal group meetings and through informal interaction. On the other hand, therapeutic communities may need to build on the firm base of recent empirical advances by taking into account developments in the design and content of effective rehabilitation programmes. It is interesting to note that specific cognitive-behavioural programmes and even individual interventions are being considered as important additions to traditional therapeutic community programmes. This volume covers a range of important issues regarding therapeutic programmes, including ethics, politics, programme design, and training, and provides much food for thought. We are grateful to Eric Cullen, Lawrence Jones and Roland Woodward for drawing together the material for this specialist text, which is a valuable addition to the Wiley Series on Offender Rehabilitation.

Mary McMurran
Clive R. Hollin

Preface

As this preface was being written, there was a growing division in the British criminal justice arena between in the one camp those who clarioned a renaissance in treating offenders and, in the other, those who demanded an escalation of the need to contain prisoners in increasingly austere, secure prisons. In Germany, as in Britain, a rehabilitative approach to offending remains a luxury for a small minority of prisoners, with fewer than 1200 places in Therapeutic Community (TC) style regimes in the two countries combined where over 110,000 people were imprisoned. Even this is a relatively small-scale 'skirmish' when contrasted with the American prison industry with over one million 'clients'.

Take a step back from the figures. Place them in a societal context and consider what they say about both the apparent incidence of serious crime and our response to it. Where on the continuum between severe punitiveness and ultra-liberal treatment does the equilibrium lie? At several levels, the issues of treating criminals raises questions of conscience as well as process and efficacy, and it is essential for anyone involved in criminal justice and administration to have reference to both, for the later to be informed by the former.

This book attempts to do more than present programmes which are variations on the theme of therapeutic communities for offenders. It sets out to help the reader to an appreciation of the concentric circles of influence on citizens' behaviour, moving in from a national 'mentality', through a cultural 'press' of regional influences, to the immediate community, the peer groups and family influences, to the individual. This deliberately ambitious aim is promulgated on an understanding that communities should be nurturing but often are not, and that therapy does not have to be curative, i.e therapeutic communities are relevant to non-Personality Disordered prisoners (and ultimately are just as relevant to normal, non-prisoners in terms of their message).

The language of therapeutic communities is replete with valued-laden terms, such as 'liberal' and 'permissive'. It would be possible to update the terminology of TCs to make it more 'user friendly'. Already, in the 1990s, the move is towards referring to treatment rather than therapy and to programmes of intervention rather than treatment. This linguistic transition is attractive not only because it reduces the apparent stigmatization of a medical model, i.e. therapy is for 'nutters, nonces and grasses' (the mentally disordered, sex offenders and informants), but also because it serves to satisfy the concerns of pragmatic prison managers that the activities are not 'soft' options. The book also attempts to make TCs and their language more accessible. Nevertheless, therapeutic community remains the best, and therefore most appropriate description of what this book is about and, while TCs may be much enhanced by other programmes of intervention, it is the 'culture of enquiry' which remains at the heart of the experience. This concept is concerned with both the language of cultures, e.g. mores, elders and customs, and with the essence of enquiry or seeking the answers to questions long-held or recently framed.

The book is divided into four loosely-linked parts. Part I is concerned with setting the scene in terms of the history and development of therapeutic communities. Jeff Roberts, a psychiatrist and psychotherapist, places the information squarely in a political and societal context. The former is presented in terms of how different political ideologies influence cultural maturation and attitudes, and the latter explores how crime may be one result of the 'derailment' of the socializing process. Roberts goes on to outline the evolution of British TCs from their origins in post-war trauma therapies. In Chapter 2, Roger Sapsford addresses the ethical contradictions inherent in TCs, particularly those based in prisons or secure hospitals. His exposition centres on the paradox between advocating self-sufficiency and autonomy for individuals whose success is then made contingent upon professional judgement as expert (the 'Scientific mode') and the 'Economistic' framework which obliges the process to occur in the least expensive manner possible. This debate could hardly be more topical.

Part II forms the bulk of the book, with four examples of British TCs for offenders. Bridget Dolan summarizes the development of what most people regard as the first TC in the UK, the Henderson Hospital (although Roberts records that it was predated by the Northfield Hospital in the 1940s). The historical significance of the development of a psychotherapeutic approach to TCs placed this treatment indisputably within a medical model from which it has never completely evolved. Dolan explains that the bridge between the Henderson and prison TCs has its foundation in the works of Copas, Whitely and Norton (in particular) establishing the relevance of this model to personality disordered and 'psychopathic' individuals who frequently have criminal histories. In Chapter 4, Cullen poses a number of questions about the viability of a total prison approach to TCs. In describing the programme at Grendon Underwood, he acknowledges the debt of gratitude to the TC legacy and confirms the qualified efficacy in both personality and criminological outcomes, but challenges the continuing powerbase of doctors and governors which determines the direction for future TC developments. David Cooke chronicles the conception, life and untimely death of Barlinnie, the most famous (and only!) therapeutic regime in Scottish prison history to date. The unique nature of this small unit for the most violent prisoners in the country is a salutary lesson in both how to treat men at the heaviest end of the 'market' and in how, if the culture does not change and continue to challenge, it may atrophy— or be put to death. Cooke concludes with signal learning points and some optimism for new proposals, especially for a National Induction Centre for all long-term prisoners. Lawrence Jones writes about the first small TC regime in the United Kingdom, The Max Glatt Centre. This contemporary of the Barlinnie Unit is also threatened with closure at the time of writing. Jones reviews the success of this small unit embedded within a much larger maximum security prison from three perspectives. First, he reviews work establishing a non-linear response to therapy, i.e. men getting worse before they get better, and then explores TIBs, or therapy interfering behaviours, by way of explanation. Compliance and non-compliance themes are explored before providing one of the most comprehensive catalogues of interpersonal dynamics within TCs extant.

Part III gives two examples of best practice in the American and German experiences of treatment in prisons. Harry Wexler summarizes the recent history of growing credibility for community and prison-based TCs for drug and other substance-abusing offenders. He highlights one of the fundamental differences between US and European TCs in prisons. While American correction has reduced recidivism as *the* goal, many British practitioners still regard this as inappropriate, focusing instead on the reintegration of dysfunctional personalities as sufficient and realistic. Wexler critiques the success of the concept-driven model of TCs in American prisons as having established their efficacy and credibility but goes on to outline a number of areas for improvement, including the need to train staff better and develop more community-based support and follow-up programmes. Fredrich Lösel and Rudolf Egg provide a thoroughly impressive description and evaluation of the social-therapeutic prisons in Germany. The development of these non-psychotherapeutic regimes, and their proven efficacy, are a significant harbinger to the future of TCs in prisons. Lösel's meta-evaluations of outcome comparisons not only add further support to the findings that early leavers represent highest reoffending risks but also, and most importantly, develop the key issues of outcome effect and multimodal models of treatment.

The final part of the book deals with the cluster of themes to do with staff—their recruitment, training, motivation and retention. Peter Lewis explores the myriad difficulties inherent in sustaining therapeutic principles in an indifferent, even hostile, environment. His psychotherapeutic insights into the roles and dilemmas of prison staff, and of the therapeutic alliance essential for personal change, form the platform for a lucid exposition of the nature of the transitional process from the unconscious to the conscious, concluding that this is the exclusive domain of the qualified therapist. Roland Woodward, on the other hand, provides a generalist's view of 'how to' set up and run a therapeutic community in prison with minimal reference to the professional nomenclature and qualifications required. His chapter is closer to a practitioners' guide, summarizing the qualities, preparation and integration of new members to TCs staff teams.

There are a number of critical and contentious passages in this text and the authors, while still practising civil servants, make no apologies for this. Therapeutic Communities based in prisons, or in the community, can only survive by continuing to adapt to treatment innovations of proven efficacy and by continuing to challenge threats to their professional integrity or practical capacity to deliver. The text therefore sets out to present not only descriptions of programmes and proof of efficacy, but also the range of threats and opportunities for the future.

Although little mention is made of the part the inmates and patients play in therapeutic communities described, it is of course essential. People rooted in criminal or antisocial patterns of behaviour, and of life, must want to change and must then submit to the most rigorous and painful scrutiny of their innermost feelings and thoughts and, most of all, of what are often the worst of crimes. All of their work, all of the contributions of thousands of committed staff, is towards reducing suffering and enhancing life. Such work, such commitment, deserves support and perhaps through this text, greater acknowledgement.

PART I

History, Development and Ethical Issues

CHAPTER 1

History of the Therapeutic Community

Jeff Roberts

The Group Analytic Practice, London

A HISTORY OF THE THEORIES AND PHILOSOPHY OF SOCIAL THERAPIES

Forensic science embraces a range of theories attempting to explain or understand offender behaviour. One field of investigation has been the relationship between the individual and the society in which he or she lives. The therapeutic community movement implicitly adopts the view that deviant behaviour, much of which is deemed criminal, represents a breakdown of the relationship between the individual and the structured society of which he or she is, by virtue of time and place of birth, a member. It is as if the 'offender', when presented with the 'social contract' (Hobbes, 1651) says 'I never signed that'. Hobbes developed a materialistic, pessimistic philosophy with a bleak picture of people in the state of nature where life is 'nasty, brutish and short'. Fear of violent death was the principal motive that caused people to create a state by contracting to surrender their natural rights and submit to the absolute authority of a sovereign. Entry into and passage through a therapeutic community represents a second chance voluntarily to accept social values and enter 'the social contract'.

Durkheim (1897) in *Le Suicide* attempted to research the relationship between an individual's behaviour and the societal phenomenon

Therapeutic Communities for Offenders.
Edited by E. Cullen, L. Jones and R. Woodward. © 1997 John Wiley & Sons Ltd.

of 'anomie', a state of disconnected alienation from other people. In *Le Suicide*, Durkheim's pioneering sociological study, suicide, an extreme piece of destructive behaviour, is identified as apparently having social origins. Suicide arises in Durkheim's view from the state of anomie. This and subsequent studies have led to a view of deviant, delinquent and frequently criminal behaviour being a consequence of some form of alienation from the main body of society. Durkheim was a pioneer who produced research findings on a large canvas to support a fundamental thesis. This theory points the way towards understanding human behaviour in its social context. It places human behaviour in a frame which can theoretically be modified in ways that will influence behaviour.

Durkheim's work was very much at the interface between psychology and sociology and as such represents an early venture into social psychology. This discipline has continued to develop in the 20th century in attempting to understand human behaviour in its group and social contexts. Freud (1922) ventured once into group psychology and proposed that in crowds we are likely to relinquish our consciences to one identified as a leader. There have been more research-based studies in this field. Murray (1938), for instance, proposed that behaviour is the resultant of personality needs and environmental pressure. This is a useful concept. Norbert Elias (1937), an early influence on S. H. Foulkes, the founder of Group Analysis (Roberts & Pines 1992), studied the Civilising Process. Kurt Lewin was also influential in his attempts to understand human behaviour on the basis of interactional fields. There are a range of studies looking at the provoking and constraining influences of group and society on their members. Hobbes is said to have been pessimistic; none the less, more recently, C. P. Snow (1980), a literary chronicler of academia and the corridors of power in the 20th century wrote a final crime novel in which he referred to our civilized behaviour as a 'coat of varnish'.

Sociology and psychology give clear indications that destructive behaviour is almost always a consequence of a failure of the restraining, constraining, or preventive effects of social relationships. Deviant behaviour can thus be thought of as either a primary failure of socializing or civilizing processes or a secondary breakdown of earlier socialization.

Developmental studies are aimed at understanding and hopefully pointing the way towards methods of modulating human behaviour. These studies tend to look at the ongoing interplay between internal world and external world as the person develops from infancy to old age. This is a complex area which can be addressed from a variety of points of view. The richest and most detailed developmental study of the human psyche has been contributed by psychoanalysis. Treading the narrow path between a broad social canvas and restricted biological theories, psychoanalysis has two contributions to make. It was the first rational attempt to understand human behaviour at the interface between our biological substrate and the human environment (Freud 1916–17; 1933). This interface is occupied by human self-consciousness! The second contribution of psychoanalysis, as mentioned above, is that it follows human behaviour developmentally from the cradle to the grave (Erickson, 1960).

Early psychoanalytic studies came to focus on the triangular relationship between mother, father and child. The resolution of the emergent Oedipal or Electra conflict represents a successful passage through the gateway to social participation. Only the child who is able to disentangle itself from the Oedipal triangle is ready for social relationships. From this point psychoanalysis has little more to contribute to the mapping of development. It is primarily devoted to the study of relationships which are accessible through a 'bi-personal field'.

When a child goes to school he/she enters for the first time the world of group and social relationships. If development in the family has proceeded satisfactorily he or she can energetically enter a world of multiple relationships. In the Freudian developmental schema he or she will be in the latency phase, relatively conflict-free and ready for learning.

The psychology of the group and the successful entry of the individual child into an increasingly complex network of relationships are probably the keys to later social and antisocial behaviour. Successful socialization gives an ability to empathize with and place a value on other beings.

HUMAN SOCIAL DEVELOPMENT

There are a number of levels in the process of developing from intrauterine unawareness to being a citizen of the world, an outline of which is given below.

A child is born having been for months effectively part of the mother's body. The process of being born and the previous captivity may or may not have been traumatic. The final conversion from watery to terrestrial life often seems to be something of a shock. It is generally not long after this initial shock before the human infant is offered an experience of total care by a mother or maternal substitutes. Something like 'mummy' is experienced with a more or less intimate relationship with her. This caring situation, with its intimate mother–child relationship is perceived as a kind of psychological symbiosis, substituting for the previous somatic host–parasite relationship of pregnancy. Psychologically speaking it would appear that the child moves rapidly from a state of symbiosis to separateness or individuation (Mahler et al., 1975; Winnicott, 1971). All subsequent development is dependent on there being a successful 'psychological birth of the human infant' (Mahler et al., 1975) by around the age of 2. From this point all human beings will encounter opportunities of developing relationships encompassing growing numbers of other human beings. This is a socializing process and also a civilizing one. The sequence of development might proceed as follows:

- *small groups* — the three-person relationship (mother, father and child), the greater than three-person family relationship (siblings and then grandparents, aunts, uncles, etc.), extrafamilial small groups.
- *median groups* — e. g. the classroom.
- *large groups* — the school, village, town, city, county, country, continent, world.

People vary in how much of the external social world is understood and seen as friendly, neutral or hostile. The closest and earliest crimes are visited on siblings and parents, the most distant and later crimes are those committed at war.

Outside the home is a complex labyrinth of potential relatedness. Human beings as a result of both constitutional, developmental and environmental factors are variably equipped to explore this labyrinth. Those who cannot find their way will fall by the wayside and in one way or another become either ill or deviant, experience themselves as ill or be labelled as ill or mad by others. There is a growing body of research identifying increasingly accurately which kind of social factors promote psychological disorder. Brown and Harris (1978) document the early development of work demonstrating that social isolation is closely correlated with at least one form of depression. There is also important work on the contribution of family and social factors to the development of schizophrenic states. Research has shown clearly and repeatedly that recovered schizophrenics are vulnerable to high levels of expressed emotion in their families (Vaughn and Leff, 1976). Observations of patients in outpatient clinics and in psychiatric hospitals also strongly suggest that the schizophrenic condition tends to deteriorate in the context of low levels of stimulation. These observations are less well documented, however, and research is needed.

RESEARCH AND EXPERIENCES LEADING TO SOCIAL THERAPEUTIC APPROACHES

Social Therapy to Promote and Repair Social Development

The argument of the social therapist is that those who have been damaged by adverse social process or who have been unable to engage in social processes should benefit from a reparative socializing experience. From 1946 until approximately 1960 social therapy for the mentally ill was actively developed in a variety of settings, including large mental hospitals. However, one of the best known British therapeutic communities developed methods aimed at people originally labelled as psychopathic and later as personality disordered. This, coupled with the relative failure of the mental hospital therapeutic community, has led to the treatment of personality disorder being seen as the main area of efficacy of social therapy. With many psychiatrists agreeing that the therapeutic community is the treatment of choice for 'personality disorder' it has been a rational development for the psychologically disturbed offender with a personality disorder to be offered social therapy.

Criminological studies have produced some attempts to classify offending behaviour on the basis of psychological abnormality. Offending behaviour may be considered as having resulted from:

1. The effects of an abnormal nervous system, i. e. due to brain damage:
   (a) Perinatal
   (b) Developmental
   (c) Trauma, infection, tumour, etc.
2. The consequences of 'mental illness', i. e. schizophrenia or major depressive illness.
3. Non-psychotic psychological disorder, such as neurosis or personality disorder, where there is undoubted abnormality but no evidence of mental illness.
4. The understandable motivation of apparently normal personalities for whom offending is a business, a consequence of intolerable stress or a fundamental disagreement with societal values — the paedophile and a dissident in Stalinist USSR might paradoxically both fit this niche.

As a general rule only those who occupy the general category of personality or character disorder naturally fit the notions of offender behaviour, resulting from derailment of the socializing process. Such individuals are ripe for a non-coercive opportunity to discover or sometimes rediscover the advantages of 'the social contract'. It is necessary to introduce a caveat here: many people in whom discipline or teaching has been well meaning but punitive or frightening and also those who have been subjected to early trauma such as physical or sexual abuse can contain dangerously asocial subpersonalities, generally inaccessible to consciousness and concealed by an apparently normal person. Such individuals can also benefit from a social therapy but require diagnostic and psychotherapeutic sophistication.

Organizations providing social therapy have been named in a variety of ways including 'therapeutic community'. The primary task of these organizations is to heal and/or correct by offering membership of an optimized social environment, consciously designed to act as a *therapeutic instrument*.

Social Therapy to Counter Harmful Effects of Institutions

The positive reasons for developing therapeutic communities are discussed above. The history of the therapeutic community is also closely interwoven with a growing awareness of the harm done to people by unsympathetic institutional environments.

The York Retreat (Kennard, 1983) was an early precursor of the therapeutic community. This enlightened institution was established as a result of the growing awareness in the late 18th century of the appalling conditions in which the insane were treated, together with the frequently barbaric nature of the treatment itself. Tuke, who was in charge of the retreat, had noted that the lower classes contributed the majority of the mentally disordered. He proposed that immunity to mental disorder was linked to refined elements of aristocratic life (Karon and Vandenbos, 1994). He therefore introduced his patients to the pleasures of the aristocratic tea party!

The Retreat was in the vanguard of a movement promoting 'moral treatment' and was the first of many rural asylums in pleasant grounds providing healthy conditions and activities for the casualties of urban development and the industrial revolution. These enlightened asylums, with a few exceptions, which included the Retreat, were to become the full and overflowing mental hospitals of the 1920s and 1930s.

The two World Wars in the first half of this century combined to accelerate scientific development and application and led to what now appears to be exponential technological progress. They also contributed to a great deal of social re-evaluation. In both wars there was a demand for the rapid treatment of psychological casualties. This forced the development, refinement and application of effective psychiatric treatment. Between the wars it became clear that mental illness could be treated and this was juxtaposed with an awareness of full and overcrowded asylums. There has been progress through this century and since the mid-1930s there has been a dramatic reduction in the number of people living out their lives in incarceration (Scull, 1961). This has been accompanied by a number of important studies of these and other total institutions, seeking to explore their social structures and the effects they have had on their inmates.

A classic study comprised four essays by the sociologist Irving Goffman (1961) entitled *Asylums*. These rich works describe in detail, using quotes from literature and a range of direct experiences including that of being a researcher living the life of an inmate, all of those processes whereby the individual is absorbed into the total institution and systematically deprived of his/her individuality and his/her ability to maintain any experience of being a worthwhile, responsible, autonomous self. Goffman graphically demonstrated that whatever the reason for spending time in a total institution (one in which an individual lives continuously, which provides for all aspects of his or her life), the outcome is likely to be major additional disablement and stigmatization, albeit physically invisible. The findings of Goffman and others, particularly in the case of State Mental Hospitals in the United States, were graphically, if somewhat belatedly, illustrated in the film *One Flew over the Cuckoo's Nest*.

A number of important studies of British psychiatric hospitals were published in the 1950s and 1960s. These indicated that the so-called Schizophrenic Defect state could be understood as being in part a consequence of institutionalization (Rees, 1957; Barton, 1966; Wing & Brown, 1970). In the famous 'three hospitals' study (Wing & Brown, 1961) it was clearly demonstrated how the day-to-day practice within the hospital would profoundly influence the patient's behaviour. On the whole the significance of this work was misunderstood. It did not mean that there is no such thing as a schizophrenic defect state. It meant that a toxic environment ensures a more profound development of schizophrenic disintegration and loss of sell. Thus this work has been used, not to promote the imaginative development of therapeutic environments but to justify an attempt to develop an entirely community-based, non-residential treatment for the entire spectrum of psychiatric illness (see below).

During the second World War and prior to the development of the second Northfield experiment Main (1977) studied sickness and absenteeism in army battalions. He found that different battalions had very different patterns of illness and availability for service. He concluded that the most important variable in these situations was morale, and that this in turn was a function of the type of interpretation by the officers of their responsibilities in matters of authority and discipline.

Some 20 years later Isobel Menzies (1960) carried out important studies on hospital wards. She was investigating particularly the function of nurses and their management structure. A clear conclusion emerged. Some hospital wards provide a therapeutic environment, some an anti-therapeutic environment. Again the most important variable appeared to be the interpretation by senior staff of the nature of their authority and management roles in these wards.

There is thus a substantial body of literature indicating the potential damage to the physical and mental health of individuals of inappropriately conducted human environments. The harm done can extend from short-term damage to physical health and long-term impairment of personality development. Furthermore, it is now equally clear that a well designed human environment can contribute a great deal to improve human health, happiness, self-expression and stability.

THE SOCIAL AND POLITICAL CONTEXT OF THE THERAPEUTIC COMMUNITY MOVEMENT

We will now examine the place of the therapeutic community in the contemporary development of psychiatry and society. We are witness to a progressive loss of interest in the therapeutic community, partly evidenced by a withdrawal of funding, and compounded very often by a shortage of 'suitable' clients. Recent restructuring of the British National Health Service and Social Services has created purchasers pressed to seek lowest cost treatment. Mental health services are also bought in bulk. In addition, it is also now the case that local and locality resources are favoured while resources with regional or national catchment areas are not.

There is also a strong social and ideological tide running against the therapeutic community. One aspect of this is a cult of individualism, to be discussed later. The other is a government policy of relocating mental health provision to the family and community setting. Community mental health services are the core of today's provision. One view of this movement is that it represents a decision to look again at the unacceptable side of society and integrate it into the community rather than attempt to dispose of it. The current push towards a predominantly community-based psychiatry seems to be the result of an overreaction to knowledge concerning institutionalization. There is no evidence of thought given to improving in-patient provision. A decision was made that it would always be bad and therefore should be closed down. Perversely this policy change has chosen to ignore all the work which had been done in developing therapeutic communities and environments. This work was treated as if non-existent or invisible. There has been little place for the development or even maintenance of high-quality therapeutic community provision in a situation where residential and long-term treatment has been largely discontinued.

Finally, the therapeutic community is likely to create persecutory anxiety in the administratively inclined. For instance, the high degree of personal freedom and choice allowed in a therapeutic community prison which encourages self and social management of behaviour, will create painful anxiety in those who believe that offenders should be locked up and punished. (Editor's note: Therapeutic communities in prisons, however, are still expanding in spite of these apprehensions.)

The Community

If 'community psychiatry' is to work it will no doubt require an appreciation of the nature of community and the kaleidoscopic changes in community over time. Nisbet (1953) in his book *The Quest for Community*, points out that by mediaeval times rich and complex social structures had developed providing meaningful and protected social environments for all those willing to abide by society's rules. From the Renaissance onwards, it seems, we have seen the emergence and rise of the individual. Slowly the guilds, churches, monasteries, extended family, villages, small towns, local councils, societies and even the unions have lost their power, influence and meaning. There is increasingly less to belong to, unless it is through the post or by way of a cable. It seems that for many people it is increasingly hard to identify sources of communal experience or Koinonia (de Mare et al., 1991). We have seen the emergence of the individual with little to belong to and limited impact on the social world in which he or she lives. Nisbet suggests that this feeble creature is readily manipulable and thus politically desirable. One of Nisbet's conclusions is that government fears community and groupings of people, preferring individuals since these are less powerful and more governable. Politicians do indeed appear wary of large groupings of people that are not directly under their control.

Governmental Undermining of Society

Margaret Thatcher was heard to say: 'There is no such thing as society.' Thus she appears to voice the very anti-community statement that Nisbet (1953) would have predicted from a politician.

This attitude inevitably weakens the 'social contract', which is an imaginary construct explaining the reason for the development of social structures by human society. In the words of Hobbes (1651) life outside societal privilege is 'Nasty, brutish and short', which is why the majority of us have entered into a social contract. In so doing we have agreed to sacrifice self-interest and thoughtless personal and narcissistic gratification in order to be looked after and protected by society or at least the instruments of society. The way in which governmental encouragement of individualism can destabilize the social contract and tend towards a restoration of the nasty, brutish and short aspects of life is perhaps seen most starkly in the former Soviet Union, where male life expectancy has declined by six years since 1992 (Shapiro, 1995). Of this decrease, 21.4% was contributed by violent death! The crimes against humanity on which this society was built are now common knowledge (Volkogonov, 1991) but in more recent times some aspects of the social order which had been established were more effective in sustaining decent human life than the often anarchistic capitalism which has replaced it. It seems reasonable to hypothesize that a highly individualistic society without other constraints and a humane social safety net will generate more crime. This situation will be exacerbated if unthinking punishment is the response to an increasing tendency to live outside the law.

My belief is that the cult of individualism dangerously weakens the social contract, tending to restore a 'nasty, brutish and short' tendency in life. Promoting individualism above social and communal values is likely to lead to more crime and increasingly vigorous attempts at stamping it out. In the UK there is currently a perceived law and order problem, coupled with one of the highest *per capita* prison populations in Europe.

The Development of Human Individual Consciousness

The development of human consciousness took place in the context of an extraordinarily complex social matrix of a multiplicity of groups, movements and institutions. This social framework provided a matrix, skeleton or scaffolding for human individual consciousness.

As indicated above Margaret Thatcher believes that there is no such thing as society. On the other hand S. H. Foulkes (1973) said, in effect, that: 'there is no such thing as an individual' without a matrix within which dialogue may occur. In short, my understanding of Foulkes is that human individual consciousness is entirely dependent on dialogue with another or in groups for its stability and integrity.

An Experiment at Removing Social Scaffolding

It follows from the foregoing that the emergence of individualism has contained within it a potentially self-destructive time bomb. The stronger the drive for individual freedom of expression and independence, the less its social framework is valued. The result appears to be that we are in the middle of a long-running unplanned social experiment in the removal of significant elements from the scaffolding which over many millennia has enabled human consciousness as we know it to evolve. While this is in part the responsibility of central government, we are all playing a role. It remains uncertain what will happen when the disassembly is complete and our social heritage is entirely removed. We neither know the result of the experiment nor whether it will be pursued to its conclusion. We do know that the therapeutic community is an experiment which opposes the tide of individualism.

A DEVELOPMENTAL HISTORY OF THE THERAPEUTIC COMMUNITY

The history of therapeutic communities is that of humane and far-sighted individual providers of treatment who were prepared to swim against the tide of public opinion and political pressure. This history goes back a long way: before the development of therapeutic communities one sees the development of a number of 'proto-therapeutic communities'.

The Retreat (Kennard, 1983), and other early asyla had, in their respect for the individual and expectation of normal behaviour arising in the context of general social and peer pressure, many features of the therapeutic community embedded in their day to day working. However, they lacked any operationalized method and any social or psychological theories which might have led to a stronger legacy to be handed down to later 'therapeutic communities'.

Another and much later proto-therapeutic community is the famous Chestnut Lodge, whose methods were strongly influenced by Harry Stack-Sullivan. This small private asylum in Rockville, Maryland has an enduring fame for the psychotherapeutic and psychoanalytic treatment of schizophrenia, but it is most particularly remembered for a period during the 1930s when it claimed to achieve a 90% success rate with young 'first break' schizophrenics.

The arguments for establishing treatment centres adopting group and social therapy methods had been steadily accumulating since the time of Durkheim. The social and psychological sciences, however, are perceived as 'soft sciences'. The application of their findings is thus assumed to be optional rather than obligatory. Current societal dynamics, processes and fashions tend to dictate what is applied. Thus, during the period of heightened camaraderie and enormous emotional trauma of the Second World War, two significant social therapeutic enterprises were developed. These marked the earliest beginnings of the 'Therapeutic Community' method. The eponym was given retrospectively (Main, 1946).

First Wilfred Bion, and later Main, Foulkes, Bridger and de Mare, worked in the early 1940s at the Northfield Military Hospital in the UK. The developments at the Northfield Hospital are interesting in a number of ways. Wilfred Bion (Bion, 1961) was an extraordinary man of great intelligence who appears to have also been something of a maverick. For a short period he was in charge of psychiatric treatment at the Northfield Military Hospital where he personally designed a therapeutic structure that was group-based and represented an attempt to treat socially the social elements of the patients' neuroses. Senior army officials were undoubtedly uncomfortable with these developments. Bion was quite rapidly removed from his post. Officially, men were being allowed to be insubordinate and to avoid military discipline; unofficially there may have been riots. This experiment was none the less regarded as worth repeating. A team of talented young doctors and psychiatrists was assembled. Their commanding officer was Harold Bridger (1946.) They also included: E. J. Anthony, S. H. Foulkes (1946 and 1948), Patrick de Mare, Ronald Casson, Tom Main (1946) and Martin James. At the time Foulkes was the only qualified psychoanalyst on the team. This group of people plus Bion were to make a major contribution to psychotherapeutic development in the second half of the 20th century. The fields they advanced were psychoanalysis, group psychotherapy, the therapeutic community and organizational training and consultancy. They had worked together, with the exception of Bion, in what was a very effective and successful therapeutic community in all but name.

At the same time in the Mill Hill Neurosis Unit, set up in London for the treatment of 'effort syndrome' or 'cardiac neurosis', Maxwell Jones (Jones, 1968) rediscovered the power of the group and social processes. Jones was a research psychiatrist who had done extensive work on the physiological manifestations of 'effort syndrome'. At Mill Hill, to which parts of the Maudsley Hospital were transferred, he set out to lecture men on these findings with a view to improving their neurotic conditions. He quickly discovered, however, that the most therapeutic part of this activity was group discussion and the teaching of the new members of the unit by the senior members. He was to transfer this discovery to the Belmont Unit for the rehabilitation of the chronically unemployed, which rapidly evolved into the Henderson Hospital. In most people's minds this hospital was the prototype therapeutic community.

After the war, Tom Main was employed at The Cassel Hospital, where he pioneered a therapeutic model, combining life in a therapeutic community with ongoing psychoanalytic psychotherapy. It was Main who coined the phrase 'therapeutic community'.

By 1954 TC ideas were infiltrating mental hospitals. A series of psychiatric hospitals developed a therapeutic community approach (Clark, 1965), notably Fulbourn (Cambridge) (Clark, 1964), Littlemore (Oxford) and Claybury (East of London) (Martin, 1962). There was also the rather less well known Halliwick Hospital, where Patrick de Mare and Lionel Kreeger collaborated in a therapeutic community ward.

In 1954 chlorpromazine was introduced as a treatment for schizophrenia. Suddenly it was possible to mitigate the symptoms of this condition in many patients, in a very short time. It was also realized at around this time that a significant contribution to the Schizophrenic Defect State was made by 'institutionalization'. A window of opportunity had opened for the development of an effective multilevel, multidisciplinary approach to the treatment of schizophrenic states. Unfortunately policy makers, apparently driven by financial and commercial considerations, have in my opinion misunderstood and misused research findings and statistical analysis, the result is that we now have a rather uniform, uncreative and suboptimal service.

A key example of mistaken interpretation and extrapolation of statistics is to be found in the use of those concerning the falling population in mental hospitals obtained by Tooth and Brook (1961). Tooth and Brook carried out a statistical study of the population of psychiatric hospitals and saw a progressive fall in this population. They then rested a ruler on their curve and drew a line. This extrapolated line indicated that by the late 1990s the population would be zero. This was a single study and the prediction was made with suspect methodology. The government of the day enthusiastically adopted this study and began to develop a mental health policy based on its implications. Community-based psychiatry would be the method of the future and large mental hospitals would be closed and the land they occupied put to alternative uses. The closures are now in full flood. There has been extensive debate in the pages of the *British Journal of Psychiatry* concerning 'the new long stay' and a need to continue to provide asylum for the mentally ill. Nevertheless the pressure to move entirely towards community psychiatry now seems irresistible.

The outcome of all this has been short stays in impoverished hospital environments (so as not to encourage dependency), with remission of the condition or suppression of symptoms promoted by high doses of medication. There has been a half-hearted adoption of elements of Therapeutic Community practice with little true understanding of why this was being done and how the methods could be appropriately modified for the schizophrenic client group. Many psychiatric wards have weekly or even daily ward meetings which are rather poorly understood and conducted.

There has been an important but limited development of therapeutic community day care and hostel care in the community. For example, there was a 'model' service (Blake et al., 1985) provided by Kensington and Chelsea Social Services. This consisted of four therapeutic community day centres, each providing for a specific client group, plus a hostel for largely schizophrenic clients which attempted to provide a therapeutic community approach.

The growing governmental embracing of community psychiatry is an understandable end-point of these developments. Some psychiatrists and other professionals have also begun to find community niches. Maxwell Jones (1982), in his book the *The Process of Change*, gives a lively, personal account of developing a pioneering community psychiatric service, with methods derived from his therapeutic community experience, in the Borders, based at Dingleton Hospital. None the less 'community psychiatry' is often developed in the context of a progressive degradation of the quality of the 'communities' in which the enterprise is to be practised. Moreover, there has been no collective agreement on the part of communities that they will provide social and psychotherapeutic facilities for their least effective members. Many psychiatrists who are expected to lead these developments are poorly trained in the fields of social and community-based therapies. In hospital the patient may have had to keep his/her clothes in a cardboard box, in the urban community he/she seems often to have to sleep in one.

The importance of these developments is that they have virtually killed off the hospital-based therapeutic community. Thus by the beginning of the 1960s it was becoming increasingly clear that the TC was not to become a core provision in the field of mental health. There were only small pockets of self-consciously designed social therapy. A conclusion had effectively been reached that the sole significant area of application of the therapeutic community would be in the area of personality disorder. The most damning statement of all was made by Walmsley (1983) in a respected psychiatric textbook, when he referred to the therapeutic community as a 'sport'.

Maxwell Jones left the Henderson Hospital in 1959 and travelled as a visiting professor to the United States. Here he became involved in the development of therapeutic communities by the California Corrections Agency, for whom he was a consultant. Eleven therapeutic community prison projects were established (Jones, 1962; 1979). In the United States, Chino, the best known therapeutic community in a prison, was established by Dennie Briggs, who was a psychologist (Briggs, 1972).

At about this time, in the early 1960s, offender programmes guided by therapeutic community principles were first developed in the United Kingdom. This followed legislation, namely the 1959 Mental Health Act, which itself was influenced by research and clinical experience. This act did not grant the status of mental illness to psychopathy and personality disorder, but granted these conditions the status of psychological abnormality which could be susceptible to treatment. Grendon Prison was built specifically to provide a series of therapeutic community wings as an experiment in the social and group treatment of psychologically disturbed offenders. Its remarkable success is documented in *Grendon: A Study of a Therapeutic Prison* (Genders & Player, 1995).

Other therapeutic communities in British prisons have been set up in Wormwood Scrubs and at the special unit at Barlinnie Prison in Glasgow. The latter had success with very disturbed offenders and also has a degree of fame arising from consultation to it from Maxwell Jones.

CONCLUSIONS: THE CHANGING SOCIAL CONTEXT AND THE CHANGING THERAPEUTIC COMMUNITY

The developments in mental health provision described above will inevitably have a considerable influence on the demography of offender behaviour and the actual location of offenders. The mental hospital population is indeed now diminishing towards zero. This follows the trend of closing large mental hospitals and replacing them by care in the community. This has been paralleled by a not entirely surprising rise in the prison population. Whatever ideals govern psychiatric care, troublesome behaviour in the community needs to be managed. Moreover, as indicated in various parts of this chapter, social conditions (i.e. conditions in our communities) are not such as to protect vulnerable or developing egos. There will be casualties of a cult of individualism, particularly if it is coupled with psychiatric treatment dependent on care in the community. Some of the casualties end up in prison.

The vicissitudes of the therapeutic community can be understood in the context of current trends in mental health provision and its socio-cultural context. The therapeutic community has developed in the context of adverse social change. This may perhaps be best described as the rise of individualism. The tide in favour of overvaluing the individual's rights and expectations has been coming in in the West now for around 1000 years. The past 50 years have perhaps seen the greatest movement in this direction. The individual has a right to privacy, confidentiality, an individually tailored programme and a diet for his/her own special needs. He or she may also come to expect to retain the advantages of individualism at the cost of others with whom he or she works, lives or plays. This has deep implications for the current nature and future development of the human psyche. One can explore ways in which we have attempted to order ourselves and our experience. It seems that an emergent property of the interaction between the human genotype and need to order ourselves and experience has led to the phenomenon of Human Individual Consciousness. Paradoxically it seems likely that this individual consciousness depends for its continuing existence and health on group and social matrices. The therapeutic community is an approach to deviance in all its forms which fully takes this into account.

There is evidence indicating that therapeutic communities in prison can have striking success (Genders & Player, 1995). The philosophy and method of the therapeutic community unfortunately run contrary to cultural expectations and aspirations of Western individualism. Therapeutic communities offer pockets of communalism and sanity, promoting a genuinely healthy and sustainable individualism in a communal context, as an antidote to disconnection and anomie which are present to excess in our current post-Thatcherite society.

In prisons the quality of practice is variable. This is not unexpected since any large and widespread organization will inevitably comprise centres of excellence, centres of mediocrity and centres containing bad practice. The British prison service is no exception. It is currently, moreover, subjected to a number of factors that worsen the situation: overcrowding, underfunding, and confusion between the three functions of punishment, custody and correction. There is much evidence to indicate that custody and punishment tend to make matters worse.

Treatment or correction is ambitious and rarely results from punishment but can be achieved by a range of therapeutic approaches of which the therapeutic community (conducted with enlightened and vigorous integrity) can be among the most effective. In the therapeutic community we have a good, partially proven method that can be relatively expensive and arduous. The method, however, is not the holy grail, which we still seem to seek, so it is overlooked while something more technical, more magical and perhaps more punitive is earnestly sought.

The Henderson hospital has long been the home of some of the best therapeutic community practice. It is one of the best known and most rigorous therapeutic communities working with people diagnosed on the whole as having personality disorders. To enter the Henderson one must also show genuine motivation to change, as judged by a selection group of clients and staff. In *Community as Doctor* Robert Rapoport (1960) reported a thorough sociological study of the hospital and its practice. A conclusion of this study was that the clinical practice confused treatment with rehabilitation. This was a more damaging conclusion than might have been apparent at the time, although Maxwell Jones was not happy about it. However, an even more troubling criticism was and still is that the TC is neither rehabilitation nor treatment, but a comfortable if eccentric way of life, like that in a monastery, which keeps its members happy but does not help them with real life in the real world. This is a valid criticism if staff are not aware of the problem. It is also the criticism most eagerly taken up by those who have other therapeutic enthusiasms. A therapeutic community will survive best and get best results if it takes care to be open to interchange with wider society and if it consciously seeks to create bridges between its social environment and that in the wider community.

A well run TC introduces social, ethical and moral values not always obvious in an individual's real world. So long as these are those aspired to by the main body of society this is a powerful intervention. Moreover, these values within the TC are constantly under attack and therapeutic work is about dealing with a tendency to corrupt. The inmate can learn about the dangers of corruption and how personally to manage self in such a context. Most well run TCs are not comfortable places to be. They do need to be open to societal process in a critical and self-critical way.

It has been failure in these areas which has made the therapeutic community vulnerable to attacks from clinicians, public and politicians. The TC has fallen with other residential contexts to an attitude which says that the best university is the university of life. In other words, the pragmatist might say—The best place for the mentally ill is the community, the best place for the offender is a strict prison with a fiercely punitive culture and a realistically tough underculture.

REFERENCES

Barton, R. (1966) *Institutional Neurosis.* 2nd edn. Bristol: Wright.
Bion, W. R. (1961). *Experiences in Groups.* London: Tavistock.
Blake, R., Millard, D. & Roberts, J. P. (1985) Therapeutic community principles in an integrated local authority mental health service. *International Journal of Therapeutic Communities,* 5(4), 243–273.
Bridger, H. (1946). The Northfield experiment. *Bulletin of the Menninger Clinic,* 10(3), 71–76.
Briggs, D. (1972). Chino, California. In S. Whiteley et al. (eds). *Dealing with Deviants.* London: Hogarth Press, pp. 95–171.
Brown, G. W. & Harris, T. (1978). *The Social Origins of Depression: A Study of Psychiatric Disorder in Women.* London: Tavistock.
Clark, D. H. (1964). *Administrative Therapy.* London: Tavistock.
Clark, D. H. (1965). The therapeutic community concept, practice and future. *British Journal of Psychiatry,* 111, 947–954.
Anon. (1989, 1991). Extract from article on Thomas Hobbes. *Concise Columbia Encyclopedia.* New York: Columbia University Press.
De Mare, P., Piper, R. & Thompson, S. (1991). Koinonia: From Hate through Dialogue to Culture in the Large Group. London: Karnac Books.
Durkheim, E. (1897). *Le Suicide* (Suicide, a Study in Sociology) (reprinted 1952). London: Routledge and Kegan Paul.
Elias, N. (1937). *The Civilising Process* (reprinted 1978). Oxford: Blackwell, 1978.
Erickson, E. H. (1965). *Childhood and Society.* Harmondsworth: Penguin Books.
Foulkes, S. H. (1946). Principles and practice of group-therapy. *Bulletin of the Menninger Clinic,* 10(3), 85–89.
Foulkes, S. H. (1948). *Introduction to Group-Analytic Psychotherapy, Studies in the Social Integration of Individuals and Groups.* London: Heinemann. (Reprinted 1983. London: Karnac Books.)
Foulkes, S. H. (1973). *The group as matrix of the individual's mental life. In L. R. Wolberg and E. K. Schwartz (Eds). Group Therapy, an Overview.* New York: Intercontinental Medical Books.

Freud, S. (1916–17). *The Introductory Lectures on Psychoanalysis*. In the Standard Edition, XV & XVI (1964). London: Institute of Psychoanalysis and Hogarth Press.

Freud, S. (1922). *Group Psychology and the Analysis of the Ego*. London: International Psychoanalytic Press.

Freud, S. (1933). *The New Introductory Lectures on Psychoanalysis*. In the Standard Edition, XXII (1964). London: Institute of Psychoanalysis and Hogarth Press.

Genders, E. & Player, E. (1995). *Grendon: A Study of a Therapeutic Prison*, Oxford: Oxford University Press.

Goffman, E. (1961). *Asylums: Essays on the Social Situation of Mental Patients and other Inmates*. New York: Doubleday.

Hobbes, T. (1651). *The Leviathan*. Harmondsworth: Penguin Classics.

Jones, M. (1962). *Social Psychiatry in the Community, in Hospitals and in Prisons*. Springfield, IL: Charles Thomas.

Jones, M. (1968). *Social Psychiatry in Practice*. Harmondsworth: Penguin Books.

Jones, M. (1979). The therapeutic community, social learning and social change. In R. D. Hinshelwood & N. Manning. *Therapeutic Communities, Reflections and Progress*. London: Routledge and Kegan Paul, pp. 1–9.

Jones, M. (1982). *The Process of Change*. London: Routledge and Kegan Paul.

Karon, B. P. & Vandenbos, G. R. (1994). *Psychotherapy of Schizophrenia: The Treatment of Choice*. New Jersey: Jason Aronson, pp. 11–12.

Kennard, D. (1983). *An Introduction to Therapeutic Communities*, pp. 15–24. London: Routledge.

Mahler, M. S., Pine, F. & Bergman, A. (1975). *The Psychological Birth of the Human Infant*. London: Hutchinson.

Main, T. F. (1946). The hospital as a therapeutic institution. *Bulletin of the Menninger Clinic*, **10**(3), 66–70.

Main, T. F. (1977). The first S. H. Foulkes Annual Lecture. *Group Analysis*, **X**(2), 1–16.

Martin, D. (1962). *Adventure in Psychiatry*. London: Cassirer.

Menzies, I. E. P. (1960). A case-study in the functioning of social systems as a defence against anxiety. *Human Relations*, **13**, 95–121.

Murray, H. A. (1938). *Explorations in Personality*. New York: Oxford University Press.

Nisbet, R. (1953). *The Quest for Community*. Oxford: OUP.

Rapoport, R. N. (1960). *Community as Doctor*. London: Tavistock.

Rees, T.P. (1957) Back to Moral Treatment and Community Care. *Journal of Mental Science*, **103**, 303–334.

Roberts, J. & Pines, M. (1992). Group-analytic psychotherapy. *International Journal of Group Psychotherapy*, **42**(4), 469–494.

Shapiro, J. (1995). *The Health of Russia*. Presented at a Seminar for Grant Recipients, promoted by the Know How Fund.

Scull, A. T. (1961). *Museums of Madness*. London: Allen Lane.

Snow, C. P. (1979). *A Coat of Varnish*. London: Macmillan.

Tooth, G. C. & Brook, E. B. (1961). Trends in the mental health population and their effects on future planning. *Lancet*, **i**, 710.

Vaughn, C. & Leff, J. (1976). The influence of family and social factors on the course of psychiatric patients. *British Journal of Psychiatry*, **129**, 125–137.

Volkogonov, D. (1991). *Stalin: Triumph and Tragedy*. London: Weidenfeld & Nicholson.

Walmsley, T. (1983). Historical introduction. In R. E. Kendell & A. K. Zealley (Eds). *Companion to Psychiatric Studies*. Edinburgh: Churchill Livingstone.

Wing, J. K. & Brown, G. W. (1970). *Institutionalisation and Schizophrenia. A Comparative Study of Three Mental Hospitals*. Cambridge: Cambridge University Press.

Wing, J. K. & Brown, G. W. (1961). The social treatment of schizophrenia: a comparative survey of three mental hospitals. *Journal of Mental Science*, **103**, 303–334.

Winnicott, D. W. (1971). *Playing and Reality*. London: Tavistock.

CHAPTER 2

The Ethics of Therapy in Prison

Roger Sapsford

The Open University, Milton Keynes

The area of psychiatry, psychotherapy, counselling, 'mental medicine' —call it what you will—is well known for the ethical dilemmas which it occasions, and nowhere more so than in 'therapeutic communities'. Some of the problems arise from the history of such communities and their internally contradictory nature. In 'the outside world' they are characterized in principle by democracy—power-sharing and freedom of information—and by a collectivist strand which makes patients into adjunct therapists and gives power and authority over the individual to the group. They abolish the power of staff and promote patients to the status of joint directors of the programme, but at the same time they are there for a purpose and are necessarily shaped by those who are considered expert in that purpose—generally the trained staff. This leaves the staff facing, uncomfortably, in two directions as professionals.

Unwittingly the dilemma was well expressed by one of their original advocates, Tom Main, in 1946:

> The anarchical rights of the doctor in the traditional hospital society have to be exchanged for the more sincere role of member in a real community, responsible not only to himself [sic] and his superiors, but to the community as a whole ... He no longer owns 'his' patients. They are given up to the community which is to treat them. (Main, 1946).

The 'giving away of patients' conflicts with the requirements of professional responsibility, however, and it is difficult to see how the

Therapeutic Communities for Offenders.
Edited by E. Cullen, L. Jones and R. Woodward. © 1997 John Wiley & Sons Ltd.

therapist can be responsible for patients to his or her superiors if they have been given away to the community. Where there is an element of control in the recruitment process—in state psychiatric hospitals and above all in prisons—democracy as a rhetoric and a therapeutic tool has inevitably to give way to some extent to control as a required purpose of the institution, which again puts staff in a dilemma of conflicting roles.

Beyond and beneath these confusions of styles and roles, however, I want to argue in this chapter that the whole of 'mental medicine' or 'therapy' is strewn with ethical minefields because it is informed by four different and, largely, incompatible conceptual frameworks which I have labelled here 'the scientific', 'the rationalistic', the 'service model'—the dominant and received view on professional activity in this area, which straddles the first two of these frameworks—and 'the economisitic'. These can be broadly defined as follows.

1. The 'scientific' framework presents the therapist as knowledge-able expert, drawing on a corpus of knowledge not available to 'lay people'. The therapist is therefore the person best placed to determine the *means* by which a desired end shall be achieved. Therapists are also considered to have the best vision of what *ends* are desirable; their knowledge encompasses how human beings can function to best advantage and how much (or how little) deviation from the norm is functionally acceptable.
2. The 'rationalistic' framework draws on the moral values of 19th-century liberalism—self-sufficiency, self-governance and the autonomy of the individual. In this framework, it is perhaps permissible to take inadequate, degenerate or damaged workers and home-makers and return them to competent functioning through therapy. The framework is prone to internal contradic-tion, however, because the dominant rhetorical values are autonomy and self-sufficiency, and there is a paradox entailed in making authoritative interventions into people's lives in order to render them autonomous and self-sufficient. In other words, there is a conceptual mismatch of ends and means.
3. What I have called 'the service model' resolves this paradox by conceding both the authority of the patient ('customer', 'client') and the authority of the therapist ('expert', 'technician'). The client is assigned the right to determine ends, and the therapist has the determination of means for achieving these ends. The model therefore combines features from both frameworks.
4. The 'economistic' framework has its roots in economic liberalism (but has mutated beyond it into modern 'managerialism'). It

differs from the other frameworks in that it does not centre on a model of the patient–therapist relationship and is not directly concerned with the setting of ends. Its original version would have taken these for granted as agreed. The modern 'managerial' version questions whether they are necessary at all; having accepted the necessity, however, it applies to their fulfilment the same 'commercial' critique as has been applied in the last two decades to, for example, schooling, policing and public health provision. It asks what is the most efficient and effective means of delivering the service—how to optimize outcomes in a *cost-effective* way. (All too often, however, it degenerates into a *cost-cutting* exercise that seeks to find the minimum that can be cheaply delivered.)

Each of these frameworks has something sensible to say about mental therapy, about therapeutic communities and about therapy within penal institutions. The problem is that they do not have the *same* things to say. Sometimes they are in outright conflict. Sometimes, more confusingly, they appear to be saying the same thing, but it comes to mean something very different within the different conceptual maps. Each framework leads us to prescribe action which follows both logically and ethically from how it describes the social area, but we are baffled by the fact that we are issuing contradictory prescriptions.

THE SCIENTIFIC FRAMEWORK

What I am calling 'the scientific framework' combines two elements to give authority to the practice of therapy: the authority of science—which in this case means psychology on the one hand and medicine on the other—and the role of 'scientific practitioner', which in this case means borrowing the professional authority of medicine and psychology. The scientific framework deals with the treatment of 'mental health' in the same unproblematic way that general medicine aims at the treatment of physical health. By this I do not mean that the treatment itself is unproblematic, but the *idea* of treatment is not in dispute. People may be conceptualized as being in some way ill (in psychology, malfunctioning). This may be seen as a biological fault or one with ultimately a biological basis. Alternatively, it may be seen as something faulty in their socialization. It may be seen as a stress response to irresistible pressure in the immediate environment. Something is wrong, however, which needs the knowledge of an expert to put right.

The underlying view of the social order is a functionalist one. While there may he disputes about detail, in general we are in agreement that the nature and value of the social system are in most people's interests—in the same way, for example, that we may dispute the value or validity of particular laws but uphold the law in general as in the interests of all. The therapist works from a consensus position, therefore: we all 'naturally' want people to be able to function in the society as it is, and it is the job of the therapist, among others, to ensure that they are able to do so.

The rise to power of modern medicine is a comparatively recent historical process; it is only during the last two centuries that medicine as science has come to dominate health care in the Western world and that medical doctors have achieved their high social esteem and their power over everyday life (see Foucault, 1963). In the Victorian era the great rise of medicine came from a two-pronged attack on the diseases and disabilities of the poor. On the one hand a 'hygienic movement', spearheaded by prominent doctors and scientists, campaigned successfully for large-scale public works to improve the health of people in towns by improving water supplies and sanitation to eradicate endemic diseases such as cholera and typhus. At the same time child death rates and the unfitness of the (working-class) population, revealed by, for example, the large numbers of recruits for the Boer War who had to be sent away as unfit to serve, focused medical and charitable attention on the health of children, and the health-visiting service grew up to oversee child-rearing. At the turn of the century and in the years up to the First World War, those who advised and monitored mothers on the well-being of their children were predominantly medical men, or were medically trained and/or supervised. From that time until the 1960s, however, a different kind of 'medicine' evolved around a different view of what was needed in child-rearing (see Sapsford, 1993). The 'individual' psychology of mental traits and psychometric measure-ment, coupled with Freudian and other 'psychiatric' ideas about the formative role of a child's early years in making affectional ties and determining affective capacities, gave us a new view or humankind, and also a new kind of expert. Between the two World Wars a psychology developed of the way in which the mother's aberrant views and attitudes were conveyed to the child and how parental dishar-monies provided an unsettling and unsound 'symbolic environment'. After the Second World War this was reworked and re-theorized by cross-fertilization with the tradition of psychoanalysis. You will now hear Bowlby's ideas, for example, bandied about in any medical discussion of pregnancy or childbirth, without even being credited to him; they have passed into the taken-for-granted knowledge of medicine and maternity and become fact and 'common sense'.

While medicine and then psychology were taking command of the child and the home, similar kinds of changes were happening in the criminal justice system. In the middle of the 18th century the punishment for crime was public and intended to inspire terror in others; general deterrence was the major purpose of sentencing. By the middle of the 19th century public punishment had more or less disappeared, and executions were carried out in private. A more probable sentence for a large range of offences, by this time, was imprisonment, reflecting a different view of what the criminal was and what it was possible to do with him or her. The offender is considered as a psychological subject, reformable in his or her own right. Increasingly the courts are asking themselves what the offence tells us about the offender, what can be added by enquiry into home circumstances or mental state. In other words, they begin to treat the evidence before them as symptoms on which a diagnostic decision is to be made—a decision about what sentence is most likely to have a reformative effect. Judgements are made by reference to a set of norms about how the 'ordinary person' would behave and therefore the direction and extremity of the offender's deviance from these norms. Psychology and psychiatry soon become involved in the court process.

Within the prisons of the 19th century, prisoners were confined under a regime of 'even less eligibility' compared with people outside, but reclamation rather than simply punishment came to be the declared aim. Work was required of all prisoners; it was, after all, precisely their inability or unwillingness to take employment outside which had led them to this situation, so work and work habits had to lie at the centre of the cure. Prison was intended above all to work on the mind—to give criminals an opportunity for repentance and reform. Religious advice was available in prisons from their early years. Charitable men and women of the middle classes visited prisoners, to talk to them and reform by conversation and example. The start of the 20th century saw welfare/probation officers helping with resettlement and advising on how life should be run industriously and honestly, and the beginning of the provision of education for prisoners. And, of course, psychologists were installed in the prisons, partly to help classify offenders, fit them to particular roles in the regime and predict their behaviour, but also with great licence to run treatment programmes from a wide variety of theoretical perspectives—analysis, group work, skills training, role play, whatever would give the prisoner a more sensitive and healthier perspective on his or her own life, past and future.

At the same time, psychology was taking over the deviant outside prison as well. Psychological and psychiatric ways of 'framing' the child penetrate two other major institutions—the schools and the courts. 'The maladjusted child' (or similar formulations) began to appear as a label within the school system from about the end of the First World War. Child Guidance clinics grew up during the 1920s and 1930s to deal with behavioural problems identified at school, in the same way that the School Medical Service dealt with physical problems. A second point of application was to those identified as 'juvenile delinquents'. The juvenile courts established by the Children Act 1908 brought within the ambit and powers of the criminal law the supervision of families with adolescent children which health visitors carried out with fewer powers on families with younger children. Several of the London courts introduced routine psychological examination of children brought before them, and the burgeoning field of forensic examination and treatment was firmly claimed be the discipline of 'individual' psychology—foremost among whose exponents at the time was Cyril Burt.

This brief and over-simplified history is intended to demonstrate the rise of psychology as a branch of legitimate expertise in the area of delinquency and malfunction, and of psychologists as 'accredited experts'. Psychology took over the business of childhood sanity and moral development from medicine, along with the assessment of juveniles for the courts and the treatment of mentally/behaviourally malfunctioning children in the ordinary schools and in youth custodial institutions. It has also gained a firm foothold in prisons for adults. In so doing it has become like medicine in two respects.

1. It rests on the basis of a science which is accepted by influential non-scientists. This element of its authority is based on science's claim to empirical validation: *treatments* have been tested and their effects shown to be more than coincidental, and *theories* have been validated by correctly predicting the outcome of treatments. In psychology and psychiatry, as in physical medicine, this does not mean that the individual practitioners have personally validated their procedures, but they are able at least in principle to draw on the science's 'corpus of knowledge' to locate such validation. (This claim to validated knowledge is not always borne out even in physical medicine, as we shall see—non-validated 'traditional' procedures persist alongside validated ones. For a variety of reasons the claim to scientifically validated procedures tends to be less defensible in the psychotherapies even than in physical medicine. The 'science card' is played more often

by, for example, the cognitive and/or behavioural therapies and 'social skills' techniques, and less often by, for example. humanistic therapies.)
2. Psychoanalysts and therapists have attained a similar expert status to that of medical doctors (and the same standard and kind of professional behaviour is now expected of them).

That this 'medical model' fits the running of therapeutic communities very poorly does not matter; the authority to set them up still rests on the warrant of science on the one hand and on professional authority on the other. The ethical problems of therapy, as assessed within the 'scientific framework', tend to concentrate around two areas.

First, there is the duty to avoid harming patients. This is not an absolute duty, however, because harm is acceptable if good follows—the surgeon cuts the patient open, for example, in order to prevent greater harm, and lasting side-effects may be acceptable in drugs if the outcome is in the patient's interest. Similarly, a degree of embarrassment, distress or even malfunction may be acceptable if on balance the patient's life and social functioning are improved. (Note that in medicine the judge of this, ultimately, is the practitioner, or at least the practitioner's profession; this is a point to which we shall return.)

Other ethical questions mimic those of general medicine and concern the duty to behave in an acceptably professional manner. The 'doctor' takes responsibility for the well-being and the cure of the 'patient' and is professionally bound not to misuse power over patients for personal ends. He or she becomes a professional adviser to the patient (see 'service model' below) and so is required to put the patient's interests before those of others, to maintain confidentiality, and so on. Again there are acute problems with this set of requirements in the case of therapeutic communities, because they assume a kind of relationship and a kind of treatment which is fundamentally alien to the aims and working practices of the community. Again, however, to plead that the ethical criteria are inappropriate does not abolish the professional requirements, because they are what is required of the practitioner by his or her own profession and what the profession guarantees to the outside world in return for the right to police its own infractions and mistakes. In winning battles against conventional medicine, less conventional therapies became *assimilated* to medicine in a number of important respects. Acupuncture, for example, opens itself up to 'scientific' validation when it becomes available through the institutions of public health, and acupuncturists develop norms of professional qualification and models of professional organization and discipline which mirror those of the medical profession. The same has been true of 'mental therapies'. The BPS MSc in Clinical Psychology or D.Clin.Psych., for example, qualifies practitioners of certain kinds, and the BPS chartering procedures put them under discipline. Somewhat similar forms of organization are to be found among systemic/family therapists, gestalt therapists and psychodynamic practitioners, among many others.

THE RATIONALISTIC FRAMEWORK

An alternative framework, contradicting the scientific one, underlies some of the resistance to general medicine and is central within 'mental medicine'. This is what I have termed 'the rationalistic framework', though historically the term 'liberal' might be equally appropriate, as it informs and permeates such works as John Stuart Mill's *On Liberty* (1859). In this framework we talk not about the cure of bodies, even if the bodies have minds, but about people taking decisions, about the information they have available and the tools they have with which to process it. The root assumption of this approach is that every 'patient' or 'client' is a rational actor with the ability to make decisions about his or her life and the *right* to do so. (Exceptions are made for those who are seen as not having this capacity or not in full measure—John Stuart Mill exempted lunatics and children from a degree of responsibility—but advocacy movements and children's rights movements have brought into question whether these exemptions may validly be made.) This framework is the backing for a number of 'prison reform' and 'hospital reform' movements which question the power of doctors and therapists. For example, the 'justice movement' of the 1980s has expressed severe doubts about any element of sentencing which is aimed at welfare/ treatment or has an indeterminate/discretionary element, as violating the rights of individuals to fair and equal treatment and putting them at risk of arbitrary administrative action.

This framework tends to lead to a different kind of treatment from the 'scientific' one—not drugs or behavioural modification, but counselling, 'talk therapy', or group work. (This is not to say that one framework or the other *requires* a given style of therapy, but there does tend to be an association.) Implicit (often explicit) in therapy framed within the rationalistic framework is the notion that if people could only learn that other ways of seeing their worlds are possible and empowering then they would be free to behave and to experience

life in a different (more satisfying, more fulfilling, more pro-social) way.
This framework is prone to three dilemmas:

1. The status of therapy framed within a 'rationalistlc' discourse raises problems for 'scientific' assessment of outcome and efficacy. As Richard Stevens (1995) has pointed out, this kind of approach might be seen as carrying with it a different kind of epistemology (a different way of claiming and testing truth) from biological psychology or from even interpretative psychology which equates people with systems of meaning. Its claim is not that such and such treatment will work or have this or that effect—or even that it will work with known probability—but that a particular approach *may* enable some people, under some circumstances, to think and act differently *if* they wish to do so. It is a sufficient proof of this proposition that a single case can be described in which this effect has been obtained, and the proposition cannot be negated: that it did not work for this or that person or group does not mean it could not work for some people.

2. The approach is fundamentally democratic—it assumes every adult competent to determine his or her best interests and act within them—and it therefore does away with the inbuilt power advantage of the therapist. In other words, informed consent is required; beyond this, indeed, those who use the techniques are seen as working on *themselves*, with the therapist present only as facilitator. This stance is explicit in full-blown therapeutic communities, where non-staff participants are effectively recruited to act as therapists and the distinction between staff and other participants is blurred, if not actually abolished. One may reasonably ask, however, whether this is a realistic position to take, or whether it involves an inherent deceit. Is it possible to 'give away' the power of the therapist in any situation where one party to the transaction is identifiable at all as *the* therapist? It may be possible in fully collaborative co-therapy, where two equal practitioners work on each other and themselves simultaneously (see. e.g. Heron, 1981), but can it ever honestly be claimed for a relationship inherently based on unequal access to 'professional' knowledge and expertise?

3. Thirdly, because the process is conceived as democratic, one may ask what gives the therapist the right to intervene. In therapeutic intervention the implicit or explicit claim is that the therapist can validly determine the outcome of therapy—that he or she knows better than the user/client what constitutes a good outcome and

can therefore validly direct the therapeutic process. This involves a contradiction within the rationalistic framework, however, because it is not clear what validates the therapist to make this claim. Indeed, it points up a dispute of long standing within the therapeutic community movement, between those who value the democratic process in its own right and those who value it as a therapeutic tool (see Kennard, 1983, pp. 53–4). As Cummings and Cummings said in 1962, 'the problem of determining whose concept of [the client's] welfare should be used is endemic in the healing and helping arts'.

There is a further conceptual/ethical/political problem concerning any work which stresses social interaction over independent decision. Much 'talk therapy' involves group work or even communal interaction— therapeutic communities are the obvious case of this, but the same considerations apply to much of what is done in groups. An essential feature of such arrangements is that hegemony lies with the group rather than the individual, at least while the group is in session (which is all the time in a therapeutic community). A purpose of the group or community is that individuals shall learn to open themselves to the group and/or subordinate their individual desires to what the group wants/decides communally to do, or at least that they should experiment with doing so. However, the right of the majority to take away the rights of the individual is not assumed within the rationalistic framework. Indeed, it is not clear in the rationalistic framework what makes the majority decision better than that of the individual; there is no basis within it for supposing that the majority must be right, when majority and individual are in conflict.

All of this poses conceptual and ethical problems which are much magnified when the therapeutic relationship (or, even more, the therapeutic group or community) is located within an institution. It is not clear to what extent full and free consent can be forthcoming even in principle in an institution to which the individual is confined against his or her will. Nor is it clear to what extent it is possible even in principle to implement a regime which presupposes the freedom of individuals or of groups/communities to 'set the rules' and experiment within them, within the walls of an institution whose fundamental purposes are at odds with this.

THE SERVICE MODEL

This is very much the conventional view of therapy—the dominant model, at least as regards privately arranged and purchased transactions—and it combines features of both the scientific and the rationalistic model. The basic metaphor is that of car servicing: I take my car to the garage for repair, my body to the doctor and my mind to the psychiatrist or psychologist. The model follows the scientific framework in acknowledging the power and knowledge of experts and seeing the person as something with 'a mind' which is separable from the rest of the person and which can have 'diseases' or 'malfunctions' which in turn are separately identifiable and treatable. At the same time, the stress on the patient as contracting client shows a strong colouring of the 'rationalistic' framework.

The Service Model has most of the strengths of both frameworks and avoids some of the pitfalls which their conjunction brings—for example, the problem of what validates the expert's intervention and his or her judgement of desirable outcomes. The intervention of the expert is validated by contract, and the knowledge of outcomes may then be validated by the expertise, which is what the client is paying for. In other words, the model grounds practitioners' expertise in the scientific framework, but it grounds the therapeutic relationship in the rationalistic framework: the client identifies a problem and willingly accepts therapeutic discipline in order to solve it.

A major problem for this model, however, is that the science on which the expert's 'expertise' is based may be open to doubt; the scientific basis of psychological medicine is less than consensual. In physical medicine what is sold as 'medical 'knowledge' may on occasions be grossly wrong—see Scully & Bart (1978), for example, for a bitterly funny account of myths about female biology and function purveyed to medical students in widely used textbooks, or Abbott & Sapsford (1987) for the myths about Down's syndrome children presented until recently in the standard textbook on the subject for doctors in training. There are well accepted and 'scientifically based' procedures, well theorized and grounded in a clear understanding of the aetiology of a condition, where the research evidence suggests that the apparently authoritative theoretical grounding is mistaken or at least not consonant with evidence—see, for example, Posner (1976) on blood-sugar normaliz-ation in diabetes. By and large, however, the body is increasingly transparent to medical science. By contrast, there are very many different theoretical formulations about 'the workings of the mind', often in conflict with each other and often requiring very different levels of theorization. Further, in physical medicine the outcomes are clear: it is clear what is meant by 'mending a broken leg' and fairly clear what is meant by 'controlling the symptoms of diabetes'. What counts as recovery from or control of 'mental illness' is much less clear—whether the emotional experience of the patient, or the ability to conform to normal social behaviour, or the ability *not* to conform but to innovate, or ... Consequently there is more scope for disagreement among practitioners and therefore less consensus about what counts as ethical treatment.

The accusation of 'pseudo-science' levelled at *any given therapy* is not necessarily a problem for the Service Model as a whole. After all, I take my car to the garage and do not understand the mechanics of what is done to it. Indeed, I may doubt the diagnosis which the engineer applied and feel that my bill has been 'padded' by unnecessary work. However, even if I believe that garages are sometimes ignorant and sometimes dishonest, I still take my car to them, because they are the only way of getting it repaired. Similarly I could have doubts about the honesty or competence of a 'mental mechanic' and still take my mind to him or her, as the only way to get it repaired. If there is any risk that *all* therapy can be seen as open to doubt, however, the model fails. Physical medicine is currently going through a crisis of confidence, as more and more of what is done at local level by General Practitioners comes to be seen as validated more by the social authority of doctors than by their supposed scientific expertise. The price paid for becoming a profession is that resentment of the profession's authority can be translated into examination of the profession's knowledge base, which leaves it vulnerable to being totally undermined just where it trusts itself to be strongest.

Another set of conceptual (and ethical) problems revolve around the concept of 'contract' which is central to the service model—the notion that the client freely chooses to undergo therapy, on the basis of available information. The least of these problems, paradoxically, is the problem of informed consent. It really is not clear to what extent the client can ever make a free choice, not knowing the psychological/psychiatric literature to the same extent as the practitioner. Further, it is not clear in what sense the decision is ever truly free; even 'voluntary patients' are present because someone or some institution—partner, work, the criminal justice system—made the alternatives to therapy, unacceptable. This is particularly the case with therapy within an institution such as a prison or psychiatric hospital, and particularly when there is any degree of indeterminacy in the prisoner's or patient's potential length of stay in the institution. We must always suppose that a desire to 'influence the judge' will affect the client's choice to some extent. However, similar problems are faced by one who takes their car to the garage—the repairs are not elective, but made necessary by the non-functioning of the car or the legal requirements of the time, and we choose our garages and agree 'courses of treatment' for our cars without much knowledge of what is involved. In therapy, however, the ethical issues remain despite the practical necessity to choose. The model is therefore able to deal as well with this problem in its metaphorical application as in the real situation from which the metaphor is drawn.

A more serious problem concerns the parties to the contract (see Goffman, 1961). When I take my car into the garage for repair, the contract is between the garage and specifically *me*, and the garage is supposed to satisfy *my* declared needs. When I take it in for its MOT test, however, there are three parties to the contract—me (in many ways the minor party), the tester, and the law/the government. The latter is a better model for most psychiatric transactions than the former. Some clients may appear because their lives or styles of thought are a problem to them, but more often they are there because they are a problem to other people. In the short range, the 'client' of the therapist might as easily be thought to be the parents or spouse or relatives, or the employer. In the long range the client might be seen as humanity at large—as the MOT certifies a car fit to be driven safely near other people, so the outcome of the therapeutic process might be seen as rendering the person fit to be lived with or near. (Where behaviour and beliefs are at stake, however, rather than just mechanical state, 'fitness to be with others' can easily become 'conformity to the existing social order', so there is a political dimension to this.) In the penal or other custodial institution the therapeutic process can also have the institution itself as one of its notional clients; 'maintaining a quiet nick' has to be one of the aims of everyone who works or lives in a prison.

Some of the ethical problems of confidentiality for therapy staff working in any institution located within the system of criminal justice and public order (a system which includes all prisons and many of the functions of psychiatric hospitals) stem from uncertainties in this notion of 'contract'. It is not clear to what extent 'the client' can ever really be the client, entitled to the right of confidentiality, when it is the therapist's duty (not just as staff member but also as concerned citizen) to make reports on inmates and contribute to decisions about release, privileges, suitability for certain types of work or accommodation, and the like. In these circumstances the inmate becomes less the car-owner, to continue the 'service' metaphor, and more the car, to be worked on and tested in the service of someone else. (Putting it another way, therapists have the privilege of speaking on behalf of clients whose voice might not otherwise be heard or at least heeded—but one man's 'privilege to represent' is another's 'breach of confidence'!) It has been argued that psychology, and particularly therapy, are social agents before they are anything else:

> Psychology—all of it—is a branch of the police; psychodynamic and humanistic psychologies are the secret police. (Richer, 1992, p. 118)

One might argue that group work has less of a policing function, because it is 'patient-driven', and therapeutic communities even less, because they function without the constant presence of the therapist. However, it would be just as fair to liken them to the 'self-examination' sessions of Russian and Chinese schools and political institutions—occasions or environments whose purpose is to extract confession of fault, by pressure from others if it is not spontaneously produced, and this is another kind of policing. (See, for example, Rapoport et al. (1960) for patients' accounts of feedback sessions as being comparable to being before a court.)

Indeed, groups and communities pose particular ethical problems in this respect for their participants as much as for the therapist. They function to induce openness of thought and feeling, and this can mean that participants get to know as much about the thoughts, feelings and behaviour of others as if they had been close and trusted friends for years—but without the duty of confidentiality and mutual protection which friendship would entail. Indeed, the basic working rules of communal therapy in prison make contradictory demands on honest participants. They are required to be open and honest and to expect a similar honesty from others. In the interests of the group, the environment or the therapy they may be required to pass on negative information about other participants. In the interests of the participants, however, they should *not* pass it on, because those to whom they pass it may have the power to harm. This leads to a second-order dilemma for those who set up and run such activities or regimes—to what extent is it ethical to face vulnerable participants with this kind of dilemma?

THE ECONOMISTIC FRAMEWORK

The final and very different, framework also helps to shape our views of therapy and to create the ethical problems which its practitioners face. I have called this 'the economistic framework', but alternative names might have used the adjectives 'capitalist' or 'managerial'. This is the view of population as a resource for the nation—for the nation's industry—and its efficient and effective management. It is the other side of 'Victorian values' and liberal political philosophy. The free, competent, contract-making individual of John Stuart Mill or of John Locke was one view which the Victorians had of men (their views of women being another matter entirely), but it is muddled up with a more Hobbesian view, the view of Chadwick and the Poor Law reformers, of man as something in need of restraint, management and direction. Psychology grew up as a discipline in the service of this more Hobbesian framework—in the service of industry, the control of the poor and the education of the young as productive and disciplined workers (see Rose, 1985, 1989; Sapsford, 1993).

Industrial manufacture rests on three elements—capital (plant, buildings), raw materials and the labour force. The essence of the capitalist system is that each has to be correctly exploited—the maximum output extracted for the minimum outlay—in order that profit shall be made for reinvestment, for the reward of shareholders and as the remuneration of the owner/managers. The overall watchword was efficiency, the most efficient use of all three elements of production: the industrialist Robert Owen prided himself that the 'animate machines' in his factories were run as efficiently as the inanimate one (Owen, 1813, quoted in Ignatieff, 1978). The 'scientific' attempts to rationalize production, and the growth of companies and consequent bureaucratic problems in the administration of individual workers, helped to define occupational psychology as an emerging discipline and to validate it as a knowledge-base for understanding and managing the most malleable element of the production process, the workers themselves. By the Second World War, psychologists and psychologically inspired ideas were well entwined in industry.

The efficient use of resource meant having a workforce that was trained, not just in the simple sense of being able to work a machine or use a tool, but in the more fundamental sense of being content to be a machine-minder or tool-user and taking pride in the work.

> Entrepreneurs concerned to 'make such machines of men as cannot err' [Josiah Wedgwood, cited in McKendrick, 1961, p. 46] soon discovered that physical threat and economic coercion will not suffice; men have to be taught to *internalise* the new attitudes and responses, to discipline themselves. (Scull, 1989, pp. 91–92)

The process started with schooling, continued through the handling and reclamation of delinquent and truant children, was impressed on the children of the poor and informed the management of workers in factories and commercial establishments. Psychology was very active in this process, and the activity in turn established psychology as a discipline and a profession (see Holloway, 1991). The same kind of thinking applied to the handling of criminals and the mentally ill. Those who were a danger—whose degenerate values would spread to the respectable poor and ultimately bring down the economy—were segregated for society's protection. Where possible, however, the efficient use of the nation's human resource—elevated to a moral principle—meant reclaiming what could be reclaimed. In the process, what we see is the development of a knowledge-base for the reformation of prisoners, simultaneously with a view of prisoners as treatable in this way—a view which makes it reasonable that this knowledge-base should be applied. It is the same knowledge-base that informs the surveillance of children, the development of educational psychology and the application of 'scientific' principles to the selection and management of factory workers.

One characteristic of recent years, within this economistic framework, has been the fast rise of the concept of 'management' as interpreted by New Right social thinkers. Over the past 10 years the concept of management in the industrial/commercial sense has been applied to institutions where its appropriateness would not seem to be immediately apparent—hospitals, schools, universities, social services departments, prisons. We are now having markets—often 'quasi-markets' whose very existence rests on a fiction sustained by state action—established in the provision of health and education and even in the criminal justice system. The aim appears to be not to provide the best service, or an effective service, or as effective a service as we can afford, but an efficient service in some absolute or moral sense—the minimum necessary, at the minimum necessary expense. Managerialism questions ends only in the sense of asking 'Is this necessary?'. If the end is seen as necessary, then the questions all centre on how to provide it at minimum expense—or, often, how to provide less in order to minimize expense. Competition between providers avoids the sin of waste—it avoids waste of resources in the sense that we find the minimum price for a given service, but also waste of provision in that the process seems inevitably to lead to establishing the minimum that can be provided without public upset. Working to the minimum means a degree of oversight and direction that would not previously have been seen as acceptable, in terms of working conditions: we are monitored and managed in ways that would not have seemed natural or appropriate even 10 years ago.

More important, the *concept* of management now holds sway; in the rhetoric of organizations, professional autonomy has given way to efficient management. At the same time, this hegemony of 'management' has an insidious political effect; managing an organiz-ation which has social consequences for people is an intensely political activity—it means setting goals and determining means—but managerialism represents itself as a set of techniques and talks about technical competence rather than political intention. The other side of this coin is that governments can distance themselves from the politics of key areas; managerialism in the health service has the effect of shifting the arena from politics to economics—we ask not what health care should be provided and to whom, but how waste can be avoided—and there is every sign that the Government are in the process of dissociating themselves from whole areas of policing, public order and penal policy (see McLaughlin & Muncie, 1994).

> ... managerialism has helped to shift the public political discourse about social policy away from traditional concerns with inputs and outputs towards an overarching concern with efficiency and the organisational means of service delivery. In the neo-conservative vision managers take on the responsibility for the delivery of services while the government prioritises, funds and evaluates. (Clarke et al., 1994, p. 231)

Prisons have been judged in the past on the basis of industrial efficiency—their efficiency as sources of cheap labour. They have been judged in terms of their longer-term efficiency in instilling 'habits of industry' and reclaiming potential workers from crime. Above all, however, they are judged quite simply by whether they manage to contain the people sent to them for containment; other aims may be pursued with the contained, but it is now clearly acknowledged that containment is their first end. This has implications for those, such as therapists, who work within prison, because they are effectively following a private goal. They may be encouraged to undertake rehabili-tative work, and they may be applauded for any success it achieves, but such work really is secondary to the main goal of containment.

The subsidiary nature of rehabilitative procedures in the penal environment poses substantial problems for therapists who work there—questions discussed above which centre around the doubt as to who the client is. The whole 'management ethos' also poses problems, however (shared with other therapists, in hospitals and in the community, who undertake state-funded work). There is of course nothing wrong with monitoring performance—we should all welcome quality checks on how we do our jobs, and on our better days we do. Individual therapy, however, thrives in an atmosphere of privacy: confidentiality and the two-person relationship are very strong elements of it. Work undertaken in groups or communities may be more open within the group, but it still does not allow the presence of 'outsiders'. What is really going on, therefore, cannot ethically (or practically) be monitored, and 'managers' lack the information they need to make rational decisions. For that reason, as elsewhere in health work, in social work and in some aspects of education, the 'need to manage' leads to the selection of of what the professional may consider irrelevant indicators, and/or to rapid vacillation between different sets of indicators, none of which is satisfactory. The method of management is also inimical to the autonomy expected by professional workers and can lead to conflicts which will be categorized by management as about techniques or efficiency but may take on an ethical character for the workers who are managed. The pressure to minimize services in the interest of efficiency (= decreased cost) will give rise to similar conflicts, with therapy and other rehabilitative and training measures taking the brunt of cuts when security can take no more without failing in the prime purpose of the institution.

CONCLUSIONS

In this chapter I have not tried to solve the ethical dilemmas of therapy, nor of therapeutic communities, nor even of therapeutic communities in prison. My aim has been the more limited one of cataloguing some of the moral problems which may trouble some therapists (and others) on some occasions and locating them within four 'frameworks' which act as moral/conceptual maps making different demands on the practitioner.

1. A 'scientific' or 'positivistic' framework has been identified which is concerned with the cure or at least amelioration of diseased states—physical diseases and handicaps, 'mental illness' and 'maladjustment', 'criminality', and so on. The knowledge-base for this framework, in relation to 'mental illness' etc., is psychology as 'the science of the mind'. Whether or not it sees itself as a branch of medicine—'mental medicine'—it takes its status and many of its working rules from the professional status and professional practices of medical doctors. Its model of the person is basic ally as a machine which may malfunction but can benefit from the practitioner's skill. Its origins can be traced to the Victorian era and the first half-century of capitalist industrialization, though it has been much modified during later historical periods.

2. The 'rationalistic' framework, it was suggested, also reaches its full modern form in the Victorian period and represents one side of liberal philosophy/politics. Its view of the person and of social relations is extreme individualism, and tacitly it posits therapy as something for the most part unethical in itself—the interference of one adult in the concerns of another, both being rational and capable of taking responsibility for their own actions. Therapy would be justified only where the individual was not capable of assuming this responsibility, and then the rules of the scientific framework would hold good—treatment for the good of the patient, but also of society, drawing on the skills of the practitioner.

3. The 'service' model, I have suggested, is a complex of ideas which draws on both frameworks and overcomes this particular problem of the rationalistic framework; it posits the legitimation of therapy carried out on a responsible adult as being a contract freely entered into by both parties. This in turn raises ethical problems, however, about the validity of the expertise which is offered and, even more, the multiplicity of parties to any supposed contract (relatives, employers, 'society' and government, as well as therapist and client). These problems are more acute in institutions and most acute of all in penal institutions.

4. I have suggested that an economistic/managerial conceptual framework, the other side of Victorian liberal values, also impinges on therapy, but from outside. The model of the person as a resource to be exploited and motivated for the most efficient and least wasteful production of wealth has become somewhat transmuted, in its applications outside the sphere of industry/commerce, by an overemphasis on the sin of waste. The goal now is not just the minimization of wasted resources and the close management and monitoring even of formerly autonomous professions to that end. Now 'efficiency' appears also to entail the minimization of wasted provision; provision at the lowest cost is becoming replaced with the minimization of provision, within the limits of what the electorate will tolerate. ('The rolling back of the state' necessarily also means the rolling back of state-provided services.)

These sometimes incompatible conceptual frameworks apply to group work and therapeutic communities as much as to more individualistic or family-based therapy, and here the ethical dilemmas can appear the most acute of all. 'Being a professional practitioner' means taking responsibility (and therefore authority) and having a knowledge-base on which to determine the best outcome; the 'scientific' framework depends on the authority of the practitioner and its solutions to ethical dilemmas depend on the authority of the practitioner. This is not compatible with the 'giving away' of the power of the therapist which is explicit in at least the rhetoric of some communities. Respect for the rights and competence of the individual—the basis of ethical solutions within the rationalist framework—is not compatible with the tyranny of the majority and the concession to other inmates/residents of the power of the therapist. Any attempt to provide therapy is implicitly at odds with the 'economistic' philosophy of minimum provision, unless it can be shown to be more cost-effective than any alternative, including the alternative of taking no action.

Thus there can be no clear-cut conclusions, because the moral dilemmas are not soluble. They exist in a clash of frameworks, and one framework cannot be established over others by logical means as better or more correct. However, this is not to say, either, that the dilemmas are in any sense unreal or 'merely the product of discourse'; they represent real, painful and intractable problems. Certainly they cannot be 'explained away'; knowing their origins and rendering them analytically distinct and therefore visible may help, but it does not abolish the problems.

REFERENCES

Abbott, P. A. & Sapsford, R. J. (1987). *Community Care for Mentally Handicapped Children: The Origins and Consequences of a Social Policy.* Milton Keynes: Open University Press.
Burt, C. (1925). *The Young Delinquent.* London: University of London Press.
Clarke, J., Cochrane, A. & McLaughlin, E. (1994). Mission accomplished or unfinished business? The impact of managerialisation. In J. Clarke, A. Cochrane & E. McLaughlin (Eds). *Managing Social Policy.* London: Sage.
Cummings, J. & Cummings, E. (1962). *Ego and Milieu.* New York: Prentice Hall.
Foucault, M. (1963). *The Birth of the Clinic.* London: Tavistock (1973).
Goffman, E. (1961). Some vicissitudes of the tinkering trades. In *Asylums: Essays on the Social Situation of Mental Patients and Other Inmates.* New York: Doubleday Anchor.
Heron, J. (1981). Experiential research methodology. In P. Reason & J. Rowan (Eds). *Human Inquiry: a Sourcebook of New Paradigm Research.* Chichester: Wiley.
Holloway, W. (1991). *Work Psychology and Organisational Behaviour: Managing the Individual at Work.* London: Sage.
Ignatieff, M. (1878). *A Just Measure of Pain: The Penitentiary in the Industrial Revolution 1750–1850.* New York: Random House.

Kennard, D. (1983). *An Introduction to Therapeutic Communities*. London: Routledge and Kegan Paul.

Main, T. (1946). The hospital as a therapeutic institution. *Bulletin of the Menninger Clinic*, **10**, 66–70.

McKendrick, N. (1961). Josiah Wedgwood and factory discipline. *Historical Journal*, **4**.

McLaughlin, E. & Muncie, J. (1994). Managing the criminal justice system. In J. Clarke, A. Cochrane & E. McLaughlin (Eds). *Managing Social Policy*. London: Sage.

Mill, J. S. (1859). *On Liberty*.

Rapoport, R. N., Rapoport, R. & Rosow, I. (1960). *Community as Doctor: New Perspectives on a Therapeutic Community*. London: Tavistock.

Posner, T. (1976). Magical elements in orthodox medicine. In R. Dingwall et al. (Eds). *Health Care and Health Knowledge*. London : Croom Helm.

Richer, P. (1992). An introduction to deconstructionist psychology. In S. Kvale (Ed). *Psychology and Postmodernism*. London: Sage.

Rose, N. (1985). *The Psychological Complex: Psychology, Politics and Society in England 1869–1939*. London: Routledge and Kegan Paul.

Rose, N. (1989). *Governing the Soul: The Shaping of the Private Self*. London: Routledge.

Sapsford, R. J. (1993). Understanding people: the growth of an expertise. In J. Clarke (Ed.). *A Crisis in Care? Challenges to Social Work*. London: Sage.

Scull, A. (1989). *Social order/Mental Disorder: Anglo-American Psychiatry in Historical Perspective*. London: Routledge.

Scully, D. & Bart, P. (1978). A funny thing happened on the way to the orifice. In J. Ehrenreich (Ed.). *Cultural Crisis of Modern Medicine*. New York: Monthly Review Press.

Stevens, R. (1996). Trimodal theory as a model for interrelating perspectives in psychology. In R. J. Sapsford (Ed.). *Issues for Social Psychology*. Milton Keynes: The Open University.

PART II

Lessons from Therapeutic Communities

CHAPTER 3

A Community based TC: The Henderson Hospital

Bridget Dolan

Henderson Hospital, Sutton, Surrey, UK

The development of the therapeutic community (TC) model in Britain comes predominantly from the work of two British psychiatrists, Maxwell Jones and Tom Main (Jones, 1946, 1952, 1956a,b; Main, 1946). Today their legacy remains within the National Health Service in the Henderson and Cassel Hospitals, the only two British NHS inpatient Therapeutic Communities specializing in patients with personality disorders. However, although the units share many similarities, Henderson Hospital tends to work with clients at the more forensic end of the spectrum, treating both men and women with psychopathic, antisocial and borderline personality disorder, whilst the Cassel Hospital aims its treatment towards the more neurotic and less severely personality-disordered client and treats predominantly women (Chiesa, 1995).

THE ORIGINS OF HENDERSON HOSPITAL[1]

Henderson Hospital, which was the first British unit to develop a therapeutic community patient-oriented approach to the treatment of psychopathic and severe personality disorder, has its origins in changes which were occurring after World War II in psychiatric hospitals, which emphasized a move away from an authoritarian

Therapeutic Communities for Offenders.
Edited by E. Cullen, L. Jones and R. Woodward. © 1997 John Wiley & Sons Ltd.

doctor–patient model to a more democratic style of staff and patient interaction including, importantly, more active participation of the patients in their own treatment (Bridger, 1946; Davidson, 1946; Foulkes, 1946). Thus, responsibility for the day-to-day running of the unit is shared among patients and staff. This collaborative and democratic style, whereby the community itself is invested with an important decision-making function, forms a cornerstone of therapy (Jones, 1952). Main, who coined the term 'therapeutic community' in 1946, suggests that it is not, however, 'the structure, but the culture which is decisive for the human relations on offer' and that the TC is a 'culture of enquiry ... into personal and interpersonal and inter-system problems' including 'the study of impulses, defences and relations, expressed and arranged socially' (Main, 1946, 1983; Norton, 1992a).

The early roots of Henderson are in the 'Effort Syndrome' unit established during the war at Mill Hill Military Hospital in London (Murto, 1991). Effort Syndrome was a psychosomatic complaint with symptomatology of breathlessness, palpitations, left chest pains, postural giddiness and fatigue (Jones, 1952). It was at Mill Hill during 1940–1945 that Maxwell Jones created the basis for a treatment model later to be called the therapeutic community, with his central realization of the strength of peer-group support in large group situations and the value of fellow patients in passing on the culture and the message to new admissions (Jones, 1942; 1946). Small group discussions were instituted, usually led by a doctor, with a selected topic. The groups were both eductional (in regard to the origin of symptoms) and philosophical in directing the patients to consider problems in the wider social milieu of their life and times. It was noticed that the older patients began to tell the new ones what they had learnt from these groups, expressed in a more understand-able language. The new patients seemed to acquire knowledge more quickly as the older patients took over the role of the staff for themselves.

From this early experimental community at Mill Hill, Jones moved temporarily to another ex-POW unit at Dartford. The Ministry of Labour showed increasing interest in Jones' communal treatment and in 1947 Jones took charge of the new 100-bedded 'Industrial Neurosis Unit' at Belmont Hospital (later the 'Social Rehabilitation Unit' and renamed 'Henderson Hospital' in 1959) The unit catered for many emotionally disturbed Prisoners of War returning from the Far East and suffering with neuroses and character disorders leading to chronic social and emotional disablement. The fear of death, hunger, torture and isolation from friends and families had led many to acquire antisocial behaviours, or adjustment problems, or to be obsessed with feelings of guilt. Although post-traumatic stress disorder was not then recognized in psychiatric glossaries, it seems likely that the traumatic experiences of war and imprisonment of many of the patients was at the root of their present disturbances.

As Jones developed his group approach it became clear that the experiment was not only useful in wartime, and many social misfits and neurotic casualties could be helped through the work to find resources within themselves to lead more fulfilling lives (Jones, 1956a). Whiteley (1980) describes how the development of the unit required internal reorganization of the traditional hospital structures to incorporate the changed status of patients; thus the treatment approach of the Unit moved away from an authoritarian, hierarchical style to one which was more collaborative and democratic. Patients were expected to take an active part both in their own treatment and in that of other patients. The traditional hierarchy between doctor/ nurse/patient became less rigid; there was more open communication among these sub-groupings and this was facilitated by daily discussion of the whole Unit, comprising all its sub-groups (Jones, 1952) . Jones later described how 'by the end of the War we were convinced that people living together in hospital, whether patients or staff, derived great benefit from examining, in daily community meetings, what they were doing and why they were doing it' (Jones, 1968).

The focus moved from 'Industrial Rehabilitation' to 'Social Rehabilitation' as it was realized that the inability to settle in a job was due more to lack of social and interpersonal skills than to any specific lack of industrial or educational expertise. Patients were referred more frequently from the Courts or through Rehabilitation Officers and Social Work agencies, and some came directly from prison to treatment. Even in these early days around 20% of admissions had criminal records (Baker, 1952). Many of the population suffered from character disorders of a kind usually considered unsuitable for psychotherapy or physical treatment methods. They were classified as inadequate and aggressive psychopaths; schizoid personalities; early schizophrenics; drug addicts; sexual perverts and chronic psychoneurotics (Jones, 1952). A proportion also had organic disorders such as epilepsy (Sandler, 1952).

In 1959 the unit, which offered a combined psychotherapeutic and sociotherapeutic approach, was renamed 'Henderson Hospital' after Professor Sir David Henderson. Henderson was the author of the classic text *Psychopathic States* (1939) and originator of the terms 'predominantly aggressive', 'inadequate' and 'creative' psychopaths; he had been Jones' mentor for 5 years during his psychiatric training in Edinburgh. The Unit was now known for its two areas of specialization: first, as the centre of the therapeutic community ideology, and second, as a unique treatment unit for psychopaths.

In the first major evaluation of Jones' unit Robert Rapoport and his colleagues spent 4 years there between 1953 and 1957. They were funded by the Nuffield Foundation to conduct an evaluative study of the treatment of psychopaths, which became an in-depth exploration of the workings of the therapeutic community. The research team consisted of anthropologists, sociologists, psychoanalysts, a psychologist, a social worker and a statistician, and their research findings are reported in the now seminal text *Community as Doctor* (Rapoport, 1960). In the book the four central tenets of the Henderson Therapeutic Community are described as: democratization (in decision-making); communalism (in sharing tasks and responsibilities); reality confrontation (of the subject with what he is doing here and now and its effects upon others); permissiveness (in tolerating behaviours and allowing mistakes).

In this early study a very limited evaluation of outcome was made by considering 64 patients one year after discharge. Patients were personally interviewed and classified according to such very basic criteria as 'improved', 'same' or 'worse' than when they entered the unit. On these criteria, 41 % of discharges were considered improved, 28% unchanged and 31% worse. The improvement rate increased with length of stay on the unit, with a good outcome reported for 52% of those who stayed more than 200 days. These initial results were encouraging; however, the mode of evaluation is far from satisfactory because it is based solely upon clinical judgement with no standardized objective measurement or control sample.

In developing the TC model, Jones had envisaged a range of treatment approaches that included open and closed units in hospitals, and a closed prison unit such as East and Hubert (1939) had described in the mid-30s. By the 1950s the Henderson's ideology and treatment methods were fast becoming renowned in the fields of criminology and penology at home and abroad. Jones contributed greatly to the debate on the inclusion of psychopathic disorder in the 'new' 1959 Mental Health Act. Professor Baan of the Department of Criminology at Utrecht drew on Jones' models to set up a Psychopathic Unit in Holland in 1955 (the Van der Hoeven Clinic); from there staff came to Belmont for initial training (Baan, 1961; Feldbrugge, 1992). The California Department of Corrections was also influenced by contact with Jones, and Dennie Briggs, after a period at Belmont, set up a therapeutic community in a maximum security prison at Chino (Briggs, 1972).

In 1959 Jones left Henderson for a one-year Commonwealth Visiting Professorship at Stanford. However, on his return to the UK he took up the post of Superintendent at Dingleton Hospital in Scotland. Under the new Director (F. H. Taylor, a former prison doctor who was appointed in 1960) the population of the Henderson became a more delinquent one as his interests were in the field of delinquency and its treatment. Even by 1960 Jones commented that the type of patient observed in Rapoport's study had 'given way to even more socially troublesome types'. The proportion of court referrals had risen from 10% in 1956 to 30% (Jones, 1960; Taylor, 1966) and by 1965 66% of patients had a history of a conviction compared with 37% in 1955 (Whiteley, 1980). Training groups were conducted by Henderson staff at Holloway Women's Prison and at a Borstal for young offenders. One of the female staff later became an Assistant Governor of Holloway Prison (Smith, 1966) whilst several nurses moved to a career in the Probation Service. The staff of the then newly opened Grendon Underwood prison for psychopathic offenders also began to attend Henderson for training placements from about 1962 onwards.

The importance of the 'rehabilitation' aspect of the Henderson community at the time is shown in two outcome studies that focused upon employment and decreased criminal activity as markers of successful treatment.

Tuxford (1961) reported one of the first outcome studies using objective data alongside clinical impressions. She followed up 86 consecutive male probation and Borstal licence cases for up to 22 months after discharge. Sending a postal questionnaire to the probation officer she obtained a response rate of 84% and found that 61% of patients traced were free of conviction on follow-up. Adjustment was assessed on a scale from 1 (increased sense of responsibility, employment and no further offending) to 4 (further offending, unemployment and lock of responsibility). On this rating, 24% and 31% fell into the first two categories respectively, i.e. 55% showed improvement. However, 28% were in the poor outcome category and a further 17% were considered 'complete failures'.

Taylor (1966) reports a similar good outcome in terms of employment history of patients discharged between 1959 and 1961. Approximately one-quarter (22%) found their own employment and a further 47% were placed by the Disablement Resettlement Officer (DRO). Those placed by the DRO were followed up 9 months later and 60% of those traced were still in work and given a satisfactory report by their employer.

In 1966 Dr Stuart Whiteley took over as Medical Director of Henderson, and a new matron was also appointed from the Cassel

Hospital whence had come the two previous senior nursing officers. Whiteley felt that by this time the Unit was now firmly regarded as a treatment centre for delinquents and the therapeutic community aspect was perhaps secondary (Whiteley, 1980). The criminological research and publications from Henderson from the 1970s to the early 1980s show how Henderson continued to be regarded as a special resource in the treatment of psychopaths (Whiteley, 1967; 1970; Copas & Whiteley, 1976; Gudjonsson & Roberts, 1981a, 1982; 1985) and many of a Whiteley's writings from the time are in the field of delinquency, although his approach was also informed by a group analytic perspective (Whiteley et al., 1972; Whiteley, 1973; 1994; Whiteley & Gordon, 1979).

Whiteley's interest in group analysis led him to investigate the therapeutic factors within the Henderson Community by applying Bloch et al.'s (1979) methods, which had originally been designed for investigating curative factors in group psychotherapy, to the entire Henderson community environment (Whiteley & Collis, 1987). Residents[2] were asked on two occasions to identify the 'most important event' in therapy that week; this was then coded according to Bloch's schema. 'Learning from interpersonal actions', 'acceptance' and 'self-understanding' were the most frequently reported types of events. Although 16% of these 'most important events' were within the small group psychotherapy sessions, it was noteworthy that over half of the events recorded took place outside the formal group therapy time and in only two reported events was a staff member cited as primarily involved in the event. Thus the study indicated the importance of the informal 'sociotherapy' and 24 hour living and learning experience, which continues alongside the formal 'psychotherapy' to make up the total therapeutic community milieu.

During Whiteley's 22 years at Henderson he was involved in a series of studies which are still some of the most important and largest scale studies of the outcome of treatment of psychopaths conducted in any institution. These early investigations all focus upon the easily 'measurable' outcome variables of recidivism and hospital readmission, on the assumption that these factors are adequate proxies for change in core pathology. Given the difficulties involved in the measurement of personality disorder and changes in internal psychological states it is perhaps understandable, particularly when it is the criminal behaviour and psychiatric service usage which initially brings the client to the attention of professionals, that in seeking to confirm the efficacy of Henderson treatment such factors would be considered.

In the first study, Whiteley (1970) followed up 122 consecutively admitted male patients. These men are described as suffering from psychopathic or sociopathic disorder with no psychosis or organic mental illness. In total, 87 (78%) had previously been convicted, 52 (46%) had served a prison sentence and 57 (51%) were on probation at admission, and 66 (60%) had a previous psychiatric admission. The men were studied 2 years after discharge and follow-up data were obtained for all but 14 men (two of whom had emigrated). Information was gained from the Criminal Records Office and the Ministry of Health Psychiatric Index and 63 (51%) were followed up by personal interview. In total 49 (40%) of patients had no further psychiatric admission or conviction at 2-year follow-up. Of those 87 men with pervious convictions, 43.6% (38%) remained free of conviction after 2 years, whilst of those 66 who had previously been admitted to a psychiatric hospital 57.5% (38) remained out of hospital over the 2-year period.

Whiteley (1970) also examined factors associated with outcome and found that good prognostic factors were: school achievement; holding a job for more than 2 years; higher social class occupation; ever being married; and affective disorder. Factors associated with bad prognosis were having: previous convictions; more than two convictions; penal commitment; probation order at referral or admission; current court proceedings; and institutionalization before the age of 15 years.

A subsequent study followed up two further cohorts, of 104 and 87 male patients respectively, to develop prediction equations for successful outcome. As with Whiteley's earlier study, outcome criteria of recidivism and readmission were used. Two-year follow-up established that 42% and 47% of the respective cohorts had no reconviction or readmission. Five-year follow-up information was collected on the first cohort of 104 and showed that 33.6% of men were completely free of conviction or admission and 12 (11.5%) cases had only one very minor relapse in the first year but had been free of conviction or admission in the following 4 years, therefore a total of over 44% could be considered to have a good outcome at 5-year follow-up. Analysis of those factors predictive of recidivism and readmission found that the effects of age and martial status were negligible, but that previous criminal and psychiatric history were both poor prognostic factors (Copas & Whiteley, 1976).

Although these studies show consistent and encouraging findings, with 40–47% of men having a successful outcome at 2 years, neither study had any control or comparison sample, which leaves questions about whether change is attributable to the admission to Henderson or simply the passage of time. In addition, both of these early studies did not examine length of stay in treatment as an outcome predictor, thus the figures presented combine the results for those who dropped out of therapy prematurely with those who completed treatment, masking any possible 'dose effect' of treatment.

However, using an improved design, Copas et al. (1984) replicated the above studies in a 5-year follow-up study which compared 194 male and female patients treated at Henderson with 51 patients referred to the unit who were not admitted. All subjects were diagnosed by their referrer as psychopathic, sociopathic or personality-disordered. Further diagnosis of psychopathy was based upon historical factors and extensive psychometric testing (O'Brien, 1976) . O'Brien describes a typography of four groups of psychopaths based upon the direction of hostility (intropunitiveness) and anxiety levels shown by subjects as follows:

1.   Neurotic (N) showing high anxiety and intropunitiveness;
2.   Extrapunitive Neurotic (EN) showing high anxiety and extrapunitiveness;
3.   Intropunitive Psychopath (IP) showing intropunitiveness and low anxiety;
4.   Psychopath (P) showing low anxiety and extrapunitiveness.

Success was again considered to be the absence of psychiatric admission or conviction in the follow-up period. At 3-year follow-up, 41% of discharged patients were free of both admission and conviction compared with 23% of the non-admitted group. At 5-year follow-up, these proportions were 36% and 19% respectively. Three-year success rates for the N, P and IP groups were similar (48%, 44%, 49%) but there was a lower success rate for the EN (extrapunitive neurotic) group (29%). This pattern was also found in the non-treated sample whose respective success rates were: N (32%); P (25%); IP (25%); and EN (8%). However, numbers in these groups are small, therefore conclusions must be guarded. The effect of gender was negligible with an overall success rate for men of 36% at 3 years and 32% at 5 years and of 38% and 34% for women over the same periods.

All the above rates of readmission and reconviction are for Henderson admissions as a group, regardless of their length of stay in treatment, thus the admitted sample included some people who left treatment within the first month as well as those who stayed in treatment for a full year. Further analysis of data showed that the success rate improved considerably with length of stay: 66% of those who stayed over 6 months were not re-convicted or readmitted to hospital in the following 3 years (compared with a 29% success rate for those who left treatment within the first month). Five years after discharge the success rates for those admitted for 6 months or more remained high at 60.5%; however, only 22% of those who left after one month were still successful (compared with a 19% success rate at 5 years for subjects referred who were not admitted) (see Table 3.1).

It must be noted that patients not admitted for treatment are not a satisfactory control group; 50% of this comparison group were assessed for admission and rejected, the remainder did not attend the assessment, did not attend for admission or were imprisoned or hospitalized elsewhere. Therefore, differences between the two groups, particularly those factors leading to non-admission (e.g. motivation to change), may have important influence upon the findings. This issue was addressed in a subsequent study with improved control samples which is reported below (see: Dolan et al. (1996a), discussed on page 66).

There is, of course, a strong argument against taking employment status, reconviction or readmission to hospital as the main criteria of

Table 3.1. Summary of studies of outcome from Henderson: Success rates in terms of no recidivism or re-admission on follow-up.

Study	Follow-up period (years)	Number of subjects	Success rate (%)	Comparison sample	Comparison success rate (%)
Whiteley 1970	2	112 (all admissions)	40		
Copas & Whiteley, 1976	2	104 (all admissions)	42		
	2	87 (all admissions)	47		
	5	104 (all admissions)	33.6		
Copas et al., 1984	3	194 (all admissions)	41	51 (not-admitted)	23
		38 (in treatment for 6+ months)	66		
	5	194 (all admissions)	36	519 (not-admitted)	19
		38 (in treatment for 6+ months)	60.5		
Dolan et al. 1996a	1	177 (all admissions)	67.2	247 (all non-admitted referrals)	48.2
		86 (in treatment for 3+ months)	80.2	44 (unfunded referrals only)	45.5

success. Although these life events are important indicators of social integration, mental health and offending behaviour, they are, at best, crude measures. The last two are, more accurately, only indicators of future service use, and psychological or psychiatric status cannot be evaluated using only subsequent hospital admission data. Similarly, reconviction data do not relate to psychological state and do not even take account of those people who reoffend but are never charged or convicted. Thus a further study of the Unit used a projective technique relying upon subject's self-report to assess psychological changes during treatment. Norris (1985) used a repertory grid to measure changes in 103 residents during treatment on five parameters: self-esteem; percept of self; percept of ideal self; aspirations regarding rule-breaking; and independence. After 3 months, 60% of Henderson residents were judged as less rule-breaking, 75% reported feeling more independent and 45% had increased self-esteem. In total, 59% of patients were assessed as 'benefiting' from therapy in that they improved on at least three of the five measures above. Norris then compared Henderson Hospital subjects with clients in two other institutions. The proportion of the Henderson sample who benefited was significantly greater than in two groups of subjects in a detention centre and in a voluntary trust community. However, the three subject groups were heterogeneous samples and thus direct comparison is limited.

The 1980s saw the advent of a new classificatory system for personality disorder within DSM-III (APA, 1980) and there was heated debate on the continued use of 'psychopathic disorder' as a category within the 1983 Mental Health Act. There was a resultant move away from the use of the term 'psychopath' as a clinical term within psychiatric research and practice and confinement of the term to its legal (Mental Health Act) usage. Today 'legal psychopaths' are specifically excluded from treatment at Henderson (as patients are never admitted under the Mental Health Act). Even so, Henderson is still considered as a specialist resource for the treatment of 'severe personality disorder,' particularly those with antisocial and borderline personality disorders, a client group who differ from, but show some overlap with, the 'Mental Health Act Psychopaths' more often found detained in high-security Special Hospitals (see section on 'residents' on p. 60).

THE HENDERSON TREATMENT PROGRAMME TODAY

The TC programme at Henderson has evolved over the past five decades, and although much of the culture and structure from Jones' days remains today, the success and longevity of the unit have in part been a result of its ability to modify the therapeutic community programme to fit the needs and mores of both the prevailing society and its own community members therein.

The treatment programme and philosophy have been described at length in several books and papers and a detailed description can be found elsewhere (Jones, 1952, 1962; Rapoport, 1960; Whiteley, 1972; 1980; 1986; Norton, 1990; 1992a; 1992b; Norton & Dolan, 1995). Although in its early days the community was as large as 100 members the present Henderson treats up to 29 patients at any one time. There are equal numbers of women and men and the maximum length of stay is one calendar year.

Active participation is central: community members are called 'residents' not patients, and no psychotropic medicine is used. Therapy takes place both informally via the social milieu and in groups: daily community meeting, small group psychotherapy, activity groups, psychodrama and art therapy (Hamer, 1993), women's and men's groups (Collis, 1987) (See Fig. 3.1 for the daily group timetable). There is no individual therapy, the aspiration is that the 'doctor' is the community itself (Jones, 1952; Rapoport, 1960).

Through a relaxing of the staff/staff and staff/patient hierarchy and the collaboration of staff and patients together in a wide range of activities, all interactions and relationships in the community can be examined. The aim is that such enquiry will lead to a better understanding of deviant or unhealthy previous behaviour (re-enacted within the treatment setting) which may then result in altered interpersonal behaviour and improved psychosocial functioning (Norton & Dolan, 1995).

Since its early days Henderson has only accepted voluntary admissions, and an essential aspect of the model is that membership of the community and engagement in therapy are voluntary. Although initially 10–20% of admissions came directly from the courts or prison, residents are never admitted under any court order of treatment or section of the 1983 Mental Health Act. At the present time, approximately 50% of admissions to Henderson have a history of adult convictions and 20% have served a prison sentence. However, in order for Henderson's community to function and social order to be maintained within it, the members must feel that they have actively chosen to collaborate in the regime. The fact that all treatment is voluntary serves to deemphasize hierarchical or authoritarian relationships, against which the residents might otherwise tend to take up, and reinforce, a complementary 'them and us' position. Thus

Time	Monday	Tuesday	Wednesday	Thursday	Friday	Saturday	Sunday
9.15 - 10.30 (45) am	"9.15"	Community Meeting					
10.30 (45) - 11.15 am		Morning Break					
11.00 -12.00 am	Small Groups	Cleaning & Reviews or Elections or Community Projects	Small Groups or Leavers Group	Welfare or Visitors or Probation	Small Groups		
12.00 - 1.30 am		LUNCH BREAK					
Surgery 1.30 - 2.00 pm	Surgery	Surgery 2.00 - 2.10 pm	Cleaning				
2.30 -4.30 pm	Psychodrama or Art Therapy	Selection or Welfare/Housing or Community Work Project 2.30 -4.30 pm	Psychodrama or Art Therapy 2.30 - 4.30 pm	Work Groups (Art, Cookery or Gardening & Maintenance) 2.15 - 4.15 pm			
Floor Meeting 4.45 - 5.00 pm		Tea 4.30 - 4.50 pm		Tea 4.15 - 4.35 pm			
		Women's Group 6.00 - 7.15 pm		Men's Group 6.00 - 7.15 pm			
7.00 - 9.00			COMMUNITY MEAL				
9.15 - 10.05 pm			Tens Group				Tens
10.15 - 11.00 pm			Summit Meeting				
11.00 pm			Night Round				Summit

Visitors Day - Thursday 9.15 am - 5.00 pm

Figure 3.1. Sample weekly programme at Henderson Hospital.

at Henderson clients on parole, suspended sentences, community supervision orders and probation orders without attached conditions of treatment are able to voluntarily to join the community. The voluntary nature of the Henderson TC model does not necessarily preclude its application within secure settings. Although in secure units participants may not be voluntarily incarcerated, TCs can be provided as a voluntary option *within* that incarceration, as shown in the similar regime at HMP Grendon (and other penal units in this volume). Indeed, other TC models that have not allowed voluntary participation in treatment but have compulsorily admitted patients have all found less favourable outcomes of treatment than voluntary units (Craft et al., 1964; Fink et al., 1969; Rice et al., 1992; Harris et al., 1994).

Selection for Admission

The task of engagement in treatment at Henderson is aided by the involvement of other patients in the interviewing process for selection of new patients (as well as in one another's subsequent treatment, including decisions concerning their discharge from the hospital).

Selection of new community members is in a group situation involving senior residents, elected by the community for the task, who have equal voting rights to the staff. Prospective residents are invited to attend a selection group consisting of nine residents and four staff (drawn from across the multidisciplinary team). The selection group is held one afternoon each week, when up to four prospective residents will meet with the group and discuss their problems and history. Following group discussion a vote is taken (one person, one vote) and the majority decision accepted. Such assessment in a group situation involves the active participation of the whole resident group in the Community (either by being in the group or by voting for those members who will make up the nine selection representatives). This is an important feature in the functioning of the unit, democratization being one of the major tenets of the Therapeutic Community approach (Rapoport, 1960). The responsibility to participate in a major decision is a factor in raising self-esteem, which has been shown to be one major beneficial effect of the Therapeutic Community approach (Norris, 1983, see below).

This setting also has the advantage that the residents are empowered to make important real decisions about their peers: this genuine empowerment recognizes residents' healthy resources. They can challenge defensive behaviours in candidates for admission in a manner which indicates that they are not taken in by any attempt to play down or rationalize this behaviour, since many of the interviewing residents may well have similar histories or behaviours. In this they may be more effective than professionals. For the selection candidate this may be the first step to developing an empathic relationship, albeit one which early in treatment is relatively brittle and unstable, with someone who has experienced and understands their problem from the 'inside'. This yields more potential for listening to and absorbing verbal feedback about the effects of acting out behaviour and suggestions for behaving (and thinking) differently in future. Hope is instilled on the basis that the client is exposed to people like themselves who have made some progress towards resolving their difficulties in the treatment situation on offer. An inability to respond to these approaches and to drop defensive non-verbal behaviour is an indicator that the client is unlikely to benefit from a psychotherapeutic community approach.

A recent study of 156 selection candidates used the SCL-90R questionnaire to assess psychological distress in those residents admitted to Henderson and those subjects rejected at admission assessment (Dolan et al., 1990). No difference was found between groups in number of symptoms reported nor the degree of distress attributable to those symptoms. However, analysis of symptom sub-scale scores revealed that those subjects not selected scored significantly higher on measures of somatization, obsessive-compulsive features and phobic anxiety. It could be argued that these three symptoms are indicative of a tendency to deny or avoid feeling emotional distress. It was suggested that the selection group may operate by identifying those candidates who are more able to verbalize their distress, i.e. those presumed most likely to benefit from the Therapeutic Community's psychotherapeutic approach.

The Residents

The majority of residents are single and unemployed at the time of admission. Typical presentations include self-damaging and suicidal behaviour in the context of severe emotional and psychosocial disturbance. Substance abuse, violence and antisocial behaviours are common. Unsurprisingly, over 80% of those admitted have had previous in-patient and out-patient therapy. The early onset of their personality disturbance is shown in that more than a quarter have had psychological or psychiatric treatment as children or adolescents and a fifth were brought up in social services care or fostered as children.

Diagnostically, the resident group can be broadly described as personality disordered. Indeed, Henderson residents' diagnoses are

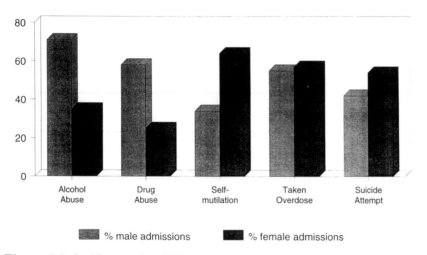

Figure 3.2. Incidence of self-damaging behaviour among 66 Henderson Hospital admissions (April 1991 to August 1992), taken from data provided at referral.

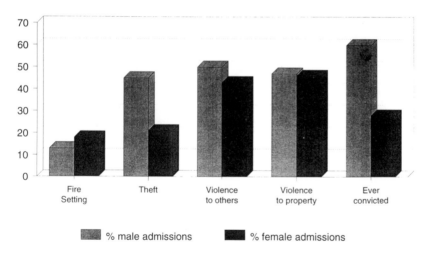

Figure 3.3. Incidence of anti-social behaviour among 66 Henderson Hospital admissions (April 1991 to August 1992), taken from data provided at referral.

mostly classifiable into Cluster B, the dramatic, erratic group of personality disorders of DSM-III-R (APA, 1987). However, in a recent study of 275 referrals to Henderson, using a self-rating Personality Disorder Questionnaire (PDQ-R: Hyler, et al., 1987), subjects averaged six DSM-III-R Axis 11 diagnoses each. Although the most prominent diagnosis is borderline personality disorder (in 86%), these sub-categories of the diagnostic group of personality disorders hold little meaning because of the large amount of personality disorder co-morbidity found in such populations. Over 60% also have antisocial personality disorder and of the 275 patients who took part in the study, only 3% scored within a single personality disorder cluster (Dolan et al., 1995a). The borderline symptomatology displayed by Henderson residents is associated with other aspects of personality psychopathology such as identity disturbances related to the separation–individuation process (Dolan et al., 1992a).

Alongside the personality disturbance there is considerable neurotic symptomatic disturbance in this group. A questionnaire study which used the SCL-90R to investigate symptomatic psychological distress in residents showed high scores on anxiety, depression, interpersonal sensitivity, psychotic symptoms, hostility and paranoid ideation (Dolan et al., 1990). Low self-esteem combined with high levels of irritability, anxiety and depression are often found (Norris, 1983; Dolan & Mitchell, 1994). Eating disorders are also a common part of the presentation in both women and men, although, particularly in men, these symptoms may be covert. A recent study found high rates of previously undiagnosed and unrecognized eating

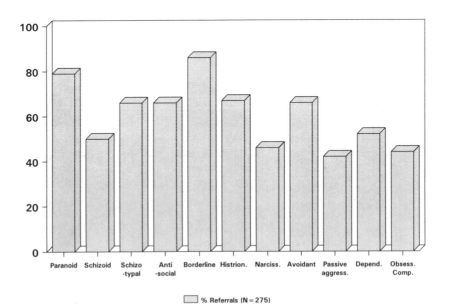

Figure 3.4. PDQ-R personality disorder diagnoses among 275 referrals to Henderson Hospital.

problems, with 37% of women and 9% of men scoring above the clinical cut-off point on the Eating Attitudes Test (Dolan et al., 1996b).

RESEARCH INTO TREATMENT AT HENDERSON IN THE 1990s

Since Henderson's first origins as an 'experimental' unit, research has always played a major role in the development and survival of the institution. Often evaluative studies have been prompted by the need to answer critics of the model who are pessimistic about the possibility of rehabilitation for this disordered client group. Research work in the 1990s has continued to investigate the characteristics of the clients and outcome of treatment. However, with the development of better measures for assessing personality disturbance the more recent research has complemented early studies of behavioural changes by considering psychological change.

Psychological Change

Dolan et al. (1992c) followed up 62 subjects after an average of 8 months from discharge (response rate 65%). They showed a highly significant reduction in symptomatic psychological distress (paired $t = 6.1$; $p < 0.0005$), (as measured by the SCL-90R questionnaire: Derogats et al., 1973) Indeed, the pre-test scores of the Henderson residents showed them to be more distressed than a comparison sample of psychiatric out-patients, whilst their follow-up scores were more similar to the general population comparison sample on which the instrument was validated (see Figure 3.5).

Although the difference as reported using group mean change scores is highly statistically significant, such average improvement scores provide no information on the effects of therapy for individual clients in the sample. In addition, the statistical 'significance' test imposes a criterion which may have little relevance to clinical change. Such 'effect-size statistics' which express difference between two group means bear little direct relation to the practical or clinical significance of the extent of the change shown by individual members of the group. Clinically it is not the 'p-value' but the extent of improvement in individuals which is of relevance. Therefore, the reliability and clinical significance of the changes in individual subjects were also assessed using the methods developed by Jacobson et al. (1984).

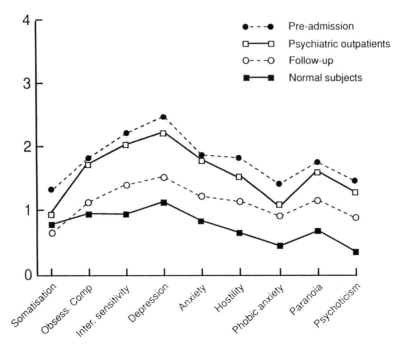

Figure 3.5. SCL-90 symptom profiles of 62 Henderson residents at admission and follow-up compared with normative data.

Using Jacobson's method it was demonstrated that on the global SCL-90R scale, 55% of subjects had improved reliably and that, in 32% this change was also clinically significant, whilst only 6.5% of subjects had deteriorated reliably since discharge. No non-admitted control group was included in this study and thus it cannot be ascertained whether the improvement found in this sample could not also be found in less intense treatment or even with no treatment at all. However, the referral process at Henderson Hospital makes it unusual for residents to be admitted in acute crisis and therefore it is unlikely that the above findings are a simple result of regression to the mean. Further data analysis considered factors related to length of stay at Henderson Hospital and found that length of stay in therapy was not related to the severity of initial symptomatology but could be predicted by psychological changes in the first 3 months. Those who stayed longer than 9 months tended to have experienced some change in symptoms (including getting worse as well as getting better) in the first 3-month period, whilst those who dropped out tended not to have changed at all on these psychological measures in the first 3 months. Again there was a non-significant tendency for those who stayed longer to improve more on psychological symptoms (Dolan et al., 1992b).

One limitation of the use of the SCL-90R questionnaire in Henderson residents is the assumption that change in neurotic symptomatology can be equated with change in the core personality disorder. The SCL-90R is not conceptually linked to the actual focus of the treatment and the underlying pathology may be unchanged. A recent study has addressed this issue using the Borderline Syndrome Index (BSI: Conte et al., 1980) to evaluate changes in borderline personality pathology of 137 subjects (Dolan et al., 1996b). Subjects completed the questionnaire on referral to Henderson and were then followed up either one year after discharge from treatment for the admitted patients ($n = 70$) or one year after referral for those who were not admitted ($n = 67$). There was no significant difference in the mean pre-test scores of the two groups. At follow-up both groups showed some decrease in symptoms over time. However, there was a significantly greater reduction in symptoms in the admitted sample than in the non-admitted group ($p < 0.0013$). The admitted group had been in treatment for an average of 7 months, although admission times ranged between one week and a year. The change in BSI score was found to be significantly positively correlated with length of stay in treatment ($r = 0.38$; $p < 0.001$), supporting previous work which has shown a similar 'dose-effect' of therapy.

As with the SCL-90 results, the reliability and clinical significance of the change for individuals were assessed following Jacobson's method. This analysis showed that 61% of the admitted group had shown statistically reliable improvement with 37% of the non-admitted group. The magnitude of this change was also clinically significant in 43% of the admitted sample compared with only 18% of the non-admitted sample. In addition, 6% of the non-admitted sample were now functioning at a reliably worse level, compared with 3% of the treated group, although this difference in proportions was not significant.

Economic Benefits

With the new purchaser/provider split in the British health service it is unsurprising that 'value for money', in terms of the cost of the treatment and decreased usage of services post-treatment, has remained an important factor in assessing the success of therapy at Henderson. The cost of service usage is of particular relevance given the high service usage of personality-disordered patients and their tendency to suck in services in a reactive and unplanned way. Menzies et al. (1993) retrospectively quantified the penal and psychiatric service usage of a cohort of 29 Henderson residents in the one year prior to their admission. They found that these residents used a total of £423,000 of services in a single year, and, as personality disorder does not spontaneously remit, they would be likely to continue to use services at a similar rate for many years if left untreated (Perry et al. 1987). However, people with personality disorders are not popular contenders for funding when budgets are tight and managers must decide upon whom to spend their limited monies. In the first year after the introduction of the NHS Bill only 36% of requests for funding of Henderson treatment were agreed (Dolan & Norton, 1992). Most worryingly, refusal of funding appeared not to be made on any clinical criteria, as those whose funding was agreed and refused did not differ in psychiatric diagnosis, psychological disturbance nor on a variety of demographic variables. However, funding was more likely to be denied to those with a history of a probation order (Dolan et al., 1994b).

The most recent cost-offset information from Henderson comes from the actual follow-up of 25 of those 29 patients in Menzies et al.'s (1993) original costing study. One year after leaving treatment the actual cost of their psychiatric and penal services had dropped from £13,966 to £1308 per person. This average saving of £12,658 per year would outweigh the (£25,000) average cost of their Henderson admission within 2 years (Dolan et al., 1996c).

Service Usage

Recently a more detailed study was made of 424 patients referred to Henderson Hospital in the period between September 1990 and December 1993 (Dolan et al., 1996c). This cohort comprised 177 admitted patients, 84 patients not accepted by Henderson, 119 patients who did not attend assessment, or whose referral was withdrawn and 44 patients who were refused treatment funding by their District Health Authority. This latter group provides an important control sample, as in previous research studies ethical considerations have precluded the random allocations of patients to treatment and non-treatment conditions. However, it is apparent that some patients who have had funding of treatment refused only differ from those admitted to Henderson in that they live in a different Health Authority area. Thus they represent a more random comparison group for research. Indeed, a separate and more detailed comparison of those referrals who were funded with those who had funding refused has shown that there were no significant differences between the groups on historical variables such as previous in-patient or out-patient psychiatric treatment, or previous convictions. Psychological measures of motivation, self-esteem, personality or dysthymia made blind to funding status also did not differ between the groups. Indeed, the only discriminating variable was being on probation at the time of referral, which was more common in the non-funded group ($p = 0.05$) (Dolan et al., 1994b).

Information about each patient's psychiatric service usage and offending history subsequent to referral was provided by the original referrer (i.e. psychiatrist, psychologist, social worker, probation officer or other therapist) and the General Practitioner of each patient. When the 177 admitted patients and the 247 non-admitted patients were compared in terms of psychiatric service usage, prescription of psychotropic medication and offending, it was found that fewer of the admitted group had subsequently had in-patient treatment or offended. However, although differences were not significant, more of the admitted group had had out-patient treatment (see Table 3.2).

To examine the effect of length of stay on outcome the admitted group were divided into those who stayed in treatment more than 12 weeks ($N = 86$) and less than 12 weeks ($N = 91$). At one-year follow-up significantly fewer of the long stayers had been admitted as in-patients following treatment (16.3% versus 33%, $p = 0.017$). Fewer of the long stay group than the short stayers had subsequently used psychotropic medication (24.4% versus 37.4%) or offended (7% versus 17.6%); however, these differences did not achieve significance.

The group who stayed more than 12 weeks in treatment were considered as a 'treated' group and were compared with those who had their funding for treatment refused. The 'treated' group tended

Table 3.2. Service usage rates at one year follow-up from referral or discharge.

	Admitted (%) (n = 177)	Not admitted (%) (n = 247)	χ^2 prob.
Out-patient	62.7	48.5	0.039
In-patient	24.8	34.8	0.037
On medication	31.0	30.4	n.s.
Other treatment	11.3	12.6	n.s.
Offended	12.4	23.5	0.006
Readmitted or reoffended	32.8	51.8	<0.001

to have had more out-patient treatment, but had had less in-patient treatment, psychotropic medication and offending than the unfunded group in the year following discharge or referral. Overall 19.8% of the treated group had either offended or been readmitted compared with 54.5% of the unfunded group. This latter difference between the groups was statistically significant ($p < 0.001$) and the findings can be more reliably attributed to the effect of Henderson treatment given the comparability of the non-funded control sample.

SUMMARY AND CONCLUSIONS

Henderson Hospital's history now spans 50 years, during which time the unit has developed a treatment model which has not only been shown to be successful within its own boundaries, but has been emulated in a whole host of units which use derivations or aspects of Jones' TC model in a range of open hospital and secure settings throughout the world.

Henderson is unusual amongst hospital units in carrying out the vast number of studies of its own treatment outcome. These have been conducted from its inception to the present day and have included evaluations of psychological changes during treatment, and follow-up investigations of both psychological and behavioural changes after discharge from the unit. The early studies which used objective 'behavioural' measures of outcome such as recidivism and readmission are now complemented by later studies of changes in psychological well-being and borderline phenomenology all of which show significant improvements following therapy.

However, it should be remembered that treatment at Henderson is not a panacea. The unit accepts only those severely personality-disordered patients who, at the time of admission: are not experiencing psychotic phenomena; do not need secure containment, and have the capacity to engage in treatment voluntarily (although 20% will have been in prison and 10% in secure hospitals previously). The treatment provided at Henderson has greatest efficacy for those who stay longer in therapy, and this model is not so successful for those with little motivation to engage in treatment or for the one-third of admitted patients who drop out of treatment within the first 3 months (Dolan et al., 1992b).

The training influence of Henderson has extended into many hospital and penal institutions directly or indirectly. Barrett, a former psychiatrist at Henderson, became Clinical Director at Grendon Underwood. Prison officers from Barlinnie Prison in

Glasgow come to Henderson to develop ideas and plans for the therapeutic community Special Unit for the most difficult prisoners in that institution (Cooke, 1989 and Chapter 5 in this volume). The incumbent of the first British post of 'Senior Lecturer in Forensic Psychotherapy' trained at Henderson for 2 years before her appointment to Broadmoor Hospital in 1994. Henderson staff continue to have both academic and clinical connections to the Regional Forensic Psychiatry Service, where the present Medical Director (Norton) is also an Honorary Senior Lecturer, and the annual Groupwork Training Course run at Henderson counts many probation and prison officers among its members.

Clinical and research expertise from Henderson continues to inform policy and practice in the areas of psychopathic disorder and mentally disordered offenders in general. The unit was recently visited by a delegation from the South African Ministry of Justice, who were reviewing their own approach to treatment of psychopathic offenders and, in 1992, Dolan was commissioned to assist with the joint Home Office and Department of Health governmental review of services for mentally disordered offenders (Reed, 1994; Dolan & Coid, 1993). The final report of the 'Reed' committee on Psychopathic Disorder (Reed, 1994) highlighted the national dearth of services for people suffering from severe personality disorders and stressed the importance of the therapeutic community approach. Indeed the final recommendations included the statement that 'more specialist units comparable to Henderson Hospital should be developed' (Reed, 1994, p. 43).

Clearly the structure and culture which have evolved at Henderson will not be appropriate to every therapeutic setting. However, the success of therapeutic communities in prisons, hospitals and eductional settings, including some which employ compulsory detention in maximum security, shows the strength of the model (as described in this volume and in: Abruni, 1975; Clarke & Glatt, 1985; Cullen, 1994; Feldbrugge, 1992; Ogloff et al., 1990; Ravndal & Vaglum, 1991; Vaglum et al., 1990). The nature of the institution in question will have an important bearing on how much of, and how far, the Henderson democratic therapeutic community model might be appropriately utilized (Norton & Dolan, 1995).

NOTES

1. Much of the following historical information in this section comes from papers by Whiteley (1980) and Murto (1991).

2. Patients at Henderson are referred to as residents as one marker of the differences between the community and the typical hospital environment.

REFERENCES

Abruzzi, W., (1975). Severe personality disorders in an institutional setting. *American Journal of Psychoanalysis*, 269–277.

APA (1980). *Diagnostic and Statistical Manual for Mental Disorders: Version 3* (DSM-III). Washington, DC: APA.

APA (1987). *Diagnostic and Statistical Manual for Mental Disorders: Version 3 Revised* (DSM-IIIR). Washington, DC: APA.

Baan, P.A.H. (1961). Some basic considerations underlying treatment policies. *Bulletin at the Menninger Clinic*, **25**: 175–185.

Baker, A. A. (1952). The misfit family: A psychodramatic technique used in a therapeutic community. *British Journal of Medical Psychology*, **25**: 235–243.

Bloch, S., Reibstein, J., Crouch, E. et al. (1979). A method for studying therapeutic factors in group psychotherapy *British Journal of Psychiatry*, **134**: 257–263.

Bridger, H. (1946). The Northfield experiment. *Bulletin at the Menninger Clinic*, **10**: 71–76.

Briggs, D. (1972). Chino, California. In Whiteley, J.S., Briggs, D., Turner, M. *Dealing with Deviants*. London: Hogarth Press.

Chiesa, M. (1995). A comparative study of different programmes of psychosocial intervention for severe personality disorders. *Proceedings of Residential Treatment of Severe Personality Disorders*, Cassel Hospital, Richmond, Surrey.

Clarke, C. R. & Glatt, M. M., (1985). Wormwood Scrubs annexe—a therapeutic community within a prison: discussion paper. *Journal of the Royal Society of Medicine,* **78**: 656–662.

Collis, M. (1987). Women's groups in the therapeutic community: The Henderson experience. *International Journal of Therapeutic Communities*, **8**(1): 175–184.

Conte, H. R., Plutchick, R. & Jerrett (1980). A self-report borderline scale: Discriminant validity preliminary norms. *Journal of Nervous and Mental Disease*, **168**, 428–435.

Cooke, D. (1989). Containing violent prisoners: an analysis of Barlinnie special unit. *British Journal of Criminology*, **129**: 129–143.

Copas, J. B. & Whiteley, J. S. (1976). Predicting success in the treatment of psychopaths. *British Journal of Psychiatry*, **129**: 388–392.

Copas, J. B., O'Brien, M., Roberts, J. & Whiteley, S. (1984). Treatment outcome in personality disorder: The effect of social, psychological and behavioural variables. *Personality and Individual Differences*, **5**(5): 565–573.

Craft, M., Stephenson, G. & Granger, C. (1964). A controlled trial of authoritarian and self-governing regimes with adolescent psychopaths. *American Journal of Orthopsychiatry*, **34**: 543–554.

Cullen, E. (1994). Grendon: The therapeutic prison that works. *Therapeutic Communities*, **15**(4): 301–311.

Davidson, S. (1946). Notes on a group of ex-prisoners of war. Bulletin of the Menninger Clinic, **10**, 90–100.

Derogatis, L. R., Lipman, R. S. & Cori, L. (1973). SCL-90: an out-patient psychiatric rating scale—preliminary report. *Psychopharmacology Bulletin*, **9**(1): 13–28.

Dolan, B. & Coid, J. (1993). *Psychopathic and Antisocial Personality Disorders: Treatment and Research Issues*, London: Gaskell.

Dolan, B. & Mitchell, E. (1994). Personality disorder and psychological disturbance of female prisoners: A comparison with women referred for NHS treatment of personality disorder. *Criminal Behaviour and Mental Health*, **4**: 130–142.

Dolan, B. & Norton, K. (1992). One year after the NHS bill: The extra contractual referral system and Henderson Hospital. *Psychiatric Bulletin*, **16**: 745–747.

Dolan, B., Morton, A. & Wilson, J. (1990). Selection of admissions to a therapeutic community using a group setting: association with degree and type of psychological distress. *International Journal of Social Psychology*, **36**(4): 265–271.

Dolan, B., Evans, C. & Norton, K. (1992a). The Separation–Individuation Inventory: association with borderline phenomena. *Journal of Nervous and Mental Disease*, **180**(18): 529–533.

Dolan, B., Evans, C. D. H. & Wilson, J. (1992b). Neurotic symptomatology and length of stay in a therapeutic community. *Therapeutic Communities*, **13**(3): 171–177.

Dolan, B., Wilson, J. & Evans, C. (1992c). Therapeutic community treatment for personality disordered adults: changes in neurotic symptomatology on follow-up *International Journal of Social Psychology*, **38**(4): 243–250.

Dolan, B., Evans, C. & Norton, K. (1994a). Eating disorders in male and female patients with personality disorders. *Journal of Personality Disorders*, **8**(1): 17–27.

Dolan, B., Evans, C. & Norton, K. (1994b). Funding treatment for offender patients: Do financial considerations trump clinical need? *Journal of Forensic Psychiatry*, **5**(2): 263–274.

Dolan, B., Murch, L. & Norton, K. (1994c). The effect of admission to a therapeutic community on subsequent service usage of personality disordered patients. *Proceedings of Society for Psychotherapy Research Annual Meeting*, Ravenscar, Yorks.

Dolan, B., Evans, C. & Norton, K. (1995). The multiple axis-II diagnosis of personality disorders. *British Journal of Psychiatry*, **166**: 107–112.

Dolan, B., Warren, F. & Norton, K. (1995b). Change in borderline symptoms one year after therapeutic community treatment for personality disorder *British Journal of Psychiatry*, (submitted for publication).

Dolan, B., Warren, F., Norton, K. & Menzies, D. (1995c). Cost-offset following therapeutic community treatment of personality disorder *Psychiatric Bulletin*, **20**(7): 413–417.

Dolan, B., Warren, F., Murch, L. & Norton, K. (1996a). Service usage following therapeutic community treatment of severe personality disorder. *British Journal of Psychiatry*, submitted for publication.

East, N. & Hubert, W. (1939). *The Psychological Treatment of Crime*. London: HMSO.

Feldbrugge, J. T. T. M. (1992). Rehabilitation of patients with personality disorders: patient–staff collaboration used as a working model and tool. *Criminal Behaviour and Mental Health*, 2(2): 169–177.

Fink, L., Derby, W. N. & Martin, J. P. (1969). Psychiatry's new role in corrections. *American Journal of Psychiatry*, 126: 124–128.

Foulkes, S. F. (1946). Principles and practice of group therapy. *Bulletin of the Menninger Clinic*, 10: 85–89.

Gudjonsson, G. H. & Roberts, J. C. (1981a). The aggressive behaviour of personality disordered patients and its relation to personality and perceptual motor performance. *Current Psychological Research*, 1(2): 101–109.

Gudjonsson, G. H. & Roberts, J. C. (1981b). Trail making scores as a prediction of aggressive behaviour in personslity-disordered patients. *Perceptual and Motor Skills*, 52, 413–414.

Gudjonsson, G. H. & Roberts, J. C. (1982). Guilt and self concept in psychopaths. *Personality and Individual Differences*, 4: 65–70.

Hamer, N. (1993). Some connections between art therapy and psychodrama in a therapeutic community. *Inscape (Journal of British. Association of Art Therapists)*, **Winter**: 23–26.

Harris, G., Rice, M. & Cormier, C. (1994). Psychopaths: is the therapeutic community therapeutic? *Therapeutic Communities*, 15(4): 283–300.

Henderson, D. K. (1939). *Psychopathic States*. London: Norton.

Hyler, S., Reider, S., Spitzer, R. L. et al. (1987). *Personality Diagnostic Questionnaire—Revised*. New York, New York State Psychiatric Institute.

Jacobson, N. S., Follette, W. C. & Revenstorf, D. (1984). Psychotherapy outcome research: Methods for reporting variability and evaluating clinical significance. *Behavior Therapy*, 15: 336–352.

Jones, M. (1942). Group psychotherapy. *British Medical Journal*, 2: 276–278.

Jones, M. (1946). Rehabilitation of forces neurosis patients to civilian life. *British Medical Journal*, 1: 533–535.

Jones, M. (1952). *Social Psychiatry*. London: Tavistock Books.

Jones, M. (1956a). Industrial rehabilitation of mental patients still in hospital. *The Lancet*, 2: 985–986.

Jones, M. (1956b). The concept of a Therapeutic Community. *American Journal of Psychiatry*, 112: 647–50.

Jones, M. (1960). Introduction to *Community as Doctor*. In Rapoport, R., *The Community as Doctor*. London: Tavistock.

Jones, M. (1962). Society and the sociopath. *American Journal of Psychiatry*, 119, 410–415.

Jones, M (1968). *Beyond the Therapeutic Community: Social Learning and Social Psychiatry*. New Haven: Yale University Press.

Main, T. (1946). The hospital as a therapeutic institution. *Bulletin of the Menninger Clinic*, 10: 66–68.

Main, T. (1983). The concept of the therapeutic community: variations and vicissitudes. In: Pines, M. (ed.) *The Evolution of Group Analysis*. London: Routledge & Kegan Paul Ltd.

Menzies, D., Dolan, B. & Norton, K. (1993). Are short term savings worth long term costs? Funding treatment for personality disorders. *Psychiatric Bulletin*, 17: 517–519.

Murto, K. (1991). *Towards the well functioning community: The development of Anton Makarenko and Maxwell Jones' communities*, Jyväskyla studies in Education, Psychology and Social Research, University of Jyväskyla, Jyväskyla, Finland.

Norris, M. (1983). Changes in patients during treatment at Henderson Hospital therapeutic community during 1977–1981. *British Journal of Medical Psychology*, **56**: 135–143.

Norton, K. (1990). The significance and importance of the therapeutic community working practice. *International Journal of Therapeutic Communities*, **II**(2): 67–76.

Norton, K. (1992a). A culture of enquiry its preservation or loss. *Therapeutic Communities*, **13**(1): 3–26.

Norton, K. (1992b). Treating personality disordered individuals: the Henderson Hospital model. *Criminal Behaviour and Mental Health*, **2**: 180–191.

Norton, K. & Dolan, B. (1995). Acting-out and the institutional response. *Journal of Forensic Psychiatry*, **6**(2): 317–332.

O'Brien, M. (1976). *Psychopathic disorder*. PhD. Thesis, University of London.

Ogloff, J. R. P., Wong, S. & Greenwood, A. (1990). Treating criminal psychopaths in a therapeutic community program. *Behavioral Sciences and the Law*, **8**: 181–190.

Perry, J. C., Lavori, P. W. & Hoke, L. (1987). A Markow model for predicting levels of psychiatric service use in borderline and antisocial personality disorders and bi-polur type 11 affective disorder. *Journal of Psychiatric Research*, **21**(3): 213–232.

Rapoport, R. (1960). *The Community as Doctor*. London: Tavistock.

Ravndal, E. & Vaglum, P. (1991). Changes in antisocial aggressiveness during treatment in a hierarchical therapeutic community: A prospective study of personality changes. *Acta Psychiatrica Scandinavica*, **84**(6): 524–530.

Reed, J. (1994). *Report of the Working Group on Psychopathic Disorder*. London: Department of Health/Home Office.

Rice, M. E., Harris, G. T. & Cormier, C. A. (1992). An evaluation of a maximum security therapeutic community for psychopaths and other mentally disordered offenders. *Law and Human Behaviour*, **16**: 399–412.

Sandler, J. (1952). In: Jones, M. *Social Psychiatry*. London: Tavistock Books.

Smith, B. (1966). Psychopaths, permissiveness or restriction? *Occupational Therapy*, **Nov**: 19–23.

Taylor, F. (1966). The Henderson therapeutic community. In Craft, M. (ed.) *Psychopathic Disorder*. Oxford: Pergamon Press.

Tuxford, J. (1961). *Treatment as a circular process*. King Edward's Hospital Fund Report, London.

Vaglum, P., Friis, S., Irion et al. (1990). Treatment response of severe and non-severe personality disorders in a therapeutic community day unit. *Journal of Personality Disorders*, **4**(2): 161–172.

Whiteley, J. S. (1967). Concepts of psychopathy and its treatment. *Medico-Legal Journal*, **35**(4): 154–163.

Whiteley, J. S. (1970). The response of psychopaths to a therapeutic community. *British Journal of Psychiatry*, **116**: 517–529.

Whiteley, J. S. (1972). Henderson. In Whiteley, J. S., Briggs, D. & Turner, M. *Dealing with Deviants*. London: Hogarth Press.

Whiteley, J. S. (1973). Deviants and their demands. *Royal Society of Health Journal*, **93**(3): 143–145.

Whiteley, J. S. (1980). The Henderson Hospital. *International Journal of Therapeutic Communities*, **1**: 38–58.

Whiteley, J. S. (1986). Sociotherapy and psychotherapy in the treatment of personality disorder. Discussion Paper. *Journal of the Royal Society of Medicine*, **79**: December.

Whiteley, J. S. (1994). Attachment, loss and the space between: Personality disorder in the therapeutic community. *Group Analysis*, **27**(4): 359–387.

Whiteley, J. S., Collis, M. (1987). Therapeutic factors applied to group psychotherapy in a therapeutic community. *International Journal of Therapeutic Communities*, **8**(1): 21–31.

Whiteley, J. S. & Gordon, J. (1979). *Group Approaches in Psychiatry*. London: Routledge & Kegan Paul.

Whiteley, J. S., Briggs, D. & Turner, M. (1972). *Dealing with Deviants*. London: Hogarth Press.

CHAPTER 4

Can a Prison be a Therapeutic Community: The Grendon Template

Eric Cullen

HMP Grendon, Aylesbury, UK

Most criminals commit crimes, with premeditation, for profit, personal gratification or both. Most prisons exist to separate convicted criminals from society as punishment rather than for rehabilitation. When in prison, most prisoners wish to pass their terms of imprisonment as quickly and comfortably as possible. These three primary assertions, while not particularly contentious, are in contrast to the purpose of therapeutic communities and in even sharper contrast, even contradiction, to attempting to create and sustain a therapeutic community in prison. The well worn truism is that people are sent to prison *as* punishment, not *for* punishment, but it is equally true that they are not sent for treatment. They have not consented to either (few consent to punishment!) and, once in prison, it is a moot point whether they can truly consent to any activity which might affect their chances of an earlier or later release, as volition implies free will. Alternatively, they consent based on contingencies which lead us to suspect that their reasons are different from those which we wish them to have, i.e. 'free will' operating within imposed contingencies.

This chapter describes the regime in the only prison in the United Kingdom totally created for, and continuing to operate as, a *collective*

Therapeutic Communities for Offenders.
Edited by E. Cullen, L. Jones and R. Woodward. © 1997 John Wiley & Sons Ltd.

of therapeutic communities. Grendon Underwood is internationally renowned for its pioneering socio-psychiatric treatment of serious offenders with histories of personality disorders. However, since it opened in 1962, a constant struggle has ensued between the medical traditions of treating 'patients' and the primary purpose of imprisonment, which is to contain and control criminals in secure prison conditions. These two themes attract different and often conflicting priorities which a total institution approach like that practised at Grendon must coalesce. This chapter describes the place, the people, the processes and the proof, while offering some of the most salient learning points from the conflicts and resolutions which spring from a dual-purpose institution with contradictory aims.

THE PLACE

Grendon Underwood is a relatively small ($n = 245$) medium-security prison in countryside about 55 miles northwest of London. When it opened in 1962 as a national resource it was officially described as an experimental psychiatric prison which was intended to 'investigate and treat mental disorders generally recognised as responsive to treatment, to investigate offenders whose offences in themselves suggest mental morbidity and to explore the problems of dealing with the psychopath'. Because of its relatively expensive regime and equivocal evidence of efficacy, the 'experimental' tag stuck and for much of the ensuing three decades, Grendon has struggled to justify its existence.

While the physical plant is unexceptional and of limited relevance to the purpose of the chapter, it is worth commenting briefly upon the limitations that the architecture imposes upon the therapeutic process, as well as affording an outline of the size parameters of the Therapeutic Communities themselves. The physical security consists essentially of a perimeter wall of minimal security specification and a standard series of secure gates and doors. The accommodation consists of an Assessment Unit for up to 26 referrals, five therapeutic community wings of between 35 and 42 residents maximum, a Pre-Release and Pre-Transfer Unit for up to 16 men and a Healthcare Unit for a maximum of 12. The Certified Normal Accommodation (CNA) or maximum agreed capacity is 245, but Grendon has an agreed therapy maximum of 235. However, even this lower ceiling obliges the communities to try to conduct therapy in small groups which can exceed 10 and in Community Meetings in excess of 50 members – staff and inmates—both higher than the maxima which professional opinion and experience recommend.

The architecture of Grendon also imposes limitations on the therapeutic process. The shape and dimensions of the rooms used for the small therapy groups and Community Meetings described later are inadequate, with the worst examples being small groups of up to 12 people—10 residents and two staff—having to meet in a room originally intended as an individual cell and a Community Meeting with up to 50 people meeting in a TV room of 30 by 18 feet. None of the five therapeutic community wings have adequate separate rooms to run all groups simultaneously without resorting to using staff offices, dining rooms and, occasionally, even the landings of the residents' cell floors. Although the general grounds of the prison within the perimeter wall are of acceptable-to-good standard, opportunities to allow residents greater access, e.g. gardening and freer movement between wings and areas, are increasingly curtailed or reduced by the imposition in 1995/6 of national operational requirements for security following from the recommendations of the Woodcock and Learmont Inquiries occasioned by escapes from two maximum-security prisons.

Issues of the architecture, structures and spatial requirements of therapeutic communities in prisons are considered in more detail in Chapter 11.

THE PEOPLE

The communities within Grendon are made up of people who are meant to share a common purpose: helping people change for the better by enabling effective therapy to take place. The reality is that there are two large groups of people, roughly comparable in size, with overlapping and sometimes conflicting agendas. While all the inmates have volunteered to come to Grendon and have affirmed a motivation to be there, the same cannot be said of all the staff. It will be seen from what follows that a great deal more is known about the inmates than is known about the staff. While it may certainly be argued that this is as it should be, given that the therapy is for the inmates, the issues and implications in terms of our expectations of both groups regarding their preparations for the enormously challenging process of intensive therapy, and more specifically for staff selection, training, support and development, are ignored at our peril.

The Staff

There are approximately 220 staff at Grendon Underwood. A career prison Governor is in overall charge, supported primarily by a

Director of Therapy, who is a psychiatrist, and a Head of Custody, who is another Governor. These three are joined by a Director of Research and Development (psychologist), Head of Finance and Audit (administrative grade), the Governor of Springhill (a minimum security prison adjacent to Grendon), a local businessman and a psychotherapist (who acts as non-executive members) to form the Management Board for Grendon and Springhill prisons.

Each therapy wing has a multidisciplinary team of staff led by a Wing Therapist, who is a doctor with a psychiatry or psychotherapy qualification. The majority of wing staff are uniformed prison officers, with two senior officers and 10 basic-grade officers given line management by a principal officer with responsibility for two wings. The composition of the wing team is completed by a psychologist and probation officer, each full-time, and a part-time wing tutor (education). Not all wings have a full complement. There is a wide range of staff in other departments, including Administration (finance and audit), the fastest growing area due to the national policy of ever-increasing requirements to monitor and control expenditure, Education (recently reduced by the imposition of budget cuts), Religion, Physical Education, Healthcare and Works (Maintenance and Engineering).

Uniformed staff, or prison officers, have been recruited locally since 1994. Prior to that, they were transferred from other prisons or the National staff college to Grendon from all over the United Kingdom. Many were transferred against their will, having been recruited and trained in prison service skills and discipline, with little or no training in, interest in or aptitude for therapy. While local recruitment has certainly improved selection in terms of interest and motivation, the paucity of adequate therapy training for uniformed grades and, indeed, all staff who join Grendon is a matter of considerable concern. This issue applies to varying degrees to all TCs in UK prisons.

There is also an Advisory Group on Grendon's Development (AGOGD), chaired by a member of the national Prisons Board and composed of a combination of four members of the Grendon Management Board and a range of external consultants in the fields of criminology, research and statistics, therapeutic communities, psychiatry, healthcare, psychology and prison management plus a successful 'graduate', i.e. ex-Grendon offender. There is also a Board of Visitors, a statutory body for all UK prisons, composed of members of the local community identified to provide an independent safeguard for the rights and privileges of the prisoners, to whom they have direct access.

THE INMATE RESIDENTS

The men come to Grendon for therapy from all over the United Kingdom. In the year ending April 1995, a total of 220 men were received from 50 prisons in England and Wales, with only seven prisons accounting for over half (52%) of all referrals. Most referrals are received from either maximum security 'Dispersal' prisons or medium security 'Category B' prisons. All but one of the referrals were serving a sentence of 3 years or more, with the average sentence length being nearly 7 years. Approximately 40% of all residents are Life Sentence prisoners, whose indeterminate sentences tend to last *at least* 13 years. Most men are referred, in accordance with policy informed by experience about optimum timings, when they are in the later stages of their sentences, i.e. 2–3 years from their parole eligibility or EDR (earliest date for release). The intention in this is to maximize the probability that as many men as possible will be able either to move from Grendon to release into the community or to make the most progressive move back into the prison system generally, i.e. to a prison of lower security classification where there are more opportunities to practise their new life skills.

The average age of the residents is around 32 years, within a range from 21 to as old as 60 in exceptional cases. Most men are between 21 and 40. Of a sample of 116 receptions in 1995, 26 (22%) were married, 71 (61%) single and 12 (10%) divorced. The main categories of offences, based on the 229 Receptions for 1994–1995, were for violence (38%—murder, manslaughter, grievous bodily harm, etc.), sex (27%—rape, indecent assault and incest), robbery (28%), dishonesty (4%—multiple thefts, e.g. houses and or cars) and arson (3%). Most of the men have previous convictions (75%, mean of 8.5). Racially, only 7% (16) of the population were black or Asian, compared with an estimated 20% in the national prison population. Table 4.1 gives details of the offence profile for 1994–1995 compared with that of 1972–1973.

Personality Characteristics

A standard battery of personality questionnaires relevant to Grendon's agreed selection criteria is given to all receptions. In the year to 30 April 1995, the receptions ($n = 212$) indicated a distinct profile, one which has changed little over the years.

1. *Intelligence.* On the Raven's Progressive Matrices (1958), a group-administered test of non-verbal intelligence, the receptions had a

Table 4.1. Main offence–Receptions 1994–1995 compared with 1972–1973.

Offence	1994–1995 ($n(\%)$)	1972–1973 (%)
Arson	6 (2.6)	5
Dishonesty		
Burglary	9 (3.9)	
Theft	0	
Other	1 (0.4)	
Total	10 (4.3)	57
Robbery/attempted robbery	65 (28.4)	8
Sexual		
Rape	35 (15.3)	
Attempted rape	4 (1.7)	
Buggery	7 (3.1)	
Indecent assault	13 (5.7)	
Incest/other	2 (0.8)	
Total	61 (26.6)	7
Violence		
Murder/attempted murder	45 (19.7)	
Manslaughter	10 (4.4)	
Wounding	16 (7)	
GBH/ABH	11 (4.8)	
Other	5 (2.2)	
Total	87 (38.1)	17
Other		
Drugs	Not known	3
Driving	Not known	3
Total offences	229 (100)	100%

    mean of 43, where the norm (for 'civilians') is 40. The range of scores for accepted referrals was 27–57, when the maximum obtainable is 60. Men who score well below average on the Ravens (a score of 25 or less) tend not to do as well in therapy.

2. *Hostility*. Scores on the Caine et al. (1976) Hostility and Direction of Hostility Questionnaire (HDHQ) indicate that receptions ($n = 216$) had significantly higher levels of self-reported Total Hostility (Grendon mean = 26.6; norms = 13.0), Extrapunitive Hostility (Grendon = 16.5; norms = 10), Self-criticism (Grendon = 6.8; norms = 3.7) and Guilt (Grendon = 4.0; norms = 1.3) than non-criminal samples.

3. *Extraversion, Neuroticism and Psychoticism*. Scores on Eysenck's Personality Questionnaire—Revised (EPQ-R 1991), support the

impression of a distinctive offender profile for Grendon Receptions. The EPQ-R is a well established measure of enduring personality, with scales for extraversion, neuroticism, 'psychoticism' or 'tough-mindedness', and criminality. Table 4.2 gives a summary comparison between EPQ-R subscale means for a Grendon reception sample of 104 in April 1995 and normative means for 'normal males' and non-therapy male prisoners.

The EPQ has more recently been revised to include scales for Impulsivity (I), Empathy, (M), Venturesomeness (V) and Addiction (A). Means for Grendon on the revised EPQ-R for 113 receptions in 1995 (with standardization norms for $n = 372$ normal adult males in brackets) were:

Impulsiveness:	10.98 (7.02)
Empathy:	13.52 (11.81)
Venturesomeness:	10.73 (8.21)
Addiction:	17.48 (norms 11.60; SD 5.5)

Clearly, the Grendon receptions are above average in terms of neuroticism, criminality and addictiveness, with additional tendencies towards impulsivity, risk-taking, solitary and disturbed behaviour than either the general male adult population or other prisoners.

This profile is supported by the psychiatric histories. Taking as a sample the first 46 receptions to Grendon in 1995, over half (56%) had a history of either psychiatric in-patient status ($n = 4$), referral to a psychiatrist ($n = 9$) or community psychiatric nurse or had received treatment in a prison hospital ($n = 11$) prior to coming to Grendon. Over half (62%) had a history of attempted suicide and the average number of doctor visits in prison prior to Grendon was 27 per man,

Table 4.2. Comparisons between EPQ means—Receptions ($n = 104$), and test norms for male prisoners and general population.

Sub-scale	Grendon (mean (SD))	Male prisoners (mean)	Male normals (mean)
EPQ-E	10.7 (5.6)	13.62	13.19
EPQ-P	6.3 (3.5)	5.72	3.78
EPQ-N	16.2 (5.0)	13.13	9.83
EPQ-C	18.1 (5.3)	15.57	3.78
EPQ-L (lie scale)	5.5 (3.7)	6.78	6.8

Comment: The Grendon sample is more introverted, neurotic, (i.e. levels of tension and stress), insensitive, and criminal than in other prisoners and significantly higher than in non-criminal males.

well above the national average. Other aspects of receptions' prior prison careers include over-representation on special protection units segregated from other prisoners, called Rule 43, either for Own Protection (OP) or for 'Good Order and Discipline' (GOAD), i.e. being unruly or violent. Grendon receptions were more likely to have been on R43-OP ($n = 19$, 41%) and R43-GOAD ($n = 17$, 38%) than the general prison population.

Personality Disorder

The prevailing methodology of referral for treatment at Grendon is via the Medical Officer in the sending prison, who is obliged to complete a form (1080) which is the responsibility of the Directorate of Health Care. While other, non-medical referring criteria have become more specific, the medical classifications of psychopathy, antisocial personality disorder or even, surprisingly, 'sub-normal personality disorder' are the only choices given. As a result, a diagnosis is not given in the majority of referrals, leaving it difficult to reach accurate conclusions as to the prevalence of either American Psychiatric Association DSM-IV (Diagnostic and Statistical Manual of Mental Disorders) or World Health Organisation ISD-10 classifications of mental disorder in Grendon's population. Dolan and Coid (1993), in *Psychopathic and Antisocial Personality Disorders: Treatment and Research Issues*, make considerable progress in bringing together the disparate threads of these diagnostic perspectives by reviewing studies of prison populations (e.g. Bland et al., 1990; Hare, 1991) and conclude that they show 'a high prevalence of antisocial personality disorder varying from 39% to 76% of subjects'.

Gunn et al. (1978) surveyed 107 'Grendon Men', and found that 48 (45%) said that they had been mental hospital in-patients at some time (this was confirmed with the hospitals concerned). They further found that 33 (31%) reported Anxiety symptoms or lack of concentration from a range of 'neurotic symptoms', including sleep disturbances 29 (27%), depression 25 (23%), and obsessions and compulsions 7 (7%).

THE PROCESS

Assessment

On arrival at Grendon, the new reception resides on the Assessment Unit. There are four basic questions which the staff team address over a brief 2-week assessment period:

- Is the inmate motivated to change?
- Is he intellectually able to deal with group psychotherapy?
- Is he psychologically minded, i.e. does he believe in the capacity for people to change and is he capable of insight into interpersonal relationships?
- What are his problems of personality relevant to Grendon's therapeutic community treatment approach?

To this purpose, all receptions are given a battery of questionnaires, a thorough matrix of offence, interpersonal, addictive/substance abuse and prison behaviour variables is collected, and are, finally, interviewed by the assessment wing staff.

The assessment questionnaires include Raven's (1958) Progressive Matrices; Caine et al.'s (1976) Hostility and Direction of Hostility Questionnaire (HDHQ), the Eysenck Personality Questionnaire— Revised (EPQ-R), the General Health Questionnaire (GHQ) of Goldberg, Battle's Culture-Free Self-Esteem Questionnaire (Battle, 1981), Gudjonsson's Blame Attribution Inventory (Gudjonsson, 1984), Nichols and Molinder's Multi-phasic Sex Inventory (Nichols & Molinder, 1984), Hare's Psychopathy Checklist (1991), the Symptom Checklist 90 of Derogatis (1975) and the Personality Diagnostic Questionnaire—Revised of Hyler (1994). The Assessment Unit is managed by a psychologist and staffed by prison officers. At the end of the 2-week assessment, a Case Conference for each new reception is chaired by the Director of Therapy and attended by the Assessment Unit staff and the Wing Therapist plus one other staff member from the new Wing to which the man is referred. Further assessment, in terms of his suitability for Grendon therapy, is then pursued on the therapy wing but the presumption at this stage is that he will be staying. If there prove to be obvious and extreme problems of adjustment to therapy, then the therapy wing team, led by the Wing Therapist, have up to 3 months (from the date of arrival at Grendon) to recommend his return to the sending prison, an option seldom used in practice. It is on the therapy wings that the true process of TC therapy begins in earnest. Before describing the programmes, however, it is essential to summarize the philosophy and principles of therapeutic communities.

Therapeutic Community Philosophy

Kennard and Roberts (1983), in *An Introduction to Therapeutic Communities*, said 'A prison might be the last place you would expect to find a therapeutic community. Prisons have traditionally been for taking away people's freedom, imposing rigid discipline and limiting their opportunity for social involvement'. Prison staff are trained to give 'good order and discipline' priority, instructed in detailed procedures for searching prisoners and their cells, controlling their movements around the prison and are carefully drilled in the correct process for disciplining, physically restraining and adjudicating upon miscreant prisoners. Therapeutic community staff, on the other hand, hold value systems which would appear to be almost antithetical. Rapaport (1960) provided in the 1950s the four principles, based on TC staffs' avowed value systems, which have become axiomatic. These are addressed here in relation to TCs within the prison system (see Cullen, 1994).

Democratization

'Every member of the community (i.e. all patients and staff) should share equally in the exercise of power in decision-making about community affairs.' Maxwell Jones (1968), in *Social Psychiatry in Practice*, revised this principle and said that democracy was giving residents 'that degree of responsibility which is compatible with their capacity at any one time'. This fundamental modification takes much of the empowerment from residents and places it in the hands of the arbiter of capacity, usually a medical practitioner. The problem with this is that, although it has the advantage implicit in most people's belief that doctors have their patients' best interests foremost, it is the doctor's rather than the patient's interpretation of this construct which most often applies. Grendon has even greater obvious difficulty with honouring this principle in that the inmates/ patients are only volunteering to be in therapy to the extent that they have chosen to be in Grendon rather than in another prison, and their exercise of power is constrained by the risk of losing their place. If they were fully enfranchised, it is reasonable to assume that the first act of egalitarian emancipation for most would be to leave the prison. Power-sharing in a prison TC will therefore presumably always be bounded by the dictates of *both* the discipline line of authority, i.e. through the Security department, via the Head of Custody to the Governor, *and* the medical/therapy line of authority, i.e. through the Wing Therapist, via the Director of Therapy to the Governor. On top of these sits the Prison Service hierarchy who, in spite of recommendations for progressive moves or release by Grendon staff, have the final power to move or release. So much for democracy.

In acknowledging these limitations, Grendon has modified this principle to: 'Empowering: Is the principle of enfranchisement wherein every community member has a direct say in every aspect of how the wing is run. He also has the power, shared democratically, to vote a community member out of therapy when he has violated one or more of the cardinal rules of abstinence from using drink, drugs, or physical violence. There are a range of other community rules and guidelines which might cause someone's position to be in question and the collective authority of the community—inmates and staff together—is sustained in order to give genuine commitment to this principle.' The compromises in this redefinition of the democratizing principle are obvious and hugely significant.

Permissiveness

'All members should tolerate from one another a wide degree of behaviour that might be distressing or seem deviant by ordinary standards.' The word *permissive*, like *liberal*, has acquired a more culturally pejorative connotation in the past decade or more due to the influence of a Conservative political philosophy. Yet the active verb in the definition is 'tolerate'. The philosophy of tolerance held within TCs is a prerequisite for allowing men to make mistakes. The new interpersonal skills that are learnt, based on courtesy and respect, often run counter to those acquired both before prison and in the long periods of imprisonment before reaching Grendon. The process is one of trial and error and successive approximations, which constantly falls foul of the more rigid, judgemental mentality of prisoners and prison staff. In prisons, behaviour which is distressing or deviant is more likely to be perceived as rule-violating and motivated by criminal intent and/or peer or staff manipulation. **It is so difficult, yet so vital, to allow people to behave as they normally behave**. If we do not, then they will learn to behave in ways which serve only to satisfy staff, not themselves, and such behaviour is neither genuine (but rather situation-specific and not enduring) nor honest. Permissiveness in this therapeutic sense is intended to tolerate the behaviour only in the sense that it is not punished by conventional prison means but turned instead back into the therapeutic process. The prescription 'take it to your group' encourages both individual and collective responsibilities to be accountable and to change.

Grendon's principles have re-named permissiveness as: 'Support: One of the first and essential dynamics for effective therapy to occur is that of acceptance. Men who are often deeply cynical, frightened and conditioned to be suspicious of any help offered by prison staff and other inmates find it difficult to honestly disclose the details of crimes and other personal experiences which are often at the darkest edges of criminality and abuse. The therapy at Grendon is very challenging, addressing things men have believed or defended for years. It means having the courage to be more honest with themselves than ever before and feeling safe to do it without rejection, insult, or abuse.'

The constant influence and fears of both the Prison Service generally and, increasingly, local prison management concerning acts of indiscipline, escapes or failures to return to prison from temporary release mean that the principle of permissiveness, however defined, is at risk.

Communalism

There should be tight-knit, intimate sets of relationships with sharing of amenities (dining room, etc.), use of first names and free communication.' Again, the emphasis is on individual and collective responsibility, with the social relationships binding community members together, reducing the inmate–staff traditional formal roles, and encouraging greater learning opportunities beyond personal, dyadic or group dynamics. In Grendon, communities elect their own management, prepare their own meals and elect (for wing-based jobs) or nominate (for off-wing positions of greater trust) their own labour allocations. Yet even here concerns have been expressed, via the Advisory Group on Grendon's Development, about the negative connotations in the wider Society about the word 'communalism'. This apparent misunderstanding of the intended definition has influenced another Grendon permutation: 'Responsibility: The regime encourages individual and collective responsibility, clearly unlike most other prison regimes which impose relatively closely supervised and structured regimes upon the population.' Grendon advocates the greatest possible assumption of accountability through a range of procedures described in the next section. Every man in therapy is also ultimately obliged to take responsibilities for his crimes. Within the separate wing communities, this principle survives relatively intact.

Reality Confrontation

'Patients should be continuously presented with interpretations of their behaviour as it is seen by others, in order to counteract their tendency to distort, deny or withdraw from their difficulties in getting on with others.' The Grendon permutation of this principle of democratic/analytic TCs is rather more directive: 'Confrontation: Although it is essential to provide a safe environment for disclosure, there is also a place for direct and candid confrontation for those who persist with defences such as denial and minimalization of their offences as well as for their behaviour towards others within the present community.' Probably the key message from these statements is that the recall of past behaviour, criminal or not, *and* the responsibility assumed for current behaviour must ultimately be challenged by observers' experiences of how they are affected by the accounts and by the effects of the behaviour upon others. This dynamic is essential to learning pro-social alternative skills and in taking the *victim* perspective for both crimes and interpersonal abuse.

Therapeutic Procedures

The principles of the democratic/social therapeutic community inform those procedures which serve to achieve the objectives. Grendon's objectives are explicit:

- To help each man who comes to Grendon to improve his self-esteem and sense of self-worth.
- To improve his behaviour towards others during his time at Grendon.
- To reduce the number and severity of future crimes.

Newell (1996) sums up the collective purpose of the therapy well: 'The TC concept is based on the assumption that prisoners and staff form the community of care and respect which is committed to the development of personal functioning, to address offending and offensive behaviour in order to change so that those who go through the process create no more victims.' The process begins when the new reception is greeted by staff in a friendly, welcoming way and on a first-name basis. The process continues with consistent messages of reassurance, information about therapy and encouragement throughout the assessment and on to the therapy wing. Once on a wing, the man is assigned a small therapy group and a personal officer and encouraged to settle in at his own pace before beginning the first stage of disclosure, telling his life story. Over a period of several hours, he will disclose his own recall of key life events including earliest memories, family relationships, the period of maturation, initial onset of criminal or antisocial behaviour, history of any alcohol or drug use/abuse, a thorough account of the current 'index' offences and imprisonment to date. Through this record, the preliminary assessment report and the man's own account of objectives for change, the Wing Therapist and team, including critically the other residents, will create a clear but malleable treatment plan. As the individual progresses, he is given more opportunities for achievement and responsibility, e.g. election to represent positions in the Community such as Wing Chairman, nomination for jobs with greater freedom of movement around the prison and outings to other institutions to represent Grendon. The cumulative effect of these opportunities, and the support and praise given for both effort and achievement, build both greater self-esteem and confidence and a stronger sense of community responsibility. Simultaneous with this process is one which explores patterns of offending.

Addressing Offending Behaviour

The justification of a Therapeutic Community approach to personality-disordered offenders in the United Kingdom comes not only from the relief of intrapsychic distress caused by the disorder itself but also by a concomitant reduction in the risk posed to others by the 'acting out' of those patient/prisoners in impulsive or premeditated destructive acts of violence, abuse or self-injury. It is not sufficient to produce well adjusted criminals.

If there is a single common characteristic for most, if not all, of our residents, it is that they have failed to sustain relationships and that they have 'resolved' their relationship conflicts in negative ways. Almost three-quarters of all primary crimes committed by our population were violence or sexual abuse of others, with fewer than one in 10 convicted of offences that were primarily profit-motivated. Of course, all crimes have victims, but the treatment premise is that the crime was a product, or consequence, of the interpersonal conflict arising from the personal disorder. Genders and Player (1995) refer to three specific elements of personal relationships:

- the men's relationships with women and children;
- their relationships with figures of authority;
- their relationships with one another.

Patterns of promiscuity, physical and sexual abuse, dominance and control, or insecurity and a sense of inadequacy are common features of inmates' accounts of their relationships with women and children. The Grendon therapy group, supplemented by conjoint therapies including Psychodrama, Social and Life Skills, Cognitive Skills and Sex Offender Treatment Programme address these key therapy themes. They are placed in a range of overlapping offence-specific issue groups. These overlapping areas of therapeutic attention include:

- attitudes to and acceptance of the primary offence, including the issues of denial, the presence of any premeditation, the perception of an ethical view, i.e. 'right and wrong', and the degree of accord between the offender's and the official accounts of the crime;
- the degree of victim awareness, including expressed capacity to feel contrition, understanding probable emotional and practical consequences of the crime for the immediate and related victims;
- the existence of any fantasies and rehearsal in the formulation of offending cognitions;
- general attitudes towards offending;
- plans and strategies for preventing future offensive, or offending, behaviour, i.e. risk and relapse prevention.

Where there are opportunities within the prison community to observe parallels between current behaviour and prior offending, these too are brought into the therapeutic process, whether the issue is women and children, attitudes to authority or generally interpersonal.

Probably the greatest opportunities for exploring attitudes to authority figures are those between the Grendon staff and residents. Norton and Dolan, (1985) address this dynamic well. They refer to violent and damaging acting out behaviour by patients causing conflict for staff, who may feel conflict between their negative reactions based either on their personal values, professional perspectives or custodial roles. If these cannot be resolved, then the authors conclude that 'the possibility of an empathic connection with the patient is lost, and without this the treatment alliance is difficult to sustain. The result may be a response which is wooden and unnatural (perhaps rational-ised as neutral or professional) or else partial, as if simply condoning or, alternatively, simply condemning.' The consequences of this dissonance may be more acting out of negative behaviour, a withdrawal by the patient from his involvement in therapy or a 'superficial appearance of compliance or co-operation with treatment'. These potential conflicts, between inmates/patients and their peers, the community staff and the prison regime, are at the heart of the therapeutic dilemma of sustaining a therapeutic agenda within a cluster of therapeutic communities within a secure prison within an increasingly proscriptive, punitive and fragmented society.

These relationships between one another within the wing community are the final area. Men imprisoned for significant portions of their adult lives inevitably acquire a complex and well ingrained repertoire of prison life skills which are frequency at odds with, and sometime antithetical to, the therapeutic agenda. Within this conflict of cultures, attitudes to taking drugs or alcohol, the hierarchy of offender groups which places sex offenders at the bottom, the code of never informing on another 'con' and the fears of returning to the conventional prison system are predominant themes for concern. Peer group influence in controlling and modifying these prison value systems are enhanced through the cultural strengthening of community 'elders', members who have successfully completed the transition themselves aided by those newer members who have either not succumbed to prison subcultural values or are highly motivated to resist temptation. The group-centred therapy rather than one-to-one treatment between inmate and therapist also serves to strengthen this countercultural press to change but only when the group's complement is balanced in favour of TC culture carriers. Other aspects of therapeutic community regimes which are potent antidotes to prison mentality include the empowering of inmates in community-based hierarchies, e.g. an elected Wing Chairman who is strongly anti-drugs, and in the ultimate sanction of being voted out of the community—by peers and staff—and having to return to a criminal culture they have voluntarily chosen to abandon. This final control on pro-criminal, anti-TC behaviour carries the double punishment of both returning to a more hostile environment and risking being labelled, e.g. in official reports, as a treatment failure.

THE PROOF

Addressing the efficacy of the therapeutic community approach in a secure prison involves four perspectives, three linked to the formal objectives stated earlier and one linked to reason:

- Changes in personality characteristics and attitudes, particularly those relevant to increased self-esteem and greater self-control.
- Changes in behaviour during imprisonment.
- Reductions in rate of offending after release from prison.
- Personal accounts of the staff and inmates regarding the value of the regime.

Personality

A large number of studies (e.g. Newton, 1973; Gunn et al., 1978; Miller, 1982; Genders & Player, 1995) have confirmed significant improvements in relevant personality characteristics, including reduced levels of introversion, neuroticism, anxiety, depression and hostility. Gunn et al. (1978) also identified significantly better attitudes to authority figures, including police, prison officers and probation officers, using Semantic Differential techniques. There had been no major studies of changes in personality for over a decade until Newton (1996) compared questionnaire scores in a sample of 99 men pre- and post-therapy (average time in therapy ~ 15 months) who left Grendon between May 1994 and December 1995, on the EPQ, HDHQ and Rotter Internal–External Locus of Control. She controlled further for change in relation to time in therapy and reasons for transfer. Data on the specific reasons for transfer, in terms of 'progressive move, own request, staff decision or voted out' were obtained for 32 of the total. Table 4.3 give the results of this most recent study.

The changes recorded are all in the direction of reduced deviance, are highly statistically significant and are related to both time in therapy and manner of release. The last finding is provisional, as the only positive transfer category, 'progressive move', has only five cases. Newton concluded 'The length of stay at Grendon appears to be a key factor, with men who stay longest tending to change most on a number of scales. This suggests a progressive treatment effect ...' While decreases in 'tough-mindedness', extrapunitive hostility and external locus of control (the tendency to blame factors other than self for crimes, etc.) are consistent with explicit aims of therapy; the additional improvements in other measures, e.g. lower self-criticism and guilt, suggest that Grendon 'graduates' may become, as Newton suggests: 'more self-accepting, less troubled and less averse to the company of others'.

Behaviour at Grendon

Sleap (1979) showed significant achievement of observable treatment goals for two samples after 6 ($n = 209$, $t = 25.3$, $p \leqslant 0.001$) and 12 ($n = 94$, $t = 27.3$, $p \leqslant 0.001$) months in therapy using a Goal Attainment Scale and calibrating the achievement of quantifiable goals, e.g. letters to prospective employers or reduction in incidents of verbal aggression towards others, using a five-point scale. Cullen (1994) confirmed that Grendon had one of the lowest rates of 'prison offending as measured by Governor's Reports (the standard category for more serious offences against prison discipline) of any prison in its category in the country'. It has to be conceded, however, that this is an unfair comparison as Grendon is also unique in being the only

Table 4.3. Test–retest scores and percentage of reliable change.

Test	n	Score on reception (mean(SD))	Score on discharge (mean (SD))	change (mean (SD))	Significance of t (two-tailed) (p)	Cases showing statistically reliable change (%)	
						reliable Decrease	reliable Increase
EPQ P	94	6.7 (3.9)	4.7 (3.8)	−1.9 (4.1)	<0.001	32	5
EPQ E	94	10.0 (5.8)	12.6 (5.7)	+2.5 (5.1)	<0.001	8	37
EPQ N	94	16.9 (4.4)	13.2 (5.9)	−3.8 (5.1)	<0.001	53	3
EPQ L	94	5.2 (3.8)	5.3 (5.3)	0.0 (3.7)	0.888		
EPQ C	51	19.0 (4.4)	15.7 (5.4)	−3.2 (4.8)	<0.001	41	0
HDHQ							
Total	94	28.3 (8.0)	21.6 (9.2)	−6.6 (9.0)	<0.001	38	3
Direction	94	2.3 (7.0)	1.3 (6.9)	−0.9 (6.8)	=0.179		
Intropun. tot.	94	11.7 (3.9)	8.6 (4.3)	−3.0 (4.1)	<0.001		
Extrapun. tot.	94	16.5 (5.9)	12.8 (6.1)	−3.7 (6.4)	<0.001		
Subscales							
HDHQ SC	94	7.2 (2.5)	5.3 (2.9)	−1.9 (2.5)	<0.001		
HDHQ G	94	4.4 (1.8)	3.4 (1.8)	−1.0 (2.1)	<0.001		
HDHQ AH	94	6.8 (2.7)	5.6 (2.4)	−1.2 (2.9)	<0.001		
HDHQ PH	94	3.1 (2.0)	2.2 (2.0)	−1.0 (2.2)	<0.001		
HDHQ CO	94	6.8 (2.6)	5.2 (2.8)	−1.5 (2.9)	<0.001		
I-E Locus	84	12.7 (3.8)	9.6 (4.1)	−3.1 (4.1)	−0.001		

'Statistically reliable change' was calculated for scales on which there was a statistically significant mean change and the necessary normative data was available.

prison in the UK which does not have a Punishment Block or Segregation Unit, and hence refers offensive or disruptive behaviour back to the individual's group and Community to deal with therapeutically rather than by traditional, formal methods. Although this is not strictly speaking proof, Grendon also has a system of regular assessments of progress using semi-structured evaluation forms for the wing to assess progress or deterioration in listed objectives. These have yet to be systematically researched.

Reconvictions

Most of the early studies of reconviction (George, 1971; Newton, 1973; Gunn et al., 1978) found that rates of offending after 2 years from leaving prison were not significantly lower than before. The first two studies, however, found that rates did drop significantly from 59% to 39.5% (George, 1971) and from 58% to 50% (Newton, 1973), controlling for whether the samples had stayed under or over one year in therapy.

No more reconviction studies were done until Cullen (1993; $n = 217$) and Newton and Thornton (1994; $n = 150$) found that although overall reconviction rates for men who had been in therapy at Grendon between 1984 and 1989 ($n = 217$; 150) were only slightly lower than rates for adult male prisoners serving similar sentences, rates were significantly lower when controlling for time in therapy and manner of release, i.e. whether released direct from Grendon or transferred to another prison and subsequently released. Half of those who left Grendon before 18 months ($n = 103$ in the second study) were reconvicted within 2 years, compared with only 19% of those who had stayed for 19 months or longer ($n = 47$), controlling for the effects of offence type, age and sentence length. The longer the term in therapy, the lower the rate of reconviction. Those paroled on License (under supervision) from Grendon ($n = 43$) were significantly ($X^2 = 8.46$, d.f. $= 2$, $p \leqslant 0.05$) less likely to be reconvicted (26%) than those transferred to other prisons and released without supervision ($n = 44$, 54%) or those released direct from Grendon without supervision ($n = 63$, 40%). The greater part of the variance was attributable to being released from Grendon than whether or not it was under supervision. These results suggest both a treatment effect and that it is better to be released direct from Grendon under supervision. Marshall (1996) expanded the sample sizes to include a 'Treatment Group' of 702 prisoners discharged or transferred from Grendon during the period of the original studies (1984–1989), one matched control group of 1425 prisoners drawn from the general prison population with 'broadly similar characteristics', e.g. offence type, sentence length and age, who were in the system during the same period, and the second 'Waiting List' control group of 142 prisoners who had been on the waiting list for therapy but did not transfer for various reasons, again during the same period. The results in terms of reconviction after 4 years showed that the prisoners selected for Grendon are a 'rather different group ... and are at higher risk of reoffending'. A comparison of the Treatment and Waiting List groups showed that both groups had higher reconviction rates than the Matched Controls and that the Treatment Group rate was 'noticeably less likely to be reconvicted' than the Waiting List Group. Although the difference was only significant at the 10% level of confidence, the trend was consistent with previous findings. This study is not yet published at the time of writing.

Accounts of Therapy

Beadle and Cullen (1994) surveyed all inmates resident on four therapy wings, asking them to rate every aspect or element of the therapy programme in terms of how important they were to therapy. One hundred (85%) of the 118 total population voluntarily complied. The main findings included:

- The majority (77%) were very or quite satisfied with therapy. Only 15% were 'not quite satisfied' and 6% were 'unhappy'.
- Almost all the inmates were very positive about Grendon, describing it as more relaxed, beneficial, caring, humane, constructive and open than other prisons in their experience. Only three individuals of 100 were negative or hostile. Examples of replies to 'How would you best describe Grendon?' included: 'Grendon offers an arena in which healing may occur', 'Grendon reaches the parts other prisons can't reach', 'your chance to stop being a chameleon', 'an oasis crowded with dirty camels' and 'Grendon may just save my or someone else's life'.

Table 4.4 gives the results of ratings for all 17 of the core and supplementary elements and programmes of the therapy regime. Those aspects of the TC regime which address men's problems directly (e.g. the core therapy groups plus the 'specialized' group therapies like Cognitive Skills and Psychodrama) and which encourage improved ties with families and the outside world, e.g. Family Days, were most valued.

The evidence is considerable that this Therapeutic Community prison is meeting or approaching all of its objectives and is, at the very least, a preferable alternative to a conventional prison regime.

Table 4.4. Inmate $(n = 100)$ survey of value of Grendon therapy elements. Inmates were asked to rate the usefulness of the following activities to their therapy.

	Don't Know/ not important	Quite important	Very important/ essential
Core element/ activity			
Small groups	2	3	95
Wing meetings	9	36	55
Feedbacks	7	28	65
Assessments	11	5	84
Other talking in general	11	18	71
Supplementary elements			
Education	13	33	54
Work	18	41	41
Psychodrama	13	9	78
Any Questions	26	50	24
Wing socials	20	24	56
Conferences	24	40	36
Life skills	9	23	68
Family Days	9	5	86
Open Days	15	14	71
Psycho-education	20	9	71
Cognitive Skills	20	18	62
Alternatives to Violence	15	6	79

SUMMARY AND COMMENT

Public risk is increased if men who are at the 'heavy end of the market' in terms of criminality and who are made less predictable by their dimensions of personality are released from prison unchanged or criminalized still further by long imprisonment. Conventional imprisonment is a hit-and-miss proposition in terms of addressing reoffending risks, with the balance clearly negative. Yet the irony is that the public, and prison service paymasters, set Grendon the unique task of proving that it works. This is in spite of Grendon being less expensive than either the average for its category of prison or for those prisons which refer men to therapy. The evidence is strong and mounting that Grendon achieves its objectives and in so doing significantly reduces the risk of releasing dysfunctional criminals to kill, rape and abuse again. The irony is thus compounded when this unique regime is threatened by the imposition of a national, security-driven manual of operation based on the fear of national escapes of notorious or political prisoners. Grendon has had one escape in 34 years and none in the past 15, the best record of security in the country, achieved by creating a place that men do not want to leave. The British Prison Service has been rocked recently by the effects of the official response to escapes from two maximum security prisons. Extremely detailed reports known as Woodcock (1994) and Learmont (1995) made over 200 recommendations about improving the security of prisons and exercising greater control over prisoners. On top of this, the Treasury has obliged the Prison Service to make budget cuts of the order of 13% over 3 years, cuts from which Grendon is not exempt in spite of its excellent track record and relatively low costs compared with similar security category prisons or alternative treatment institutions. The threats to this unique therapeutic regime are all the more ironic when viewed against the fact that the prisons that are receiving the greatest increases in funding are those with the worst records of security or that have failed official inspections! These concerns must be placed within the wider context of a host organization struggling to make coherent sense of recognizing the achievements of those parts, or institutions, which are so unlike the majority whilst appearing fair to all in terms of fiscal allocations.

Staff Issues

That Grendon has continued to function as a collective of therapeutic wings is to its credit. Yet there is another, more subtle threat which comes from within. The original treatment model for Grendon in the 1960s was a medical one, primarily psychiatric and psychotherapeutic. Over the ensuing two decades, other modalities, many with a psychological perspective such as Cognitive and Social Skills, were introduced to great effect, so that in the 1990s the therapy offered has developed into a multi-modal model of the kind which most research attests best serves a prison population. This flexible, complementary model was further enhanced by carefully introducing more opportunities to community members to test out their new interpersonal skills either within the prison grounds, e.g. more representation on committees and greater freedom of movement between wings and areas, and by greater use of Temporary Releases outside the prison to look for work, housing or build better family ties. These too are now threatened, the former by a return to the primacy of the 'medical model' and the latter by the effects of the security impositions mentioned earlier.

Redressing an imbalance in authority between the medical and governorial power bases in favour of the former was a positive collaborative initiative. The risk, however, has been to replace one hierarchical decision-making process with another. A 'doctor knows best' sense may be better than the hierarchical prison model but it is one which risks diminishing the more egalitarian tradition of flatter decision-making and collective responsibility which has distinguished British TCs for most of their history. Returning to this greater medical model in terms of the nomenclature of therapy and emphasizing the 'illness' of the 'patients' by reference to psychopathy and personality disorder risks returning to the stigmatization for prisoners of being labelled mentally ill and the concomitant fear of being transferred from the Therapeutic Community prison (if the doctor judges the patient not to have progressed in his treatment or to have worsened) to a Special Secure Hospital. Although these fears may be largely unfounded, they have always had a life in hearsay throughout the prisons. Yet, the quandary is that retaining accountability for therapy in Grendon within the Directorate of Health Care has always been perceived as a safeguard against the encroachment from the prison side of the equation. It is possible to strike a balance and, to its great credit, Grendon has managed it, more or less, to date.

One limitation of this bilateral management arrangement is that it can inherently resist innovations outside the medical sphere or even see changes in treatment modalities, e.g. to more offence-specific, programme-based methods, as threats or as inferior models to more traditional, psychotherapeutic counselling. The TC model traditionally practised at Grendon has the additional weakness of never having been empirically described and assessed in terms of how the dynamic actually works or which elements of the regime contribute to which aspects of the reintegration of the offender's personality, i.e. there is an inherent lack of cause-and-effect specificity. Another limitation is that there is a tendency for polarization of procedures and people into one of two 'camps', either the treatment staff or the discipline staff. This dynamic has accelerated recently with the imposition of obligatory changes to security arrangements within prisons nationally to comply with the 'Recommendations' of the two national inquiries into standards.

The evidence of over three decades of therapy in the total institution approach practised at Grendon is that, on balance, it has been possible to sustain a therapeutic ethos within a security-conscious institution. There are, however, many hazards—some obvious, some subtle and some insidious. Ultimately, the greatest risk may come from the imposition of arbitrary budget cuts initiated by the Treasury in order to reduce the Public Expenditure percentage. If the proposed cuts of 13.3% over 3 fiscal years are imposed indiscriminately, on successful and unsuccessful regimes alike, then Grendon will no longer be a Therapeutic Community prison by 1999. These issues are developed in more detail in the final chapter.

REFERENCES

Battle, J. (1981). The Culture-Free Self-Esteem Inventory (AD). Texas: Pro-Ed.

Beadle, P. & Cullen, E. (1994). Evaluation of all aspects of therapy. A study among inmates. Unpublished report.

Bland, R. C., Newman, S. C., Dyck, R. J. et al. (1990). Prevalence of psychiatric disorders and suicide attempts in a prison population. *Canadian Jounral of Psychiatry* **35**, 407–413.

Cullen, E. (1993). The Grendon Reconviction Study, Part 1. *Prison Service Journal,* **90**, 35–37.

Cullen, E. (1994). Grendon: The therapeutic prison that works. *Journal of Therapeutic Communities,* **15**, 4.

Caine, T. M., Foulds, G. A. & Hope, K. (1976). *The Hostility – Direction of Hostility Questionnaire.* Sevenoaks: Hodder and Stoughton.

Derogatis, L. R. (1975). *Symptom Checklist-90-Revised.* Minneapolis: National Computer Systems Inc.

Dolan, B. & Coid, J. (1993). *Psychopathic and Antisocial Personality Disorders: Treatment and Research Issues.* London: Gaskell.

Eysenck, H. J. & Eysenck, S. B. G. (1991). *Manual of the Eysenck Personality Questionnaire – Revised.* London: Hodder & Stoughton.

Genders, E. & Player, E. (1995). *Grendon: A Study of a Therapeutic Prison.* Oxford: Clarendon Press.

George, R. (1971). *Grendon Follow-up 1967–68.* Grendon Psychology Unit Series A Report No 47.

Goldberg, D. & Williams, P. (1988). *The General Health Questionnaire.* Windsor: NFER-Nelson.

Gudjonsson, G. H. (1984). *The Blame Attribution Inventory.* Beckenham, Kent: The Bethlem & Maudsley NHS Trust.

Gunn, J. Robertson, G. & Dell, S. (1978). *Psychiatric Aspects of Imprisonment.* London: Academic Press.

Hare, R. D. (1991). *The Hare Psychopathy Checklist–Revised.* Toronto: Multi-Health Systems, Inc.

Hyler, S. (1994). *Psychological Diagnostic Questionnaire-Revised (4).* New York: Scarsdale.

Jacobson, N. S., Follette, W. C. & Revenstorf, D. (1984). *Behaviour Therapy,* **15**, 336–352.

Jones, M. (1968). *Beyond the Therapeutic Community: Social Learning and Social Psychiatry.* New Haven: Yale University Press.

Kennard, D. & Roberts, J. (1983). *An Introduction to Therapeutic Communities*. London: Routledge Kegan Paul.

Main, T. (1946). The hospital as a therapeutic institution. *Bulletin of the Menninger Clinic,* **10**, 66–68.

Marshall, P. (1996). The Grendon Re-Conviction Study, Part II. Unpublished report from the Home Office Research & Statistics Directorate.

Miller, Q. (1982). Preliminary consideration of psychological test/retest scores and their bearing on criminal reconviction. Grendon Psychology Unit Series D, Report D13.

Newton, M. (1973). Reconviction after treatment at Grendon. CP Report Series B, No 1, Prison Service, Home Office.

Newton, M. (1996). Outcome of treatment at Grendon: Changes in personality (EPQ), Hostility (HDHQ) and Locus of Control (Unpublished research report).

Newton, M. & Thornton, D. (1994). Grendon Re-conviction Study, Part 1 update. Unpublished internal correspondence.

Newell, T. (1996). Grendon's future (Unpublished management briefing paper).

Nichols, X. & Molinder, Y. (1984). *The Multi-Phasic Sex Inventory*. Washington: Tacoma.

Norton, K. (1992). A culture of enquiry—Its preservation or loss. *Journal of Therapeutic Communities,* **13**(1), 3–25.

Norton, K. & Dolan, B. (1995). Acting out and the institutional response. *The Journal of Forensic Psychiatry,* **6**(2), 317–332.

Phares, E. J. (1976). *Locus of Control in Personality*. Morrison, NJ: General Learning Press.

Rapaport, R. (1960). *The Community as Doctor*. London: Tavistock.

Ravens, J. S. (1958). *Ravens Standard Progressive Matrices*, University Printing House, Cambridge. London: H.K. Lewis.

Sleap, H. (1979). Goal attainment scaling. An introduction and some limited findings. Grendon Psychology Unit Series B, Report B14.

Woodcock, Sir J. (1994). The Woodcock Report, an inquiry into the escape of six prisoners from the Special Security Unit at Whitemoor Prison. London: HMSO.

Woodward, R. (1991). Banging your head against a sponge (Unpublished article).

Yalom, L. D. (1975). *The Theory and Practice of Group Psychotherapy*. New York: Basic Books.

CHAPTER 5

The Barlinnie Special Unit: The Rise and Fall of a Therapeutic Experiment

David J. Cooke

The Douglas Inch Centre and Glasgow Caledonian University

The Barlinnie Special Unit (BSU) was established in 1973 as a regime for dealing with some of Scotland's most difficult prisoners; the unit was closed in 1995 following a detailed review of the Scottish Prison Service's strategy for small units (SPS, 1994). The BSU had an influence disproportionate either to its size or its throughput of prisoners; it obtained local notoriety and international fame. This disproportionate influence arose because the BSU became an icon, used by believers in rehabilitation to confront the acolytes of the 'nothing works' doctrine (Martinson, 1974).

The interest generated by the regime can be gauged by the number of accounts—both qualitative and quantitative—which have been published about the BSU (e.g. Boyle, 1977; Carrell & Laing, 1982; Light, 1985; Cooke, 1987, 1989; Conlin & Boag, 1986; Whatmore, 1987, 1990; Woznik, 1995) Rarely, throughout its history, was the BSU out of the media: the comments were frequently negative as these two examples illustrate; 'Porridge with cream: a life of luxury behind bars in Barlinnie Special Unit' and 'The Nutcracker Suite, more freedom for the danger men'. Other commentators were more positive. Jimmy Boyle, perhaps the most celebrated inmate of the Unit, indicated that it furnished him with a 'sense of freedom' within

Therapeutic Communities for Offenders.
Edited by E. Cullen, L. Jones and R. Woodward. © 1997 John Wiley & Sons Ltd.

the prison system (Boyle, 1977) and Russell Kerr, speaking in the House of Commons (Hansard, 1987), opined '...we owe it to our children not to turn away from a major breakthrough in penal reform'.

The recent closing of the BSU provides an opportunity to review both the achievements of the Unit and the problems which it generated; it allows a retrospective determination of the lessons which may be derived for the future containment and treatment of violent and disruptive prisoners.

THE RISE OF THE BARLINNIE SPECIAL UNIT

The BSU was established in 1973 in response to growing concerns amongst prison staff and prison management about the rate and nature of violent incidents within Scottish prisons (SHHD, 1971). Not only the number but also the seriousness of assaults was increasing, and weapons were being used more frequently. The official view at this time was that the increase in the quantity and seriousness of violence was related to an increase in the life-sentenced population. The suspension and the ultimate abolition of the death sentence for murder in the 1960s resulted in a growing cohort of young prisoners who did not know whether they would ever be released. They perceived that they had little to lose, and perhaps much to gain in terms of reputation, by being violent.

The Scottish Home and Health Department set up a working party to deal with this problem, which not only worked with great dispatch but also produced novel solutions to the problem of prisoner violence (SHHD, 1971). The primary focus of the working party was to find a method for reducing violent behaviour within prison rather than reducing violent recidivism. A regime plan evolved that was underpinned by three basic principles which were derived from the Therapeutic Community movement; the application of these principles to the management of this type of prisoner was radical.

First, it was argued that much prison violence is underpinned by inadequate or inappropriate staff/prisoner relationships. Although the 'us and them' sub-culture is the norm in most prisons, an attempt was made to move from the traditional officer/prisoner relationship towards something approaching a nurse/patient relationship.

Second, it was argued that traditional regimes frustrate certain prisoners by removing any vestiges of autonomy; they may be told what and when to eat, when to shower and change their underclothes, when to exercise, when to go to bed: particularly in the era during which the BSU was established, prisoners had little say in day-to-day decisions. In order to enhance autonomy, prisoners in the new regime were given a share of the decision-making within the Unit.

Third, prisons are inherently stressful and frustrating environments for many prisoners (e.g. Sykes, 1958; Toch, 1982); normal responses to stress and frustration, including anger, are frequently punished. The working party accepted that such responses would be common, and perhaps understandable, for the group of prisoners targeted for this Unit, and thus it was resolved, that prisoners should be given the opportunity to verbalize their feelings, their hostility and their violent thoughts, rather than resort to violence.

From this basic framework a regime evolved. The three principles were operationalized through the 'community' which evolved in the Unit. Three types of meetings were developed: weekly 'community' meetings, 'special meetings' and 'four groups'. All members of the community, both staff and prisoners, had to attend the community and special meetings. Community meetings were held every week and they focused on both the practical housekeeping aspects of the Unit and on the challenging of inappropriate behaviour or attitudes of staff and prisoners alike. Special meetings could be called at any time and they were designed to resolve conflicts or crises through discussion and debate rather than through violence. The final type of meeting—'four groups' composed of two staff and two prisoners— evolved to have two purposes: first, they were used to indoctrinate new staff and prisoners into the style and ethos of the regime, and second, they were used as a smaller forum in which to resolve serious conflicts (see Whatmore, 1987; Cooke, 1987 for more detailed accounts).

Over time prisoners in the BSU began to enjoy privileges that were very different to their peers in other prisons in Scotland. They enjoyed frequent visits in circumstances that ensured privacy, they had the opportunity to cook their own food, they could decorate their own cells and could fit these out with a television and a video recorder, they could work or not as they chose. These conditions led to much comment not just from the media but also from professional commentators. Two psychologists described it as '... the easiest, plushest prison Unit that has ever existed' (Conlin & Boag, 1986, p. 22).

The material benefits of the regime, particularly the discrepancy between the benefits in this and other contemporary regimes, were easy to perceive and easy to criticize. However, when the regime was functioning properly these material benefits were counterbalanced by less obvious physical and psychological disadvantages (Cooke, 1987).

The BSU was cramped and privacy was at a premium. Within the meetings described above prisoners were subjected to considerable pressure; men who had traditionally resolved conflicts and crises through the use of physical violence had to learn the new skills of debate, negotiation and compromise. Prisoners inured to, and frequently contemptuous of, the discipline meted out by a governor had to learn to accept the discipline imposed by the community of prisoners and staff. Those who transgressed 'norms' of acceptable behaviour would be 'sanctioned' by the community group; sanctions could entail the loss of visits or the loss of the privilege of going outside the prison. Community-imposed sanctions became a powerful control over prisoners' behaviour (Whatmore, 1987; Cooke, 1987).

GETTING TO THE BARLINNIE SPECIAL UNIT

Prisoners were transferred to the Unit because they had engaged in significant and prolonged violent, disruptive or subversive behaviour in other prisons. Once a particular prisoner was referred to the BSU they were subjected to a detailed evaluation by an assessment team composed of three prison staff, including the governor and deputy governor of the Unit, a psychiatrist and a clinical psychologist (Whatmore, 1987; Cooke, 1989). The assessment team determined whether the problems the prisoner was presenting could be resolved in the referring prison. If it appeared that transfer was required then the assessment team had to be convinced, not only that the prisoner wished to be transferred, but also that he had some motivation to engage in the BSU regime. Prisoners could be deemed to be inappropriate for the regime if they suffered from a psychiatric illness which required long-term medication, if it appeared that they might not cope with what was an inherently stressful regime or if there was a significant ongoing personal feud between the referred prisoner and a prisoner already in the regime.

The assessment team were mindful of the danger that prisoners may have deliberately sought a place in the BSU by behaving in a violent and disruptive manner: great care was taken in the assessment process to rule out this possibility.

PRISONERS IN THE BARLINNIE SPECIAL UNIT

Only 36 prisoners experienced the BSU regime, their length of stay ranging from four months to 126 months. They all had a history of serious offences generally, both within and outwith prison; 66% had convictions for homicide, 11% having convictions for more than one homicide. Consideration of the victims of these homicides suggests that the homicides were somewhat unusual. Of the 33 victims killed by this cohort of prisoners, only 15% were female compared with an average of 31% of victims of homicide in Scotland (The Scottish Office, 1993). Their relationships with their victims were also unusual; 70% of the victims were strangers and 30% were acquaintances; this contrasts markedly with the average pattern of homicides in Scotland in which 28% of victims are strangers, 40% are acquaintances and 28% are relatives. This pattern is not unusual in seriously personality-disordered prisoners: Hare & McPherson (1984) have indicated that psychopathic offenders are most likely to kill male victims who are strangers to them.

Apart from homicide most of the prisoners showed considerable versatility in their offending; most had extensive criminal records which included crimes of dishonesty as well as crimes of violence. Many had committed serious offences in prison, including assaults, mobbing and rioting and hostage taking, offences which resulted in outside adjudication and additional prison sentences (Cooke, 1989).

The majority of the prisoners suffered from psychopathy or significant psychopathic traits. The Hare Psychopathy Checklist— Revised (Hare, 1991) has been developed to measure psychopathic traits in a reliable and valid manner. The expression of psychopathic traits shows some cross-cultural variation and it is necessary to use different cut-off scores on this instrument when it is applied in Scotland (Cooke & Michie, 1995; Cooke, 1995a, 1995b, 1996). Analysis of the metric inequivalence of this instrument indicates that a score of 25 in Scotland is equivalent to the diagnostic cut-off score of 30 in North America. Using a Psychopathy Checklist Score of 25 or higher as the diagnostic cut-off, 72% of the prisoners were classified as psychopathic, and a further 25% were classified as having significant psychopathic traits.

This observation has significance in that psychopathic individuals are not only persistent in their offending (Hare & McPherson, 1984; Hare et al., 1988; Hart, et al., 1988; Serin et al., 1990; Serin, 1991; Harris et al., Cormier, 1991) but are also extremely difficult to treat (Blackburn, 1993); indeed, recent evidence suggests that treatment may make them worse (Rice et al., 1992). Psychopaths almost inevitably generate difficulties in prison settings; they disregard social control and convention, in particular, they reject authority and discipline, their behaviour does not alter in response to punishment, they have low frustration toleration and are likely to act out under minor provocation, they may engage in subversive and manipulative behaviour as a way of combating boredom and as a means of expressing duping delight. They cause problems disproportionate to their numbers.

CHANGE OF BEHAVIOUR IN THE BARLINNIE SPECIAL UNIT

This cohort of prisoners was referred to the BSU because their disturbed and disruptive behaviour could not be dealt with effectively in the referring prison. How did they respond? Did their behaviour change? In order to answer these questions the behaviour of the cohort of prisoners was examined before and after their transfer to the BSU. (See Cooke (1989) for a more detailed account of a smaller cohort of prisoners.)

Records of offences against discipline, both those offences which received adjudication within the prison and those which received adjudication in outside courts, were reviewed for all the prisoners. In order to minimize errors due to inaccuracies or differences in recording practices, only serious incidents were analysed. Two indices of violent and disruptive behaviour were derived; first, the number of people whom the prisoner had physically assaulted, and secondly, the number of serious incidents in which the prisoner had engaged. Serious incidents included hostage-taking, escaping, 'smashing up', demonstrating, barricading, fire-raising and dirty campaigns. These indices give some estimate of the violent and disruptive behaviour of these individuals, but as with all markers of criminal behaviour they must be underestimates; this type of prisoner is particularly skilful at engaging in disruptive behaviour, particularly subversive behaviour, which is difficult to prove.

Number of People Assaulted

The cohort of 36 prisoners who experienced the regime of the BSU during its existence were responsible for 181 assaults in their current sentence before being transferred to the BSU; during their time in the BSU they were responsible for two assaults. The fact that prisoners spent different periods of time in their referring prison than they did in the BSU means that it is not legitimate to compare raw assault rates. In order to correct for differences in time exposed to different regimes expected rates of assault were calculated for each prisoner using the formula below; individual figures were then aggregated.

$$A_e = T_2 \cdot A_0 / T_1$$

where A_e is the expected rate of assaults, A_0 is the observed number of assaults prior to transfer, T_2 is the time spent in the BSU and T_1 is the time spent in prison prior to transfer.

Application of the above formula reveals that the total number of assaults which would have been expected during the prisoners' time in the BSU, assuming that their behavior had not changed, would have been 131. This figure is in marked contrast to the observed rate of two assaults during the history of the Unit.

Number of Serious Incidents

The cohort of 36 prisoners were responsible for 174 serious incidents prior to their transfer to the BSU; many were responsible for particularly serious incidents, including hostage-taking. During their stay in the BSU they were responsible for 11 serious incidents, the majority of which were incidents of cell barricading. When the expected rate of serious incidents was determined using the methodology described above it was estimated to be 102.

Significant Change or Statistical Artefact?

These results suggest that the behaviour of those exposed to the the regime of the BSU, in terms of both assaults and serious incidents, changed dramatically. Before concluding that this is in any sense a 'real change' it is necessary to exclude other explanations for the observed changes.

Despite the fact that the BSU was regarded as an experimental regime, no formal monitoring was put in place when the Unit was established. Because the prisoners were particularly unusual and because they were subjected to a complex selection process it is not possible to generate an appropriate control group. Cook & Campbell (1979) indicated that the design used in the evaluation—one of the most widely used designs in outcome research—is a 'One-group pre-test post-test' design. This is a weak design and changes in behaviour may be misinterpreted as treatment effects where in fact the changes are the consequence of confounding factors. This particular design is subject to five confounding factors, the most important being confounding due to 'history' and due to 'maturation' (See Cooke (1989) for a more detailed account of confounding factors.)

Could confounding factors explain these observed changes in behaviour? Experimental designs are confounded by 'history' when some process other than the treatment produced the observed change. For example, if a group of prisoners were told that if they did not have any disciplinary offences for five years they would be considered for parole, then their behaviour may change in order to achieve parole; the change would have little to do with the regime in which they were contained. It is unlikely that the change in behaviour observed in the BSU could be attributed to external processes such as change in parole policy. The observed change in prisoner behaviour occurred at all stages of the BSU operation; to explain this process in terms of historical confounding would require the existence of a series of external events all directed towards changing the prisoners' behaviour. This is improbable.

Maturation is a more serious threat to the conclusion that the observed changes could be attributed to the regime. There is a commonly held clinical belief that psychopaths either mature or burn out in their 30 or 40s. Walters (1990) indicated that the processes of maturation and burn-out should be differentiated. Those who mature may change their mode of thinking and their values, they may develop stable relationships with non-criminal associates, they may desist from criminal activity. Those who burn out may merely lack the energy or drive to engage in criminal or antisocial activity; these activities cease but they are not replaced by any of the prosocial adaptations manifested by those who mature.

The clinical perception of maturation or burn-out is not supported by the research literature. Hare & Forth (1992) and Hare et al. (1988) have demonstrated that although psychopathic individuals' convictions for non-violent crimes decline with age, particularly in the 35–40-year age range, their propensity to commit violent crime does not appear to decline until much later in life.

Moffit (1993) has argued, in a compelling review article, that there is a small and distinct taxon of offenders who are characterized both by the early onset of behavioural disturbance and lifetime persistence of antisocial and criminal behaviour. Most of the cohort in the BSU would fall into this category.

It is unlikely that maturation or burn-out could explain the change of behaviour within the BSU; the best empirical evidence available suggests that the violent offending of this type of prisoners does not decline significantly with age. The observed change in behaviour of those in the BSU was rapid; if either maturation or burn-out were responsible, a more gradual decline in offending would be expected. The rapidity of the behavioural change can be highlighted by examining the actual and expected rates of assaults during the first 12 months in the BSU. Using the procedure outlined above the expected rate of assaults for the first year of the prisoners' stay in the BSU was estimated as being 39 compared with the observed rate of zero during this period; the expected rate of serious incidents in the first 12 months was 34 compared with the two which occurred.

It is unlikely, therefore, that the substantial changes in behaviour noted can be attributed to an experimental artefact; the BSU appears to have been successful in containing violent offenders in a manner that avoided further violence.

LESSONS FROM THE REGIME

The results of the BSU regime were notable; however, it is difficult to provide a detailed explanation of which particular elements of the regime promoted change, or at the very least desistance from violence. Perhaps one of the greatest contributions of the BSU is that it confirmed the importance of regime factors in the maintenance of a virtually violence-free regime. I will now examine the literature which demonstrates the importance of regime factors. (See Cooke (1991; 1992) for more detailed accounts.)

Although researchers such as Megargee (1976) have emphasized the fact that prison violence comes about through an interaction of the characteristics of the individuals and the characteristics of the situation that they are in, psychologists and psychiatrists still tend to focus on individual factors rather than situational factors. There is still a tendency to attribute violence to constructs including mental disorder, high internal drive to aggression, psychopathic personality disorder or low frustration tolerance.

There is considerable evidence that situational factors can affect the outcome of violent events. Felson & Steadman (1983), in their classic study of serious assaults and homicides, demonstrated that the behaviour of the victim could have a significant effect on the outcome of an incident: victims who drew a knife were more likely to be killed. There is a clear link between the availability of handguns in homes and the rate of homicide and suicide (Shepherd & Farrington, 1995). The sevenfold difference in homicide rates between the cities of Seattle and Vancouver, despite their equality of assault rates, can be attributed to differences in the availability of guns (Sloan et al., 1988).

Perhaps the most considered expression of the interactionist perspective to be found in the literature on prison violence is in the report on the Special Units in England:

> Except perhaps in the case of those prisoners whose behaviour is the product of mental disturbance or abnormality, all our experience suggests that 'troublesome prisoners' present control problems only at particular times or in particular contexts. (RAG, 1987 p.11).

Unfortunately, as Bonta & Gendreau (1990) noted, accounts of the processes of incarceration are often influenced more by ideology than by data, more by rhetoric than by empirical findings. This process is nowhere more evident in the literature on prison violence than in two commentaries on the the causes of the epidemic of prison violence in Scottish prisons in the late 1980s. The debate was polarized. Commenting on the hostage-taking and major riot which took place in Peterhead prison in 1987, three critical criminologists attributed the difficulties exclusively to situational factors and dismissed any notion that the psychological characteristics of the prisoners involved could have had an influence. Their position is clearly illustrated by the following comment:

> Violence ... is an inevitable and rational reaction to a violent and repressive regime. (Scratton et al. 1991, p. 17)

By way of sharp contrast the official explanation imputed psychological processes rather than regime factors: (SHHD, 1988, p. 11)

> ... rather than looking to changes in the way in which the Prison Service as a whole goes about its task ... a more productive approach may be to concentrate attention on the individual personality and 'repertoire' of particularly disruptive and violent inmates. (SHHD, 1988, p. 11)

Attempting to reduce prison violence by focusing on the intrapsychic processes and behaviour of violent prisoners is an enterprise doomed to failure. This is a common error:

> ...with all our attention to the individual, we tend to underestimate the prison setting as a powerful influence on day-to-day inmate behaviour. (Clements, 1982, p. 81)

Almost by definition, the prisoners who require to be influenced are not going to engage readily in treatment; they do not perceive themselves as having problems, they do not perceive a need to change. Changing regimes is probably easier than changing the habitual modes of perceiving, thinking and behaving of violent people.

It is my contention that the BSU demonstrated the power of situational factors in the maintenance of violent behaviour in prison settings. Some of these situational factors, and evidence for their influence in the literature on institutional violence will be scrutinized in the following.

Staff and the Minimization of Violence

It is a truism—perhaps a cliché—to argue that high-calibre staffing is the key to maintaining low levels of violence in an institution. Four interlinked facets of staffing appear to have significance: the quality of staff-prisoner relationships, the level of staff experience, the level of staff training and, finally, the level of staff morale.

Within the BSU good staff—prisoner relationships were perceived as critical. As ex-inmate Jimmy Boyle noted:

> What made the Unit unlike any other place was the way staff and prisoners were allowed and encouraged to sit down and talk together. This was the single most important factor of the Unit . (Boyle, 1977, p. 11)

The importance of good quality staff-prisoner relationships is not a new-fangled notion; indeed, the Inspector of Prisons for Scotland in 1844 noted that:

> ... in some prisons an unusual degree of good conduct is induced, and the number of punishments kept low, by the personal influence of the officers, and by their care in reasoning with prisoners before resorting to punishment.

This viewpoint is confirmed by experimental evidence. In their mathematical model of prison disturbances Zeeman et al. (1977) illustrated that the absence of good staff–prisoner relationships was a potent predictor of disturbance.

Examining variations in the rate of violence within Birmingham prison during the reign of four governors, Davies & Burgess (1988b) demonstrated that not only the *extent of the* but also the *quality* of the staff–prisoner interaction had a significant impact on the variation in assault rates. One governor introduced staff–prisoner committees which allowed enhanced contact between staff and prisoners and facilitated greater understanding of each others' problems.

Good staff–prisoner relationships should increase understanding, reduce the capricious exercise of authority and, thereby, avoid the desire to assault as a means of saving face (Felson & Steadman, 1983). Within the BSU, until the latter years of its operation, emphasis was given to recruiting staff who possessed experience in the management of the adult long-term prisoner; once within the regime their training in interpersonal skills, although modest, was considerably more than that provided in other parts of the Scottish Prison Service at that time.

There is evidence from a variety of sources that staff with more experience are less likely to be assaulted. Hodgkinson et al. (1985) established that psychiatric nurses under training had a greater risk of assault than qualified nurses; the difference could not be accounted for by differences in the tasks carried out by these two groups or their locations. Davies & Burgess (1988a), on examining assaults on prison officers, found that less experienced officers were more likely to be assaulted than more experienced officers; this finding was true irrespective of whether the officers were older or younger. Experience brings skills, the skill of being able to judge when to assert authority and when to be more circumspect, the skill of judging a prisoner's mood and the skill of defusing rather than exacerbating aggression.

Fortunately, these skills can be taught (Infantino & Musingo, 1985; Kratcoski, 1988; Rice et al., 1989; Cooke et al., 1990; Lanza et al., 1991). Infantino & Musingo (1985) trained staff in both psychological de-escalation skills and physical 'control and restraint' skills: they demonstrated a substantial reduction in the rate of assault amongst the trained staff compared with comparable untrained staff. The training in 'control and restraint' techniques provided the staff with the confidence that allowed them to be more subtle and flexible in their approach to disturbed patients.

The importance of training in interpersonal techniques is coherently expressed by Lerner et al. (1986). They argued that:

> Officers need to understand offenders in order to know when to confront and when to support, when to be directive and when not to, when to trust and when not to, when to recommend psychotherapy and when not to, when not to set rules (and which rules.) (Lerner et al., 1986, p. 255)

Having experienced and well trained staff is a necessary but not sufficient condition for running a regime with low levels of violence—the morale of this staff must be maintained. Within the

BSU the most significant incident of violence occurred when staff morale was at a low point because of a threat of disciplinary action hanging over staff. In studies of epidemics of violence it has been shown that low staff morale together with inter-staff conflicts are a common feature (Lion et al., 1976). Prior to this assault within the BSU the staff-management conflict not only led to staff being preoccupied with their job security, at the expense of focusing on their primary task of managing violent prisoners, but also led to heightened anxiety amongst the prisoners: they feared that staff with whom they were familiar would be replaced suddenly by new and potentially hostile staff.

More systematic evidence exists. The importance of the staff morale was highlighted in an unpublished study of Bathurst gaol in Australia, a gaol which modelled its approach, in part, on the approach developed in the BSU (Mahony, 1984). Staff at this prison were so dissatisfied that they held a 31-day strike. Prisoners who previously had created few management problems became aggressive and antagonistic to those staff who had engaged in the strike.

Experience in the BSU, and elsewhere, emphasizes the importance of management structures being in place to maintain staff morale.

Visitors

Perhaps the greatest privilege of prisoners in the BSU was virtually unfettered access to visitors. Unfortunately, frequent access to visitors can be a two-edged sword. On the one hand visitors may engender and promote the idea that the prisoner has options which do not entail criminal activity, on the other hand, visitors can be used by the prisoner as a means of avoiding meaningful interaction with other members of the community.

There is little doubt that within the BSU both processes operated. Whatmore (1987), a distinguished forensic psychiatrist who not only assisted in the development of the Unit but who also consulted there for most of the time the Unit was in operation, argued that personal visitors provided both a control over violent and disruptive behaviour and an impetus towards change in social behaviour.

Unfortunately, by way of contrast, in the latter phase of the BSU's operation, visitors were used as a barrier against engaging in the regime (SPS, 1994). Care and control is needed in allowing access to visitors; there is little doubt that positive benefits may be derived by creating access to more visitors than hitherto had been allowed in normal regimes (SPS, 1990; Woolf, 1991); however, the pitfalls inherent in a too liberal approach have to be avoided.

The Quality of the Regime

Although the BSU was housed in a cramped Victorian prison, with little access to facilities outwith the confines of the Unit, other qualities of the regime acted to limit frustration. Limiting unnecessary frustration is of fundamental importance with prisoners with a high propensity to violence. Megargee (1982) argued that the general frustrations of prison life, as exemplified by closed visits, letters going missing, lack of work, limited access to education and poor food, act as a significant situational determinant of violence.

King (1991), in an attempt to explain the different rates of assault in an American maximum security prison compared with an English maximum security prison, indicated that one factor was the greater quality of the American regime. The American regime entailed more out-of-cell activities, greater disposable income, more frequent visits, and in-cell televisions. Behaviour may be improved, not only because prison life is enhanced, but also because prisoners have more to lose.

Ideally, daily activities should be purposeful and not imposed merely as a means of filling time. Within the BSU no formal routine of activities was imposed because the sub-cultural norms which the prisoners brought to the Unit were anti-work. None-the-less, prisoners were encouraged and resourced to pursue their own interests and set their own level of stimulation. Many engaged in constructive activity, and the Unit developed a reputation for producing a disproportionate number of individuals with significant writing and artistic achievements. In retrospect, it would appear that while this *laissez-faire* approach worked for a minority, more structure was probably required for the majority of inmates.

Level of Security and Control

The vast majority of BSU prisoners were transferred from conditions of high security and control, yet, perhaps contrary to expectations, transfer to conditions of diffuse control did not lead to increased levels of violence. The relationship between security and control is not straightforward. Paradoxically, high levels of overt security and control may act to increase the probability of violence. Bidna (1975), describing the effects of strict security in an American prison, found that the greater the security measures imposed, the greater the amount of violence which occurred. Bidna (1975) found that the implementation of strict lock-down in Californian prisons resulted in an increased rate of stabbings amongst the high-security prisoners. Unfortunately, once again we are dealing with conflicting results.

King (1991) contended that the lower rates of assaults in an American prison compared with an English prison could be attributed, in part, to higher levels of control and observation—American prisoners felt safer. The optimum level of control will depend on the population.

Why is the level of control important? Much violent behaviour is predicated on the desire to 'save face'. Felson & Steadman (1983) argued that when the 'saving of face' is a critical concern, the behaviour of one antagonist is a powerful determinant of the behaviour of the other antagonist. Aggression escalates in a trial of strength. Thus, if prison management provide an overly rigid, inflexible and authoritarian style of management certain prisoners may resort to violence as a means of saving face, to show that they can resist the regime.

Evidence from regimes where control is diffuse supports this view (Robson, 1989). Within the Barlinnie Special Unit, prisoners were responsible for their daily routine, they could influence the day-to-day running of the regime and they were involved in taking decisions about their own progress and that of their peers. Prisoners whose behaviour was not acceptable to their peers could be subjected to sanctions including loss of visiting privileges. It is important to emphasize that authority was still maintained by the prison staff; however, the control was less overt and was therefore less likely to stimulate resistance.

THE DECLINE AND FALL OF THE BARLINNIE SPECIAL UNIT

If the BSU was such a remarkable regime, what went wrong, why should the Scottish Prison Service choose to close the 'jewel in its crown'?

Perhaps it is inevitable that regimes which are innovative and effective must plateau and then decline; their progenitors move on or burn out, practices become routinized, staff and prisoners embrace the comfort of ignoring negative behaviour rather than challenging it.

The regime did not fail—as many feared it would—with a bang but rather with a whimper: it gradually disintegrated. Prisoners, and perhaps staff, spent too long in the regime. Prisoners were allowed to disengage from even the tenuous community base of the regime, new prisoners perceived non-involvement as the norm and the control function of community meetings was lost. Ultimately, community meetings which previously had been used to challenge and control difficult and disruptive behaviour became routinized; more concern was expressed about why the video repair was taking too long than about the hostile and non-cooperative behaviour of a new inmate.

Failure to comply with fundamental obligations in the regime, such as attending community meetings, went unchallenged. There was a gradual loss of staff skilled in challenging prisoners, new staff lacked appropriate role models and were not only unclear about how to challenge but also when it was appropriate to challenge. The morale of new staff dropped as the image of the Unit failed to match the actuality.

Gradual decline within a regime is both the hardest to detect and the hardest to remedy. While those within the regime cannot be absolved from blame when a regime declines, this process emphasizes the need for careful and persistent outside monitoring; as Robert Burns observed in *To a louse:* 'O wad some Pow'r the giftie gie us, to see ourselves as others see us! It wad frae mony a blunder free us, and foolish notion.' [Roughly translated this means: 'Oh would some external power give us the gift of perceiving ourselves as other people see us; this would allow us to avoid mistakes and inappropriate ideas.']

Within the context of the Scottish Prison Service in the late 1980s, the senior management of the Service were preoccupied with the many significant difficulties in the rest of the system, understandably they failed to focus on the BSU which became a quiet backwater.

THE FUTURE

In the spring of 1994, in response to a critical report on the BSU by HM Inspector of Prisons (The Scottish Office, 1994) a working party was set up to review the functioning of the Unit. The working party, much to the surprise of many, advocated the closing of the BSU (SPS, 1994). Unfortunately, most of the attention surrounding this report focused on this closure and ignored the innovative and potentially exciting strategy for handling difficult and disruptive prisoners in the Scottish Prison System (Wozniak, 1995). The new strategy entails the enhancement of the regime in the Unit in Shotts prison, the establishment of a new Unit at Peterhead prison, and finally, the creation of a National Induction Centre (NIC). The NIC perhaps represents the most innovative approach. All prisoners sentenced to 10 years or more will spend between six and 12 months in the NIC; the regime is being designed in order to assist prisoners adjust to the losses and difficulties associated with serving a long sentence (SPS, 1994). It is hoped that proactive intervention will prevent the creation of 'difficult prisoners'.

While it would be wrong to suggest that the new system is a phoenix rising from the ashes of the BSU, it is firmly based on the lessons, both positive and negative, which were derived from the 22-year history of the unit. The BSU was a remarkable experiment in the control and management of violent and disruptive prisoners. In its heyday it had a substantial impact on the lives of many of the staff and prisoners who passed through it, although now abandoned, it provides valuable insights into the management of violent prisoners.

REFERENCES

Bidna, H. (1975). Effect of increased security on prison violence. *Journal of Criminal Justice*, **3**, 33–46.

Blackburn, R. (1993). Clinical programmes with psychopaths. In K. Howells & C. R. Hollins (Eds). *Clinical Approaches to the Mentally Disordered Offender*, John Wiley & Sons, pp. 179–210.

Bonta, J. & Gendreau, P. (1990). Reexamining the cruel and unusual punishment of prison life. *Law and Human Behavior*, **14**, 347–372.

Boyle, J. (1977). *A Sense of Freedom*, London: Handbooks.

Carrell, C. & Laing, J. (1982). *The Special Unit Barlinnie Prison: Its Evolution Through its Art*, Glasgow: Third Eye Centre.

Clements, C. B. (1982). The relationship of offender classification to the problems of prison overcrowding. *Crime and Deliquency* **28**, 72–81.

Conlin, B. & Boag, D. (1986). The Barlinnie Special Unit. *The Prison Service Journal*, **62**, 21–22.

Cook, T. D. & Campbell, D. T. (1979). *Quasi-experimentation, Design and Analysis Issues for Field Settings*. Chicago: Rand McNally College Publishing Company.

Cooke, D. J. (1987). Barlinnie Special Unit: fact or fantasy. *The Prison Service Journal*, **64**, 17–20.

Cooke, D. J. (1989). Containing violent prisoners: an analysis of the Barlinnie Special Unit. *British Journal of Criminology*, **29**, 129–143.

Cooke, D. J. (1991). Violence in prisons: the influence of regime factors. *The Howard Journal of Criminal Justice*, **30**, 95–109.

Cooke, D. J. (1992). Violence in prisons: a Scottish perspective. *Forum on Corrections Research*, **4**, 23–30.

Cooke, D. J. (1995a). Cross-cultural research on psychopathy. In S. D. Hart & R. D. Hare (Eds). *Criminal Psychopaths: Assessment. Patterns of Offending, and Treatment*. Harcourt Brace.

Cooke, D. J. (1995b). Psychopathic disturbance in the Scottish prison population: the cross-cultural generalisability of the Hare psychopathy checklist. *Psychology, Crime and Law*, **2**, 101–108.

Cooke, D. J. (1996). Psychopathic personality in different cultures. What do we know? What do we need to find out? *Journal of Personality Disorders* **10**, 23–40.

Cooke, D. J. & Michie, C. (1995). Psychopathy across cultures: an Item Response Theory comparison of Hare's Psychopathy Checklist-Revised. Manuscript submitted for review.

Cooke, D. J., Baldwin, P. J. & Howison, J. (1990). *Psychology in Prisons.* London: Routledge.

Davies, W. & Burgess, P. W. (1988a). Prison officers' experience as a predictor of risk of attack: an analysis within the British prison system. *Medicine, Science and the Law,* **28,** 135–138.

Davies, W. & Burgess, P. W. (1988b). The effects of management regime on disruptive behaviour: an analysis within the British Prison System. *Medicine, Science and the Law,* **28,** 243–247.

Felson, R. B. & Steadman, H. J. (1983). Situational factors in disputes leading to criminal violence. *Criminology,* **21,** 59–74.

Hansard (1987) 'Prisoners', Written Answers p. 4.

Hare, R. D. (1991). *The Hare Psychopathy Checklist—Revised.* Toronto, Ontario: Multi-Health Systems.

Hare, R. D. & Forth, A. E. (1992). Psychopathy and crime across the lifespan. In R. Peters, R. McMahon & V. Ouinsey (Eds). *Aggression and Violence Across the Lifespan.* Newbury Park, California: Sage.

Hare, R. D. & McPherson, L. M. (1984). Violent and aggressive behavior in criminal psychopaths. *International Journal of Law and Psychiatry,* **7,** 35–50.

Hare, R. D., McPherson, L. E. & Forth, A. E. (1988). Male psychopaths and their criminal careers. *Journal of Consulting and Clinical Psychology,* **56,** 710–114.

Harris, G. T., Rice, M. E. & Cormier, C. A. (1991). Psychopathy and violent recidivism. *Law and Human Behavior,* **15,** 625–637.

Hart, S. D., Kropp, P. R. & Hare, R. D. (1988). The performance of male psychopaths following conditional release from prison. *Journal of Consulting in Clinical Psychology,* **57,** 227–32.

Hodgkinson, P., McIvor, L. & Phillips, M. (1985). Patients' assaults on staff in a psychiatric hospital: a 2 year retrospective study. *Medicine, Science and the Law,* **25,** 288–294.

Infantino, J. A. & Musingo, S. Y. (1985). Assaults and injuries amongst staff with and without training in aggression control techniques. *Hospital and Community Psychiatry,* **36,** 1312–1314.

King, R. D. (1991). Maximum-security custody in Britain and the USA: A study of Gartree and Oak Park Heights. *British Journal of Criminology,* **31,** 126–152.

Kratcoski, P. C. (1988). The implications of research explaining prison violence and disruption. *Federal Probation,* **52,** 27–32.

Lanza, M. L., Kayne, H. L., Hicks, C. & Milner, J. (1991). Nursing staff characteristics related to patient assault. *Issues In Mental Health Nursing,* **12,** 253–265.

Lerner, K., Arling, G., & Baird, S. C. (1986). Client management classification strategies for case supervision. *Crime and Deliquency,* **32,** 254–271.

Light, R. (1985). The Special Unit—Barlinnie Prison. *The Prison Service Journal,* **60,** 14–21.

Lion, J. R., Madden, D. & Christopher, R. L. (1976). A violence clinic: three years' experience. *American Journal of Psychiatry,* **133,** 432–435.

Mahony, K. (1984). Effects of the February 1984 prison officer strike. Bathurst Gaol Evaluation Study. (unpublished).

Martinson. R. (1974). What works? Questions and answers about prison reform. *The Public Interest,* **35,** 22–54.

Megargee, E. I. (1976). Population density and disruptive behaviour in a prison setting. In A. K. Cohen, A. F. Cole & R. G. Bailey (Eds). *Prison Violence*, Lexington, DC: Heath.

Megargee, E. I. (1982). Psychological determinants and correlates of criminal violence. In M. E. Wolfgang & N.A. Weiner (Eds). *Criminal Violence*. Beverley Hills, CA: Sage.

Moffit, T. E. (1993). Adolescence-limited and life-course-persistent antisocial behavior: a developmental taxonomy. *Psychological Review*, **100**, 674–701.

RAG (1987). *Special Units for Long-term Prisoners: Regimes, Management and Research. A Report by the Research and Advisory Group on the Long-term Prison System*. London: HMSO.

Rice, M. E., Harris, G. T. & Cormier, C. A. (1992). An evaluation of a maximum security therapeutic community for psychopaths and other mentally disordered offenders. *Law and Human Behavior*, **16**, 399–412.

Rice, M. E., Harris, G. T., Varney, G. W. & Quinsey, B. L. (1989). *Violence in Institutions: Understanding Prevention and Control*. Toronto: Hans Huber.

Robson, R. (1989). Managing the long term prisoner: a report on an Australian innovation in unit management. *Howard Journal*, **28**, 187–203.

Scratton, P., Sim, J. & Skidmore, P. (1991). *Prisons under Protest*. Milton Keynes: Open University Press.

Serin, R. C. (1991). Psychopathy and violence in criminals. *Journal of Interpersonal Violence* **6**, 423–431.

Serin, R. C., Peters, R. D. & Barbaree, H. E. (1990). Predictors of psychopathy and release outcome in a criminal population. *Psychological Assessment: A Journal of Consulting and Clinical Psychology*, **2**, 419–422.

Shepherd, J. P. & Farrington, D. (1995). Preventing crime and violence. Preschool education, early family support, and situational prevention can be effective. *British Medical Journal*, **310**, 271–272.

SHHD, (1971). *Report of the Departmental Working Party on the Treatment of Certain Male Long Term Prisoners and Potentially Violent Prisoners*. Edinburgh: Scottish Home and Health Department.

SHHD (1988). *Assessment and Control: The Management of Violent and Disruptive Prisoners. (A Scottish Prison Service Discussion Paper.)* Edinburgh: Scottish Home and Health Department.

Sloan, J. H., Kellerman, A. L., Reay, D. T., Ferris, J. A., Koepsell, T. & Rivara, F. (1988). Handgun regulations, crime assaults and homicide. *New England Journal of Medicine*, **319**, 1256–1262.

SPS (1990). *Opportunity and responsibility: Developing New Approaches to the Management of the Long Term Prison System in Scotland*. Edinburgh: HMSO.

SPS (1994). *Small Units in the Scottish Prison Service. A Report of the Working Party on Barlinnie Special Unit*. Edinburgh: Scottish Prison Service.

Sykes, G. M. (1958). *The Society of Captives*. Princeton: Princeton University Press.

The Scottish Office (1993). Homicide in Scotland 1983–1992. *Statistical Bulletin: Scottish Office Criminal Justice Series* **5**, 1–12.

The Scottish Office (1994). *Report on HM Special Unit Barlinnie. HM Inspectorate of Prisons for Scotland*. Edinburgh: The Scottish Office.

Toch, H. (1982). Studying and reducing stress. In R. Johnson & H. Toch (Eds). *The Pains of Imprisonment*. Beverly Hills: Sage.

Walters, G. D. (1990). *The Criminal Lifestyle: Patterns of Serious Criminal Conduct*. Newbury Park: Sage.

Whatmore, P. (1990). The special unit at Barlinnie Prison, Glasgow. In P. Bowden & R. Bluglass (Eds). *Principles and Practice of Forensic Psychiatry*, pp. 1359–1362. Edinburgh: Churchill Livingstone.

Whatmore, P. B. (1987). Barlinnie Special Unit: an insider's view. In A. E. Bottoms & R. Light (Eds). *Problems of Long-term Imprisonment*. Aldershot: Gower.

Woolf, (1991). *Prison Disturbances April 1990: Report of an Inquiry*. London: HMSO.

Wozniak, E. (1995). The future of small units in the Scottish Prison Service. *The Prison Service Journal*, **101**, 14–18.

Zeeman, E. C., Hall, C. S., Harrison, P. J., Marriage, G. H. & Shapland, P. H. (1977). A model for prison disturbances. *British Journal of Criminology*, 17, 251–263.

CHAPTER 6

Developing Models for Managing Treatment Integrity and Efficacy in a Prison-based TC: The Max Glatt Centre

Lawrence Jones

HMP Wormwood Scrubs, London

Therapeutic communities are not static treatment programmes, but organizations or elements of an organization that are continually adapting in response to internal and external contingencies. As such it is unwise simply to use a standard 'how-to-do-it' model for management strategy; management in this context needs to be flexible and responsive. In this chapter an effort to illustrate this method of management is attempted.

Thematically the aims of this chapter are threefold. First, the regime of the max Glatt Centre is described in terms of its recent evolution as a dynamic response to an integral programme of 'action research' informed by the 'what works' debate currently taking place in the criminological psychology literature (e.g. Gendreau & Ross, 1987; Lipsey, 1992a; 1992b; Losel, 1995). This section highlights the importance of focusing on attrition as a critical dimension of working with personality-disordered offenders. The second aim is to detail the therapeutic community's unique potential as an environment for working with offenders with 'personality disorders' or 'interaction disturbances' (Derksen, 1995). In this section a cognitive behavioural

Therapeutic Communities for Offenders.
Edited by E. Cullen, L. Jones and R. Woodward. © 1997 John Wiley & Sons Ltd.

model of challenging interpersonal behaviours that can contribute to sabotaging the process of change, possibly leading to attrition, is formulated.

Thirdly, the organizational dynamics of a small unit, with an independent culture and set within a large 'local' prison, are explored, also with a view to highlighting the potential impact of this on treatment integrity.

THE CONTEXT

The Max Glatt Centre (MGC), previously known as the Annexe, HMP Wormwood Scrubs has been operating as a therapeutic community for 22 years. During this time it has seen a variety of managements attempting to implement a range of models of what a therapeutic community should be. Resources, particularly staffing and accommodation, have also varied over time.

The initial culture of the unit has to a large extent survived and is described in Glatt (1974, 1985). Initially only catering for inmates with addiction problems, it went on to take inmates with other compulsive behavioural problems including people with long-standing problems with gambling and sexual offending. More recently the criteria have been extended to include offenders with 'personality disorders' and problems with violent offending. The basic formula of community meetings, small groups and a variety of cognitive-behavioural programmes has continued since the unit's inception. Intervention focusing on both offending behaviour and underlying problems has also been a core feature of the regime. An emphasis on inmates escaping from the culture of dependence, engendered by some non-therapeutic regimes, and developing skills in self-policing and taking independent initiatives has been maintained and has developed since the unit opened. The underlying philosophy of intervention has, however, changed significantly over time, ranging from primarily psychodynamic to, more recently, a cognitive-behavioural orientation. The current timetable is shown in Figure 6.1.

MANAGING ATTRITION

Reconviction Study

An essential management requirement for any intervention programme is feedback as to the efficacy of the intervention. From the

MONDAY	TUESDAY	WEDNESDAY	THURSDAY	FRIDAY	WEEKEND
GYM	GYM	GYM	GYM	GYM	FREE TIME
COMMUNITY MEETING	SMALL GROUPS CRAFTS WORKSHOPS	SMALL GROUPS CRAFTS WORKSHOPS	OFFENCE FOCUSSED ROLE PLAY + RELAPSE PREVENTION	SEX OFFENDER GROUP + SUBSTANCE ABUSE GROUP	
DEBRIEF	DEBRIEF	DEBRIEF	DEBRIEF	DEBRIEF	
STAFF MEETING		STAFF MEETING			
LUNCH	LUNCH	LUNCH	LUNCH	LUNCH	LUNCH
SMALL GROUPS CRAFTS WORKSHOPS	THINKING SKILLS + EMOTIONS GROUP	GYM LIBRARY	SMALL GROUPS CRAFTS WORKSHOPS	GOAL SETTING COMMUNITY MEETING	VISITING GROUPS E.G. NA AND AA
DEBRIEF	DEBRIEF	EDUCATION	DEBRIEF	DEBRIEF	
				STAFF MEETING	
	EVENINGS USED FOR EDUCATION, ASSOCIATION AND EXTRA-CURRICULAR ACTIVITIES				

All groups for 1.5 to 2 hrs, debriefs 30 mins

Figure 6.1. Max Glatt Centre timetable.

earliest days (see Jones, 1976) the notion that it is essential to have a continual process of evaluation of the regime, to which it is then obliged to respond and adapt, has been a central precept of Maxwell Jones' theoretical conception of therapeutic community practice. Jones (1989) highlights the necessity of an action–research model along the lines of Pattons (1986) account of an 'utilization-focused' evaluation procedure where information from statistical analyses of relevant variables is combined with qualitative information based on a continuing dialogue with the 'stakeholder' (i.e. those for whom the evaluation is being conducted) in order to create a picture of the kinds of change that are taking place, thus facilitating informed decision-making.

A primary concern for 'stakeholders' at Wormwood Scrubs prison was to ascertain whether time spent in treatment on the unit had any impact on reconviction rates. In order to answer this question Jones (1988) analysed a data set representing the two-year reconviction rates for a sample of 122 treatment graduates. Regression analysis controlling for age and criminal history revealed that reconviction rates were significantly linked with two key variables: time in treatment and reason for leaving—whether the inmate left the unit because therapy had been completed or because they had exhibited serious behavioural or motivational problems that could not be contained on the unit, such as drug use or violent acting out.

Regression analysis also explored non-linear change processes over time. Change processes are often not linear, a finding not uncommon in the clinical literature (e.g. Barkham et al., 1989) and in sociological accounts of change processes in prison (e.g. Lewis, 1973). Lewis describes deterioration in positive 'attitudes' and 'perspectives' during the middle stage of prison sentences, with an upturn prior to release. The results of this study are represented in Figure 6.2. This shows the key finding that reconviction rates appear to be higher for those spending brief periods of time on the unit and significantly reduced for those spending a year or more on the unit.

This study was followed by an investigation by Jones (1989) designed, in part, to explore the change process using careful assessment of changes in construal of self and others using the role construct repertory grid (RG) technique (Kelly, 1955). Results revealed significant non-linear changes in a variety of RG measures over time. Focusing on self-esteem, Jones (1989) found that both the RG measure of self-esteem—the distance between the 'self' and the 'ideal-self'—and a brief self-esteem questionnaire (the Self Esteem Questionnaire—Thornton, 1988) showed an identical pattern of deterioration during the initial stages of therapy and improvement in

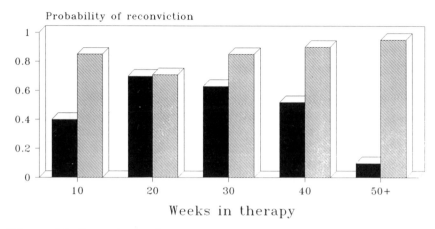

Figure 6.2. Dependence of probability of reconviction on time in treatment. Solid, Treatment completed; hatched, treatment terminated due to breach of unit rules.

the later stages. This change was paralleled by a similar non-linear change in perception of self as being aggressive—as measured by the distance between the 'self' and 'aggressive person' elements in the RG—the self being construed as increasingly aggressive during the initial stages of therapy and less aggressive during the later stages. Jones (1989) proposed a model of the therapeutic change process on the unit, suggesting that change was brought about by confronting core criminogenic beliefs about the self and others, inducing a degree of cognitive dissonance, and that this challenging was accompanied by a deterioration in self-esteem. At this point in the therapeutic process the individual *either* developed new self-esteem enhancement strategies and, if these proved successful, incorporated the value system that came with these alternative strategies, *or* resorted to old self-esteem enhancement strategies (e.g. various types of offending behaviour and substance abuse) thereby reinforcing the criminogenic value system and increasing resistance to and disillusionment with the therapeutic process itself, now construed as painful and ineffectual and perhaps even punitive. Figure 6.2 also shows the common finding that dropping out of treatment for inappropriate behaviour is a good predictor of future reconviction. This group of inmates also score highly on various other measures frequently shown to be predictors of reconviction, such as number of previous convictions. This group may include the more 'psychopathic' inmates, such as those found by Hemphill (1991) to be at a high risk of dropping out of therapeutic community treatment and to go on to do badly when released.

Management Implications

Length of Stay

This research, along with research such as that of George (1971) and Cullen (1991), clearly indicated that a recommended minimum length of stay should be introduced. In the past inmates with only six months of their sentences left to serve had occasionally been accepted onto the unit, as had inmates who had parole applications being processed at the time of admission that could—and occasionally did—result in premature termination of therapy. A screen was consequently introduced to ensure that an absolute minimum of 12 months of an inmate's sentence was still left to do—even if this meant voluntarily forgoing parole.

Identifying Potential 'Drop-outs'

The research clearly indicated that treatment drop-out meant a poor prognosis and also reflected a higher level of risk prior to being accepted into treatment. An algorithm was established in order to select out high-risk inmates. First, psychometric information about potential treatment drop-out was explored. Jones (1988) identified the 'extrapunitive hostility' score on the HDHQ (Caine et al., 1967) as a correlate of eventual drop-out. In further research Jones (1992) suggested that the EPQ (Eysenck & Eysenck, 1975) 'P' score in combination with the number of previous convictions was a good predictor of eventual drop-out—work on this is still in progress. Secondly, an assessment instrument was devised to identify potential treatment drop-out. This was devised for use at interview stage and assessed the following dimensions:

- *Poor motivation.* Shows little or no interest in changing. High level of denial of problems. Expects therapy to be a magical process which he passively undergoes at the hands of therapists. Expresses unwillingness to self-disclose.
- *Ulterior motives.* Clear ulterior—i.e. not explicitly therapeutic—motives expressed, e.g. visits, lighter regime, to get away from current prison due to debt, violence, drug use, quality of regime or wanting 'good reports'.
- *Manipulative.* Staff in referring prison indicate that he meets needs by manipulating staff. Has conned people into giving him what he wants.
- *Evidence of previous drop-out from therapy.* Consistent record of having dropped out of treatment or breached probation orders.

- *Number of previous convictions.* Significant history of offending starting at an early age.
- *Seriousness of drug history.* Long-standing class 'A' drug addiction characterized by multiple episodes of detoxification and relapses.
- *Aggression.* More than two prison reports for violence. Previous convictions include violent offending. Evidence of bullying on the wing in referring prison.
- *Blaming cognitive style.* External locus of control. Blames others for most of problems. Feels picked on unjustly or persecuted. Accepts responsibility for little. Shows little understanding—to the point of appearing like a genuine mental block—of the concept of 'taking responsibility'.
- *Lack of empathy.* Shows little evidence of a capacity for empathy.
- *Poor capacity for maintaining relationships.* Has no long-standing relationships.
- *Absence of guilt.* Shows no remorse or guilt about offending behaviour.
- *Polarized thinking about people.* All relationships and significant others seen in extreme terms—either idealized or derogated.
- *Rigid thinking.* Fixed, rigid, inflexible or stubborn thinking exhibited in interview in more than one subject area.
- *Distractable.* Thoughts loosely linked. Unfocused.
- *Emotionally flat or absence of variation in emotion.* Shows little emotion or seems to be stuck in one emotional mode and unable to show other feelings—e.g. continually hostile or depressed throughout interview.
- *Shows no curiosity about reasons for offending or strategies for avoiding offending.*
- *Interested in controlling others.* Evidence of trying to 'take charge' of relationships. Tries to dominate interviewer and interrupts interviewer frequently.

Items were generated by systematically contrasting individuals who had stayed the course on the unit with a sample of inmates who had been discharged for misbehaviour. Differences between the two groups were characterized using constructs frequently found in the literature as predictive of drop-out or relapse along with constructs that were suggested by examining the cases themselves. Clearly many of the items individually are indications of treatment need; collectively, however, they form an index of the chances of dropping out of treatment. Although this instrument is still being assessed, preliminary investigation looks promising. Literature on treatment drop-out in non-custodial settings (Backalead and Lundall (1975) and

Stark (1992)) can be useful in developing models for application in the custodial setting.

Targeting Treatment Drop-out

In response to these findings a basic strategy for dealing with treatment drop-out was developed based on the work of Linehan (1993). This approach argues that it is important to prioritize targets for intervention in terms of the seriousness of the immediate threat to the client. Linehan proposes the following hierarchy of target behaviours:

1. Suicidal behaviours.
2. Therapy-interfering behaviours.
3. Quality-of-life interfering behaviours.
4. Increasing behavioural skills.

As a model developed primarily for working with 'borderline' personality-disordered clients the strategy needed to be adjusted for work with a personality-disordered offender population.

The part of this model that proved most useful in the TC context is Linehan's concept of therapy-interfering behaviours (TIBs). Adapted for working with offenders in a TC these are:

1. Patient or therapist interfering behaviours likely to destroy therapy. Examples of these are: leaving, using drugs, and violence.
2. Immediately interfering behaviours of patient or therapist. Examples of these are: not turning up for groups, talking about issues not relevant to offending behaviour, and colluding with distorted thinking.
3. Patient, therapist or group interfering behaviours functionally related to offending behaviour or drug abuse behaviours. For example: Albert threatens people in the large group in order to get his own way. He creates an atmosphere of fear and ends up getting his own way. His offence is armed robbery.
4. Inmate TIBs similar to problem behaviours, not directly related to offending behaviour or drug abuse, outside therapeutic context. For example: Bill keeps expressing ambivalence about therapy and asks periodically to leave. When at liberty he spent little time in one place and regularly moved to a new locale when things got difficult. Both in therapy and outside he felt frightened of getting close to others and would characteristically switch between trying to make relationships and withdrawing from them.

5. Lack of progress in therapy. For example: Chris keeps talking in his small group about the need to address his anger but keeps exploding with anger in the large group. In spite of being contracted by the staff group and the community to focus on and control his hostile behaviour he continues to lose his temper in the large group. Staff and inmates have begun to reach the end of their tether with him.

A prediction of possible future TIBs is made early in therapy by staff and sometimes the community or small group. The prediction of TIBs is developed from the behavioural assessment and risk factor identification strategy described by McDougal and Clark (1991) Clark et al. (1991) and McDougal et al. (1994) where a similar approach is taken to the prediction of offence—related behaviour in an institutional setting. For instance, an inmate whose offences were primarily armed robberies to gain money to maintain a heroin habit might be expected to show instrumental aggression towards other inmates and/or staff and might be expected to relapse to drug use during therapy. This area is then targeted as the initial area for intervention. Exploration of these issues is undertaken early in therapy and TIBs are established as a priority area for intervention. Informing inmates, on group, of the potential strategies of self-sabotage can also have the effect of a paradoxical intervention provoking a countervailing effort to prevent the prediction from becoming reality. Previous experiences of therapy are also examined to establish what kinds of TIBs led to therapy being terminated. TIBs in similar programmes are more relevant to establishing treatment targets than TIBs in dissimilar programmes. TIBs that have been repeated in several contexts are also more relevant. An example of the relevance of past TIBs is an inmate, Derek, who had been in therapy on the TC at Glen Parva and had been discharged for making threats to sex offenders on the unit. He later went to Grendon where he was again discharged for threatening other inmates and eventually was referred to the Scrubs Annexe TC where he again made threats to sex offenders and was discharged. Two interpretations can be made of this example, either that he was an inappropriate candidate for TC intervention or that his TIB was not identified and dealt with as soon as he arrived on the unit—or prior to arrival—and that prompter intervention might have enabled him to have stayed without repeating his TIB. A final strategy for identifying TIBs from past behaviour is to look at personal and working relationships that have broken down and see if there are any recurring themes—e.g. a fear of getting emotionally close, issues with people in authority.

Some TIBs are almost universally found and predictions about them need to be tailored for the individual. Two types of TIB that fall into this category are ambivalence and the urge to repeat aspects of offending behaviour.

Ambivalence

The uniquely social context of a TC enables work on the critically criminogenic dimension, highlighted by Marshall (1989) for sex offenders, of intimacy skills deficits, or the lack of motivation to use such skills. Ambivalent motivation to engage with others socially is often also reflected in ambivalence towards both the self and aspects of the change process itself. The PCL-R (Hare et al., 1990) items looking at frequent changing of jobs and relationships also point towards this area as relevant to tackling behaviours which in themselves are not offending but which may underpin offending behaviour. Motivational interviewing strategies (Miller & Rollnick, 1991) highlight ways of fostering change by working with ambivalence in Prochaska and DiClemente's (1986) contemplation stage of the change process. An interesting exposition of this model for use in milieu therapeutic settings is given by Van Bilsen and Van Emst (1989), who highlight the futility of coercive and hard confrontational approaches when working with motivationally ambivalent substance abusers.

An exploration of the various types of ambivalence towards the treatment culture, in this case the TC culture, encountered in an institutional setting is, however, useful in developing a systematic approach to the issue of treatment drop-out. Whilst the Prochaska and DiClemente model has good heuristic value it does not take into account the secondary gains of engaging in treatment. A key motivational feature of interventions in a penal setting is the inmate's perception of the possible non-therapeutic benefits contingent upon engaging in therapy; for instance, being in therapy can mean increasing the chances of getting released, getting parole, better visits, being less susceptible to violence and having a better regime. A more detailed formulation of the pre-contemplation and contemplation stages, more relevant to the penal setting, can be derived from Woods' (1979) typology of 'modes of adaptation' to an organization. Originally developed in an educational setting (see also Furlong (1985) for a review of this and other models of deviance in the school setting) Woods' typology looks at both motivation to change (the ends of therapy) and motivation to do that changing in a particular way (the means of changing). Woods proposes nine characteristic modes of adaptation based on the individual's position in relation to the *goals* of change and the *means* of achieving these goals. This model can be usefully generalized to other settings and cultures—e.g. the goals and means of pro-offending cultures (Figure 6.3). Adapted to the TC context these modes are listed below.

- *Compliance*
  1. Optimistic compliance. The individual takes on the goals of therapy in an air of expectant hope. This is sometimes manifested as an *over*optimistic approach—often in new arrivals—with an idealized view of therapy. It can also be seen in individuals towards the end of their stay who adopt an unrealistic 'I've got there, I'm better now' attitude.
  2. Instrumental compliance. Here the individual takes on therapeutic goals as a means to an end—e.g. to get 'good reports' to aid parole, to stay in a liberal regime, getting visits, staying away from drug debts.
- *Ingratiation*
  The ingratiator's main aim is to maximize benefits by earning the favour of those in power—e.g. staff or more powerful community members—and is not usually affected by unpopularity with peers.
- *Ambivalence or opportunism*
  Characterized by ambivalence towards both therapeutic goals and the means of achieving them. This often proceeds from earlier optimistic compliance as a result of disillusionment after realizing that there is no 'quick fix', and as a 'trying out' phase in which more 'deviant' coping strategies are frequently, but momentarily, revisited. Effort is still put into therapy albeit with less enthusiasm.
- *Ritualism*
  This is characterized by lack of interest in therapeutic goals but still continuing to 'go through the motions' of accepting norms of behaviour. This is not unlike some forms of institutionalization where the capacity for independence has been whittled away. The structure provided by therapy may be intrinsically rewarding. This also describes the strategy of behavioural compliance while actively engaging in cognitive non-compliance to change.
- *Intransigence*
  The intransigent individual rejects therapeutic means and is generally cynically indifferent to its ends. Assertion of autonomy is important for this individual.
- *Rebellion*
  Individuals often move from intransigence to rebellion. This is characterized by substituting their own goals for those of therapy.

		ATTITUDE TO THERAPY					GOALS	
			Indifference	Indulgence	Identification	Rejection without replacement	Ambivalence	Rejection with replacement
M		Indifference	Retreatism			Retreatism		
E		Indulgence		Ingratiation	Ingratiation			
B		Identification	Ritualism	COMPLIANCE	Compliance			
A		Rejection without replacement	Retreatism			Retreatism		
N		Ambivalence	Colonization				OPPORTUNISM	
S		Rejection with replacement	Intransigence					Rebellion

Figure 6.3. Types of response to therapeutic community ethos. Adaptation modes in capital letters are the most frequent, those in small print the least frequent.

This can either be substituting alternative therapeutic goals—e.g. opting for the 12-step AA programme and asking to leave—or substituting overt or covert offending or prison culture goals for goals relating to change. Such individuals may choose to stay in a particular regime as long as it provides opportunities to pursue the alternative goals, e.g. as long as there is an opportunity to exploit weaker people, use drugs, attend AA meetings. As soon as these goals are challenged or the opportunity to pursue them is taken away the TC ethos no longer holds the attraction that it had before and the individual seeks to leave.

- *Colonisation*
  This is characterized by ambivalence about formal rules with indifference to therapeutic goals. This individual accepts the therapeutic ethos and tries to 'work the system' by maximizing available gratification, whether officially permitted or not. For example, there are those who comply with the aspects of the programme that are 'enjoyable' but do not comply with therapy if they have, for instance, to deal with painful issues.

- *Retreatism*
  The individual is no longer committed to therapeutic goals or the means of achieving them but also has no alternatives. The strategy thus employed is to retreat, i.e. to truant either literally or psychologically by withdrawing.

This conceptual model is not about establishing 'right' and 'wrong' adaptations but, rather, is an aid to developing strategies to deal with ambivalence-based TIBs. In this context it is essential to recognize that switching between more and less compliant adaptations may be necessary for certain individuals as they experiment with various ways of coping without offending and establishing independent identities. Woods' original formulation emphasizes the fact that particular individuals move from one adaptation strategy to another and that local variations in ethos, e.g. authoritarian or permissive, would provoke different adaptation strategies. Adaptation strategies will inevitably switch during the therapeutic process. Particular interpersonal styles will also predispose individuals to particular strategies. An interpersonal theoretical approach (Blackburn, 1990) can be used to hypothesize about adaptation strategies that might prove attractive to individuals with different interpersonal styles (Figure 6.4). Identifying the adaptation mode enables both more effective prediction and prioritization of TIBs 1 to 4 (see above) and work on TIB 5, lack of progress in therapy. In particular it is important to identify overtly non-problematic adaptations that

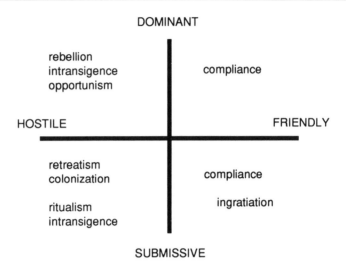

Figure 6.4. Characteristic modes of adaptation of different interpersonal styles.

nevertheless reflect lack of progress, e.g. ingratiation, superficial forms of compliance, ritualism and retreatism.

Ostapiuk and Westwood, (1986) remind us that care must be taken not to lose sight of the goal of developing skills in adapting to the real world—described by them as unpredictable, lacking fixed boundaries and with low structure—and to facilitate the evolution of a capacity to meet basic needs of self-control, freedom and independence. To develop adaptation strategies for meeting management needs of control, containment, compliance and institutional routines in a secure, predictable, artificial and highly structured environment would be of only marginal use to the future ex-offender at large. Similarly, adapting to TC life can prove to be irrelevant to future living environments if sight is lost of the transitional nature of the therapeutic environment. In this respect the adaptation strategy of rebellion may be an important strategy for somebody preparing for re-entry—though it might backfire and result in premature discharge or reversion to past offence-related coping strategies. Rebellion in this context means rejection of the therapeutic ethos and the adoption of a maintenance—following Prochaska and DiClemente's model—stance towards a newly adopted feasible non-offending life-style. Each transition between motivational stages, e.g. contemplation to action and action to maintenance, involves a process of switching from rebellion to compliance to a new set of values.

The relative flexibility of structure in some TC contexts provides the opportunity to experiment with new behaviours. Highly structured environments prevent this kind of experimentation and make learning from mistakes relatively impossible as there is little scope for making mistakes. This also prevents adequate assessment of problem behaviours. Walters & Chulmsky (1993) found that the Lifestyle Criminality Screening Form failed to predict prison behaviour in highly structured environments but succeeded in less structured environments, thus giving empirical evidence for this kind of environmental inhibition of offence-related behaviour in prison. The best place to assess offence-related behaviour in prison is in relatively unstructured environments, TCs offer one kind of environment where the reins can be systematically loosened and tightened to meet the varying needs of assessment, change through experimentation with alternative behaviour and containment. As we have seen, however, this has to be a delicate balancing act if premature discharge or counterproductive permissiveness is to be avoided.

Working with lapse and relapse

One manifestation of ambivalent motivation is lapse (temporary) or relapse (repeating pattern of behaviour) to either drug use or aspects of offending behaviour.

Sole reliance on self-disclosure and confrontation of other relapsers. The initial strategy for dealing with drug use on the unit was to ensure that there was a culture where inmates were encouraged to disclose their drug use voluntarily or to challenge and confront drug use by fellow inmates when this occurred—behaviour that in most other prison environments would be construed as 'grassing' i.e. a behaviour that would lead to social ostracism and possibly violence from fellow inmates. Although this approach worked to an extent it failed to control drug use on the unit. When urine testing was eventually introduced onto the unit some 60% of inmates produced samples positive for cannabis. Prior to the introduction of urine testing there were alternately cultures that were anti-drug use and collusively silent about drug use. When the anti-drug culture was ascendant individuals would bring lapses to the community or staff group and this would be worked with. In addition inmates would challenge drug use in others on the unit. This was felt to be important for their own development of skills to resist temptation to use. In the collusively silent phase inmates would sometimes confront each other about drug use and would have their challenges met with outraged denial and accusations of 'grassing'. Some inmates would 'split off' staff by bringing them information about other drug users on the unit and at the same time refusing to confront them openly for fear of reprisals—or this was part of a more sophisticated strategy to take the scent away from their own drug use.

At this time it becomes increasingly easy to use key markers in group behaviour to identify nascent 'malignant' cultures. Collusive silence about drug use often correlates with absence of self-disclosure generally and with community meetings characterized by either unrealistic self-congratulation and 'sweet-talking' the staff or strong scapegoating of less popular members of the community or staff for not providing an adequate regime. This is also accompanied by the emergence of stronger hierarchical divisions between 'stronger' and 'weaker' inmates. There is a general shift towards a prison culture where everyone knows their 'place' in relation to the 'strong arms' and 'Barons' on the wing who are running the black economy—using a currency of tobacco and drugs—and where staff are 'bought off' by a covert bargain in which the wing is policed by the Barons in exchange for turning a blind eye to the Barons' activities. Typically this kind of culture moves through the stages shown in Figure 6.5. The beginnings of a prison culture would be marked by fragmentation into subgroupings, e.g. sex offenders, armed robbers, lifers, uniformed staff, non-uniformed staff, dominance displays and attempts to intimidate—sometimes disguised as 'confrontation' of less dominant inmate's denial of offending behaviour. Hinshelwood's (1987) notion of the vicissitude of the boundary gives a useful account of this kind of dynamic. This culture is particularly exacerbated by the introduction of a significant number of new members *at the same time*. Evidence for this comes from Mcpherson (1973) and from Jones (1989). Mcpherson investigated the relationship between the number of inmate movements, which he saw as a crude measure of what he termed 'wing stability', and reconviction rates for inmates at Grendon TC. The only movement variable that was significantly different for those who went on to be reconvicted was whether an inmate's reception coincided with that of another inmate; those arriving accompanied went on to reoffend more frequently than those arriving alone. Jones (1989) also provided evidence for the negative impact of arriving with others on the hypothesized enculturation process of revising self-esteem enhancement strategies. In addition, new arrivals with drug abuse problems often bring drugs with them to tide them over the first few days on the unit (standard practice for addicts moving from prison to prison).

Another cause of the development of this culture can be the sudden enhanced availability of harder drugs. This can lead to, initially, one

Figure 6.5. Responsibility for policing wing.

or two inmates relapsing and eventually to a 'domino' effect where large numbers of the substance abusers on the wing can relapse (Figure 6.6).

Guilt and loss of self-esteem (through the Abstinence Violation Effect (AVE), i.e. the exacerbating consequences on drug use, or offending behaviour, of lowered self-esteem and self-efficacy after relapsing) at having relapsed can often express themselves as either unrealistic suspicion and or denigration of staff. Alternatively staff and inmates identified as potentially threatening to the developing prison culture are attacked and challenged as a way of silencing them or as a means of creating 'red herrings'.

An additional indicator of evolving prison culture is the increased ambivalence of more motivated community members, in terms of the typology proposed above beginning to *retreat* from or *rebel* against

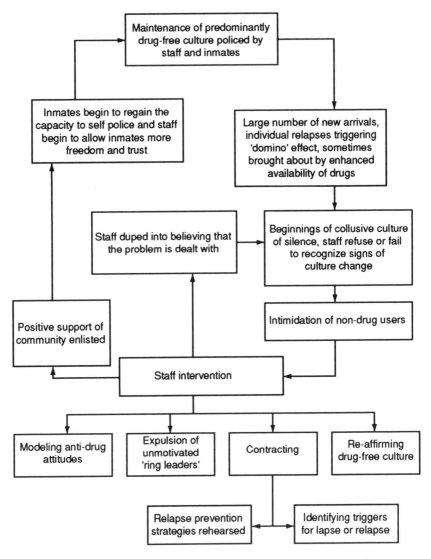

Figure 6.6. Intervention strategy for re-establishing drug-free culture.

the emergent culture. The drug-free members show increasing cynicism and withdraw from confronting and challenging.

Besides the obvious physical signs of drug use these group behavioural and cultural markers are the only method available for identifying relapse on the unit. In the absence of high levels of staffing this monitoring process is inadequate and the chances for regression back to the prison culture are amplified. Disclosed relapse is dealt with by either discharge or contracting. Staff try to get a commitment to explore the relapse from inmates that they and the community feel are capable of learning from the experience and who pose little threat to other community members. Returning to a drug-free culture entails staff being more pro-active initially, followed by a careful fostering of self-policing skills in the community (see fig b.).

Dealing with relapse constructively. Figure 6.6 outlines some of the issues involved in deciding whether or not to discharge inmates who have broken the basic rules of the unit (e.g. using drugs). In terms of the earlier discussion about TIBs this is what happens when work on *potential* TIBs has failed.

Choice of strategy is usually based on trying to maximize advantages for the individual and the community and to minimize the disadvantages. As such the critical factors to explore are:

1. The community's view of the matter.
2. The chances that the individual has been or is likely to involve others in relapsing (e.g. has dealing been a major part of drug-abuse behaviour in the past?).
3. Were the drugs obtained from inside or outside the unit? If inside, what are the implications for the strategy to be used with co-relapsers—can you keep them both? Is it 'fair' to discharge one and not the other?
4. Attitude of inmate to relapse; this can range from complete denial through cannabis is not a problem for me, I'm here to deal with my heroin problem' to 'I could see it coming and I didn't do anything about it; I'm afraid about what that means for when I am released'.

If it is deemed necessary, the possibility of taking the inmate back at some stage in the future needs to be explored. Those who are felt to be capable of benefiting from staying, and with whom the risk of contaminating other members of the community is deemed to be minimal, are then put through a behavioural contracting procedure—formulated by staff and community—which focuses on what led to the relapse (e.g. triggers such as feeling as if control has been lost, negative or positive mood states and environmental triggers) and identifying high-risk situations for possible future relapse. In addition motivational interviewing techniques (Miller & Rollnick, 1991) are used in order to re-establish motivation. The contract is written and fed back to the community where the issues leading up to the relapse are collectively explored. In addition urine

Implications			
For individual		**For community**	
Positive	Negative	Positive	Negative
Contract Identify and work on aspects of the relapse process. Feeling accepted in spite of weakness.	No / little sanction or deterrent, unless contract stipulates negative consequences for further infractions.	Opportunity to learn from others' relapse and to explore the collective role in relapse process, e.g. collusion.	Loss of deterrent effect and may put others at risk through 'domino' effect or if relapser engages in dealing drugs to others.
Discharge Clear message that behaviour is destructive and not compatible with commitment to change.	A. V. E. May move to wing where drugs are freely available. May develop a hostile view of therapy generally.	Enhances the deterrent effect of threat of discharge. May prevent 'domino' effect.	Collective A.V.E., loss of confidence in ability to change and in therapy.

Figure 6.7. Factors influencing response to relapse. AVE, Abstinence violation effect.

tests are increased for the individual over a prescribed period and clean results—when obtained—fed back to the community. A second relapse is currently seen as indicating a need to move, either temporarily or indefinitely.

More recently this model has been extended to other kinds of offending or offence-related behaviour such as child sex offenders 'grooming' 'weaker' members of the community to obtain favours. The core theme in this process is establishing links between the individual's relapsing behaviour and patterns of relapse when at liberty, finding parallel processes to the offending behaviour, e.g.

Offence:
Rejection-induced → tension/anger, → violent offence
stress from female   'paranoid' thinking   against woman
                                                partner

On unit:
rejection stress → tension/anger, → aggressive outburst
from female staff   'paranoid' thinking   in which staff are
refusing request   verbally abused.

Other areas in which offence-paralleling behaviour is explored are early experiences of, or witnessing of, abusive caregiver and peer behaviour, fantasies of offending, and large and small group behaviour.

Once identified the pattern is explored by the group to establish both the meaning of the behaviour (e.g. Was it an attempt to feel powerful after being humiliated? What was the history of this vulnerability to rejection? Was the rejection provoked as a defensive-distancing strategy? How often has this behaviour chain been repeated in the past?) and alternative strategies for dealing with the various stages along the behaviour chain identified collectively. The advantage of the TC context is that this pattern of thinking can be identified in parallel forms and coping responses rehearsed. Dealing with the offence-paralleling interpersonal interaction pattern is a more inclusive approach than merely focusing on the interaction pattern that ended in the offending behaviour.

PERSONALITY-DISORDERED OFFENDERS IN TCs: A COGNITIVE-BEHAVIOURAL FORMULATION

Attrition or attrition-related behaviour is also one of the key behavioural characteristics of 'personality—disordered' offenders.

People who either find other people too difficult to cope with or who behave in such a way as to drive others away (or provoke them into pushing them away) are often the most difficult to hold on to in a therapeutic context.

Cognitive-behavioural Formulation of 'Personality Disorder'

The recent development of cognitive-behavioural formulations of the domain of 'personality disorder' offers some useful models for working in a TC context. In the past this domain has been the preserve of psychodynamically oriented clinicians such as Kohut (1971) and Kernberg (1984). Interestingly, cognitive-behavioural theorists such as Beck and Freeman (1990) have drawn extensively from the psychodynamic literature in their work; as is often the case many useful innovations come from the interaction between different paradigms. Space does not permit a thorough review of this rapidly developing area. The interested reader is referred to Derksen (1995) for a recent review. In this section a brief description of the MGC population will be presented, in terms of the classical notion of personality disorder. This will then be followed by an exploration of the domain of 'personality disorder'—without buying into the classical formulation of that domain—in terms of the two critically attrition- and offence-related issues of *interpersonal behaviour* and *countertransference* (i.e. the effect of the client on the therapist).

The Incidence of Personality Disorder in the MGC Population

Dolan and Coid (1993), in reviewing the treatment of offenders with personality disorder (PD), point out that the descriptions of the various populations in the literature have very few measures of PD. This clearly makes comparisons between treatments or meta-analytic summaries of the literature difficult. Partly in response to this need the incidence of the various PDs in the MGC population were assessed using the Personality Diagnostic Questionnaire, Revised version (Hyler et al., 1987, 1988). While this instrument has its limitations—it overdiagnoses PD and does not correlate highly with structured interviews assessing DSM III-R PD, see Derksen (1995)—it has been used extensively and has the advantage of not making the theoretical assumptions of the only other questionnaire assessing DSM III-R axis II, the MCMI-III (Millon, 1991) which is based on Millon's model of personality disorder. Of a sample of 72 inmates accepted onto the unit the following percentages of cases met the criteria for the PDQ-R criteria for PDs: schizoid 28%, schizotypal

40%, paranoid 78%, passive aggressive 49%, avoidant 49%, dependent 22%, obsessive compulsive 21%, self-defeating 40%, narcissistic
62%, histrionic 57%, borderline 78%, antisocial 85%, sadistic 22%.
The mean number of PDQ-R diagnoses per inmate (not including
sadistic PD and self-defeating PD which were, at the time of testing,
PDs proposed for inclusion in DSM-IV) was 5.4, roughly 1 fewer than
the population at the Henderson described by Dolan et al. (1992).
Figure 6.8 shows these results.

Only 2.8% of the population obtained no PD diagnosis on the PDQ-
R. Overall the population is more antisocial and narcissistic, equally
paranoid and passive-aggressive, and less schizoid, schizotypal,
dependent, histrionic, avoidant and obsessive compulsive than the
Henderson referrals described by Dolan et al. (1992). Looking at some
subpopulations, substance abusers ($n = 43$) tended to have a higher
incidence of paranoid PD (86%), borderline PD (90%) and antisocial
PD (95%) and had an average of six PD diagnoses. Inmates with rape
offences ($n = 6$) all had paranoid PD diagnoses, incest offenders
($n = 8$) had relatively few diagnoses (mean number of diagnoses = 2)

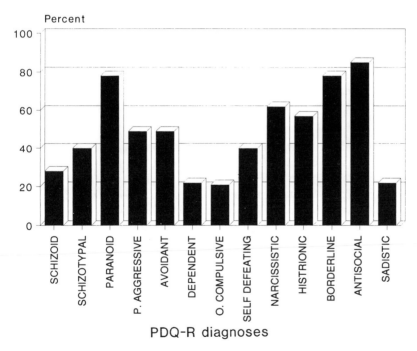

Figure 6.8. Incidence of personality disorder on the Max Glatt Centre
($n = 72$).

and had a high incidence of avoidant PD (50%). Dolan et al. (1992) argue that multiple Axis II diagnoses of PD are common and have often been overlooked in the literature. Their finding of a correlation between the number of PDQ diagnoses and the score on the impairment distress scale was replicated with the MGC sample ($r = 0.65$, $p = 0.001$). These results support their contention that it is important to take into account the multiplicity of diagnoses rather than select the single most salient diagnosis when assessing this domain.

The Interpersonal Behaviour Approach to the PD Domain

It is critical to working with offender PDs in a TC context to have a model of how community behaviour reflects offending behaviour. The cognitive-behavioural literature offers some formulations of PD that can be of use here. One of the key defining characteristics of PDs is what Derksen (1995) has termed 'interaction disturbance'. This area has been highlighted by many as the defining characteristic of PDs. Three main types of formulation of interpersonal behaviour can be identified in the cognitive behavioural (CB) literature:

1. Translations of psychodynamic object relations theory, e.g. Ryle (1985) and Horrowitz (1988), into a cognitive behavioural framework.
2. The schema-focused approaches of Young and Swift (1987) and Beck and Freeman (1990).
3. The interpersonal formulations of Leary (1957), Kiesler (1983) and, more relevant to the offender population, Blackburn (1989, 1990).

Ryle (1985) reformulated the psychodynamic notion of 'object relations' into a cognitive framework using the notion of 'reciprocal role procedures', learned procedures for interacting with others developed from past experiences of interaction that incorporate strategies for anticipating the interpersonal behaviour of others. Horowitz (1988) similarly attempts to define 'object relations' in terms of role relationship models '... a mental schematisation of the relative characteristics of self and others, and a sort of script of what each might do to the other in a sequence of interactions'. He also locates the origins of these schemata in early relationships. Both of these constructs are developments from the early Bowlby (1977) attachment theoretical notion of 'the internal working model'.

Starting from a primarily cognitive framework the schema-focused model (e.g. Beck et al. 1990; Young and Swift 1987 ; Young 1990) emphasizes the importance of schemata. Beck et al. (1990) argue that schemata are '... structures with a highly personalised idiosyncratic content that ... when hypervalent ... displace and probably inhibit other schemas that may be adaptive or more appropriate to a given situation. They consequently introduce a systematic bias into information processing. The typical schema of personality disorders ... are operative on a continuous basis in information processing'.

Guidano and Liotti (1983) and Mahoney (1991) highlight the importance of meta-cognitive processes, such as beliefs about and attitudes towards change, thinking itself and what kinds of evidence can be used to refute particular beliefs about self and others, in determining interpersonal behaviour.

The interpersonal approach of Leary (1957), Carson (1970), Kiesler (1983) and Blackburn (1990) is based on empirical analysis of interpersonal behaviour that has identified two basic dimensions: dominance versus submission and hostile versus friendly (Figure 6.9). Moreover this model postulates a formula for identifying reactions to these kinds of social behaviour: '... a particular behaviour' writes Blackburn (1990) "pulls" a reaction from the other person, within a limited range of possibilities, and this is governed by principles of *complementarity*. Along the dominance–submission axis, this is held to be reciprocal, i.e. a dominant response "pulls" a submissive reaction, while along the friendly–hostile axis the relation is corresponding or congruent, i.e. a hostile response invites a hostile reaction, and a friendly overture elicits a friendly reaction.

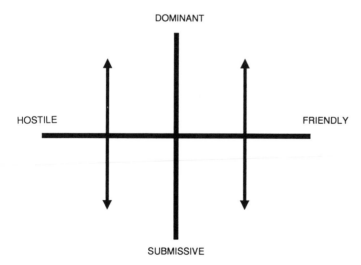

Figure 6.9. Complementarity: dominance pulls submission, submission pulls dominance, hostility pulls hostility, friendliness pulls friendliness.

The effect of a rigid interpersonal style will be that the person produces many anti-complementary reactions in situations where they are inappropriate and aversive to other people'.

Together these models when applied to interpersonal interaction indicate the following.

1. Each individual has a characteristic pattern of interpersonal behaviour and strategies for the anticipation of others' responses.
2. Interpersonal behaviour is mediated by core beliefs or schemata which affect both the content and the process of perception and interaction with others.
3. It is possible to predict—following the principle of complementarity—characteristic responses of others to particular kinds of interaction. Dominance pulls submission, submission pulls dominance, hostility pulls hostility, affiliation pulls affiliation.

Community meetings are a good place for exploring these dimensions of behaviour. They tend to amplify any pre-existing interpersonal style. In particular the dominance–submission dimension is played out. This behaviour can then be used to identify the individual's current position on this dimension and help to identify alternatives when this is too extreme, i.e. too dominant or too submissive. A recent study looked at the hypothesis that dominance bids on community meetings would reflect the notional status of the individual's victim at the time of the offence. To test this, two group workers rated all community members on a three-point scale: $0 =$ submissive, $1 =$ neither predominantly submissive nor dominant, and $2 =$ dominant. Interrater reliability proved to be high ($n = 20$, $r = 0.92$, $p = 0.0001$) and a combined score was obtained by averaging their scores. This score was then correlated with a nominal victim status scale ($0 =$ child victim, $1 =$ individual adult victim, $2 =$ more than one victim present in single offence (e.g. armed robbery)); a significant correlation was obtained ($r = 0.63$, $p = 0.0029$). Similarly ratings on a three-point affiliation scale ($0 =$ friendly, $1 =$ neither hostile nor friendly and $2 =$ hostile) were scored for each individual on their community meeting behaviour. This correlated ($r = 0.45$, $p = 0.04$) with ratings of the extent to which violence was involved in the offence ($0 =$ little overt violence used, $1 =$ violence clearly involved, $2 =$ serious violence using a weapon). Interestingly the variance accounted for in the violence ratings by hostility on community meetings was added to by entering victim status as a covariate in regression analysis. This suggests that severity of violent behaviour is determined by victim status (and presumably the higher degree of violence required to have an impact on higher status victims) independently of interpersonal hostility.

Clearly then, the interpersonal model—even when used in this crude manner—is useful for assessing offence-related and offence-relevant social interaction. Large-group behaviour can significantly mirror aspects of offending behaviour. Changes in behaviour in the large group can be an indicator of changes in behaviour in other domains.

The schema-focused approach can then be useful in examining the kinds of cognitive content and cognitive process that support and maintain this meeting behaviour. Blackburn (1990) indicates that a critical strategy in helping individuals to change their position on the hostile–friendly dimension is to challenge core beliefs about self and others by *not* confirming assumptions that the individual is making about the potential responses to his behaviour. In interpersonal terms this means responding in an anti-complementary way, i.e. meeting hostility with friendliness or, conversely, meeting gullible over-affection (designed to provoke acceptance) with a degree of hostility. 'To react to hostile behaviour with punishment is not only to provide confirmation for hostile expectations, it is also more likely to perpetuate hostility as an interpersonal style' (Blackburn, 1990).

It is exactly this issue of behaving in an 'anti-complementary' style that highlights the importance of having a clear conception of countertransference issues when working with PD offenders. The term 'countertransference' has evolved, in the psychodynamic literature, to mean the various aspects of the therapist's response to the client's behaviour. Typically these responses are used as important information about the individual's interpersonal style.

Countertransference Issues in TCs with Offenders

Countertransference as a construct has begun to be used more widely in the therapeutic literature where there are several useful explorations of this area. Some of the more salient issues will be touched on here. Linehan (1993) emphasizes the importance of identifying staff/therapist therapy-interfering behaviours i.e. therapist behaviours that can lead to premature termination of therapy or to stagnation in the therapeutic process. The other critical factor here, of course, is staff well-being; it must be ensured that they do not suffer from 'burn out'. Many of the issues described in the literature can be usefully reformulated in interpersonal behavioural terms.

Staff fear and appeasement cultures. Wishnie (1977) describes the signs of what might be termed an appeasement culture in the staff group: '... staff members were terrified and sought to appease patients rather than confront and deal with their fears in more constructive ways. Unacknowledged fear reactions should be suspected when there are unusual staff behaviour patterns, such as calling in sick, forgetting appointments, using excessive seclusion and restraint ... or early discharge of patients. In order to enhance staff capacity to cope with fear producing situations staff members, as a group, must be allowed to openly express fear ... including fear of litigation'. This is an example of staff behaving in a complementary way in response to domineering behaviour. It is particularly important that hostile dominance bids are met by friendly counterdominance from staff or community members, for example, non-punitive confrontation and presenting the individual with choices.

Helplessness and guilt. Strasburger (1986) describes various responses to antisocial PDs who show no signs of progressing in therapy (Figure 6.10). He identifies the way in which this can provoke feelings of helplessness and guilt in staff—and other group members—which can be dealt with in various counterproductive ways. Emotional withdrawal, characterized by cutting off and avoiding emotional contact, can then provoke a stepping up of the original behaviour. Assuming 'over-responsibility' (sometimes reinforced by other agencies such as the media that might hold workers responsible for inmates' future behaviour) can lead to embarking on rescue attempts that are doomed to failure or which smother the inmate and provoke countervailing behaviour. The solution to these situations, Strasburger argues, is to show the individual their responsibility for themselves and not to assume responsibility for them. In interpersonal terms the irresponsible behaviour of the inmate is designed to 'pull' responsible behaviour by staff.

Inmate behaviour	Staff emotional reaction	Staff behaviour
Lack of progress or active expression of contempt for therapy	Staff feel helpless and/or guilty	Respond with: Emotional withdrawal Indifference Retaliation Rage at inmate Submission Over-responsibility 'Heroic' rescue attempts

Figure 6.10. Staff responses to lack of progress.

Feelings of invalidity and loss of identity.   With individuals with a characteristically blaming cognitive style and an external locus of control it is not uncommon for the therapist—and other group members—to be held accountable for the individual's problems. Strasburger (1986) writes : 'as the patient disowns his problems and ascribes them to the therapist the therapist may come to feel that he owns them ... All therapists require validation. Devaluation is devastating, producing feelings of worthlessness, depression, fear, rage, guilt, shame and envy... The patient who tells the therapist his own professional doubts are correct touches on a vulnerable spot'. It is easy to underestimate the extent to which inmates, individually and collectively, can impact on the TC worker's behaviour by shaping it with rewards and punishments.

Denial.   Strasburger (1986) identifies denial of fear of violence, and the minimization of the probability thereof, as leading to overly confident and imprudent interventions. The classical account by Hare (e.g. 1993) of the psychopath's unusual ability to dupe staff into releasing them on home-leave may involve playing on this tendency in staff to overconfidence as a manipulative strategy.

Special problems of settings.   Strasburger (1986) also points out the dangers of either assuming an overidentification with anti-ther- apeutic staff cultures—often expressed as 'jokes' designed to test out 'whose side you are really on '—or an overidentification with inmates perceived, sometimes realistically, as being on the receiving end of cruelty and injustice at the hands of the 'system', which then provokes indignant anger in the worker. This overidentification, Strasburger reminds us, 'makes it hard to identify the role inmates play in incidents or to help them to accept responsibility'.

Aversive emotional reactions.   Groves (1978) identifies four types of inmate behaviour that provoke aversive feelings in workers. These he describes as:

- *Dependent clingers*: inmates who provoke aversive feelings through their overdependent behaviour. Groves recommends challenging unrealistic expectations of therapy and the therapist for this group.
- *Entitled demanders*: inmates who demand 'entitlements' whenever they have an opportunity can provoke feelings of anger and possibly a wish to counterattack. For this group he suggests limit-setting: acknowledging the entitlement to care, but not to other things.

- *Manipulative help rejecters*: these inmates can provoke feelings of helplessness and depression, Groves argues. For this group he suggests acknowledging that the inmate's pessimism is shared.
- *Self-destructive deniers*: these inmates can provoke feelings of malice and frustration in workers; for this group Groves suggests the worker needs to reduce his/her expectations of their own capacity to care or have an impact on the inmate.

In all of these cases, if the therapist acts, unthinkingly, on the aversive feelings provoked by the inmate the problem behaviour is simply reinforced.

Denial of the inmate's need to test out.   Shamblin (1986) argues that

> '..understanding the patient's need to test the integrity of the system before working in treatment is very important. The mistrustful, manipulative and dishonest patient cannot at first believe that an honest situation, which is very clear and which values the patient, could exist. In the first few months especially, patient behaviour may be designed to ask:
> - Can I make them dislike or reject me?
> - Can I turn staff against me and thereby discredit them?
> - Can I catch them being dishonest or breaking the rules?
> - Can I overwhelm them with my pathology?'

All of these behaviours are examples of an inmates response to *anti-complementary* behaviour (Blackburn, 1990) from the therapist and are designed to provoke the behaviour most anticipated by their interpersonal style. Extinguishing these behaviours must entail cessation of reinforcement.

Therapeutic nihilism.   This is a complementary response of the therapist to the hostile inmate's or group's behaviour (i.e. hostility pulling a hostile reaction). As Meloy (1988) notes, therapeutic nihilism is a response to the '...behavioural pathology of the psycho-path' for whom devaluing and dehumanizing others is a core interpersonal style. Therapeutic nihilism, he argues, is simply '... the clinician doing to the psychopath what the clinician perceives the psychopath doing to others'. Another complementary response to offenders is deception such as 'ghosting' inmates out of therapy without explaining why they are being moved on.

The illusory treatment alliance.   We looked above at the potential power of aversive conditioning on staff. Inmates are equally capable of manipulating staff and other community members with the use of reinforcement. Meloy (1988) describes this appositely as being '... taken in by the chameleon-like ability of the patient to *mirror* what is expected of him'. In this strategy the inmate, for instrumental reasons, is making an effort to obtain a complementary response from the worker. As soon as the desired outcome is obtained (e.g. the parole report, the home leave) the behaviour changes back.

ORGANIZATIONAL ISSUES: BEING A SMALL UNIT IN A LARGE PRISON

In-group, Out-group Dynamics

A feature of many sub-regimes (not just TCs), with a distinct and independent culture, set within the context of a large prison is that they attract the kind of distorted and often hostile perceptions characteristic of in-group, out-group dynamics. Typically the unit receives a mixture of responses from diverse other regimes and 'subcultures' within the prison. For this process not to become destructive it needs to be monitored and managed carefully at both the unit level and at the senior management level. At the unit level it is important that staff and inmates do not personalize the various critical or devaluing responses and respond in a retaliatory mode. This only serves to feed the process by both confirming assumptions about the general hostility of the unit and by communicating a basic misunderstanding of the origins of the criticism. Often criticisms have a kernel of truth that can be important to the staff group as one source of feedback—the danger of becoming over-isolated, inward-looking and out of touch with current issues is high in TCs generally; this risk can be exacerbated by being in a prison setting. Much as in dealing with 'personality-disordered' inmates it is wise to explore which types of therapist behaviours pull what kinds of inmate behaviours (following the cognitive-interpersonal model (Blackburn 1990), it is also useful to conceptualize how subcultures within the larger organization pull particular kinds of response from other subcultures. From the outside TCs often appear to be élitist and pampering environments and therefore can provoke countervailing behaviour designed to address these perceptions. At its worst this can be active sabotage and at its best this can be, as has already been mentioned, a valuable source of information. In the following vignettes these two potential effects of countervailing behaviours are illustrated.

Hypothetical Vignettes

John's visit. John had been worried about making contact with his mother as he had heard that she was ill and might be dying. He initially avoided addressing the issue in the group meetings but was eventually persuaded by his group to try to get his mother to visit. He asked the staff to ensure that he had an extended visit in order to explore various issues with her. The staff agreed and contacted the Visits department to arrange this. The officer in Visits reluctantly agreed to the arrangement. His view was that this inmate was being treated differently and that this was not fair on other inmates in the prison who were not engaging in treatment. In the event John's visit was curtailed after half an hour. He protested but to no avail. Staff on duty had not been informed of the extended visit.

Paul's home leave. Paul had been asking staff relentlessly for support for a home-leave application. He had succeeded in getting the community to back him and had spent long periods of time on community meetings haranguing the staff group for not acting quickly enough. Other inmates were also jumping on the home leave bandwagon and asking for home leave. Staff, beaten into submission, supported the home-leave application for Paul.

The security department, however, argued that he was a risk for absconding and turned down the application. Initial reaction in the staff group was hostile as they knew that they would have to convey this information to Paul. After further consideration, however, staff identified that they were relieved that Paul was not going on home leave as they shared some of the concerns highlighted by the security department. Following this staff explored the overemphasis on home leave in the community and their own anxieties about having to say 'no' to home leave applicants. Paul's threatening behaviour and manipulativeness and the group's collusion with this was explored in the next community meeting.

The first vignette illustrates the occasional sabotaging behaviour that is a feature of prison life. Unfortunately, behaviour like this can distract from the therapeutic goal of helping the individual to own responsibility for his role in offending behaviour and problem situations. If staff overreact they simply prolong the problem. As with individual hostile reactions the knack is to respond in an anti-complementary fashion, i.e. with a positive and constructive problem-solving approach. A retaliatory response or using the management structure to get things changed can provoke further hostility disguised as incompetence or the implementation of previously unimplemented rules. Staff training should include a session on managing relations with the rest of the prison and dealing with the mild social ostracism that will inevitably meet them from their peers on other wings. Persistent sabotage does, however, need to be met with firm action at a managerial level. Inmates need to explore the dynamic between the unit and the rest of the prison and a positive stance needs to be taken by them where possible. Inviting other professionals from the prison, such as the chaplains and the Board Of Visitors, to get involved is also fruitful.

The second vignette illustrates the important principle that interaction with the rest of the prison can provide the practitioner with positive information about the current state of things on the unit. Managers involved in the rest of the organization who are aware of the various issues faced by the unit can help to provide impartial information from the outside.

Occupancy Dynamics

Pressure to maintain occupancy can have a detrimental rebound effect on the unit if mismanaged (Figure 6.11). This can be particularly true if the criteria for acceptance are loosened for the purposes

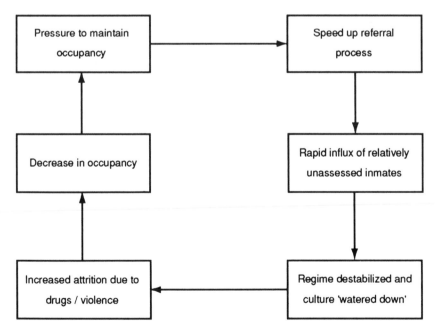

Figure 6.11. Occupancy dynamics.

of increasing occupancy, as this can destabilize the regime. Management of this dynamic involves developing systematic screening strategies linked to acceptance criteria. The best strategy when under pressure to fill up quickly is to take inmates with a relatively low level of need. The screening instrument described above can be used to help identify level of need.

CONCLUSION

In this chapter, then, various strategic responses, derived from an action–research methodology, to the problem of managing treatment integrity and maintaining efficacy have been outlined. In particular the various intrapersonal, interpersonal and organizational attrition-engendering contingencies have been examined. Rather than presenting the reader with a treatment manual for working in a prison-based TC, it is hoped that this chapter has helped the practitioner to develop an empirically informed practice based on evolving models to meet the specific needs of the community at any particular moment.

By focusing on attrition and attrition-related issues it is hoped that the significance of this issue as a challenge to effective intervention is recognized. The reconviction data point in this direction. Traditionally TCs have had a reputation for having a high rate of attrition. One of the reasons for this is the high incidence of personality-disordered offenders in this population. This group are also at higher risk of reoffending (see Sapsford and Fairhead, 1980). More importantly, it is hoped that the reader has been armed with a battery of models and intervention strategies with which to impact on this critical area. If nothing else, it is hoped that the reader has been provoked into recognizing the importance of holding the offender client in treatment long enough to have an impact on his/her behaviour.

REFERENCES

Backalead, F. & Lundall, L. (1975). Dropping out of treatment: A critical review. *Psychological Bulletin* **82**, 738–783.
Barkham, M., Shapiro, D. A. & Firth-Cozens, J. (1989). Personal questionnaire changes in prescriptive vs. exploratory psychotherapy. *British Journal of Clinical Psychology* **28**, 97–107.
Beck, A. T., Freeman, A. & associates (1990). *Cognitive Therapy of Personality Disorders*. New York: Guilford Press.

Blackburn, R. (1989). Psychopathy and personality disorder in relation to violence. In Howells, K. & Hollin, C. R. (Eds). *Clinical Approaches to Violence*. Chichester: Wiley.

Blackburn, R. (1990). Treatment of the psychopathic offender. In Howells, K. & Hollin, C. (Eds). *Clinical Approaches to Working with Mentally Disordered and Sexual Offenders*. Issues in Criminological and Legal Psychology, Vol 16, pp. 54–66. London: British Psychological Society.

Bowlby, J. (1977). The making and breaking of affectional bonds: I. Etiology and psychopathology in the light of attachment theory. *British Journal Of Psychiatry* **130**, 201–210.

Caine, T. M., Foulds, G. A. & Hope, K. (1967). *Manual of the Hostility and Direction of Hostility Questionnaire*. London: University of London Press.

Carson, R. C. (1970). *Interaction Concepts of Personality*. London: Allen & Unwin.

Clark, M. A., Fisher, M. & Thomas, M. E. (1991). The assessment of risk: a guide. HMP Wakefield, (unpublished manuscript).

Cullen, E. (1991). The Grendon reconviction study. HMP Grendon internal document (unpublished).

Derksen J. (1995). *Personality Disorders, Clinical and Social Perspectives*. Chichester: Wiley.

Dolan, B. & Coid, (1993). *Psychopathic and Antisocial Personality Disorders. Treatment and Research Issues*. London: Gaskell.

Dolan, B., Evans, C. D. & Norton, K. (1992). Never mind the quality, feel the width; multiple Axis-II diagnoses of personality disorder. Paper presented at Royal College of Psychiatrists Annual Meeting, Dublin.

Eysenck, H. J. & Eysenck, S. B. G. (1975). *Manual of the Eysenck Personality Questionnaire (Junior and Adult)*. London: Hodder & Stoughton.

Furlong, V. J. (1985). *The Deviant Pupil*. Milton Keynes: Open University Press.

Gendreau, P. & Ross, R. R. (1987). Revivification of rehabilitation: Evidence from the 1980s. *Justice Quarterly* **4**, 349–407.

George, R. (1971). A study to measure the effect of certain variables on reconviction rates of men who left Grendon prison in 1967 and 1968. (Unpublished manuscript).

Glatt, M. M. (1974). An addicts' therapeutic community in a London prison. Lecture presented at International Council on Alcohol and Addictions, Copenhagen Institute.

Glatt, M. M. (1985). The Wormwood Scrubs Annexe: Reflections on the working and functioning of an addicts' therapeutic community within a prison. *Prison Care* **November**.

Groves, J. (1978). Taking care of the hateful patient. *New England Journal of Medicine* **298**, 883–887.

Guidano, U. F. & Liotti, G. (1983). *Cognitive Processes and Emotional Disorders*. New York: Guilford Press.

Hare, R. D., Harpur, T. J., Hakstian, A. R., Forth, A. E., Hart, S. D. & Newman, J. P. (1990). The revised Psychopathy Checklist : Reliability and factor structure. Psychological assessment. *Journal of Consulting and Clinical Psychology* **2**: 338–341.

Hare, R. D. (1993). *Without Conscience*. London: Warner Books.

Hemphill, J. (1991). Recidivism of criminal psychopaths after therapeutic community treatment. Unpublished Masters Thesis, Department of

Psychology, University of Saskatchewan, Saskatoon, Canada. [Referred to in Hare, R. D. (1993). *Without Conscience*. Warner Books.]

Hinshelwood, R. D. (1987). *What Happens in Groups*. New York: Free Association Press.

Hyler, S., Reidler, R. & Spitzer, R. L. (1987). *The Personality Diagnostic Questionnaire*. New York : New York State Psychiatric Institute.

Hyler, S., Rieder, R., Williams, J., Spitzer, R., Hendler, J. & Lyons, M. (1988). The Personality Diagnostic Questionnaire: Development and preliminary results. *Journal of Personality Disorders* 2: 229–237.

Jones, M. (1976). *The Maturation of the Therapeutic Community*. New York: Human Sciences Press.

Jones, L. F. (1988). *The Hospital Annexe: A Preliminary Evaluation*. Directorate of Psychological Services, Series II Report.

Jones, L. F. (1989). The use of the repertory grid as a tool for the evaluation of a therapeutic community. M.Sc. Thesis, Birkbeck College London.

Kelly, G. (1955). *The Psychology of Personal Constructs*. New York: Norton.

Kiesler, D. J. (1983). The 1982 interpersonal taxonomy for complementarity in human transactions. *Psychological Review* 90: 185–214.

Kernberg, O. (1984). *Severe Personality Disorders: Psychotherapeutic Strategies*. New Haven: Yale University Press.

Kohut, H. (1971). *The Analysis of the Self*. London: The Hogarth Press.

Leary, T. (1957). *Interpersonal Diagnosis of Personality*. New York: Ronald Press.

Lewis, P. S. (1973). The prisoner's perception of himself and his world. PhD Thesis, University of Leeds.

Linehan, M. M. (1993) *Cognitive Behavioural Treatment of Borderline Personality Disorder*. New York: Guilford Press.

Lipsey, M. W. (1992a). Juvenile delinquency treatment: a meta-analytic inquiry into the variability of effects. In T. D. Cook, H. Cooper, D. S. Corday, H. Hartmann, L. V. Hedges, R. J. Light, T. A. Louis & F. Mosteller (Eds). *Meta-analysis for Explanation: a Casebook*. New York: Russell Sage Foundation.

Lipsey, M. W. (1992b). The effect of treatment on juvenile delinquency: results from meta-analysis. In F. Lösel, D. Bender, & T. Bliesener (Eds). *Psychology and Law: International Perspectives*. Berlin: Walter de Gruyter.

Lösel, F. (1995). Efficacy of correctional treatment: a review and synthesis of meta-evaluations. In J. McGuire (Ed) *What Works: Reducing Reoffending. Guidelines from Research and Practice*. Chichester: John Wiley.

Mahoney, M. J. (1991). *Human Change Processes*. New York: Basic Books.

Marshall, W. L. (1989). Intimacy, loneliness and sexual offenders. *Behaviour Research and Therapy* 27, 491–503.

McDougal, C. & Clark D. A. (1991). A risk assessment model. In S. Boddis (Ed). *Proceedings of the Prison Psychology Conference*. London: Her Majesty's Stationery Office.

McDougal, C., Clark, D. & Fisher, M. (1994). Assessment of violent offenders. In McMurran M. and Hodge, J. (Eds). *The Assessment of Criminal Behaviours in Secure Settings*. London: Jessica Kingsley.

Mcpherson, R. H. (1973). Wing stability and success rate. HMP Grendon (unpublished document).

Meloy, J. R. (1988). *The Psychopathic Mind: Origins, Dynamics and Treatment*. New York: Jason Aronson.

Miller, W. R. & Rollnick, S. (Eds) (1991). *Motivational Interviewing: Preparing People to Change Addictive Behaviour*. New York: Guilford Press.

Millon, T. (1991). *Millon Personality Type Questionnaire*, Manual. Minneapolis: National Computer Systems.

Nutall, C. P. et al (1977). *Parole in England and Wales. Home Office Research Study No. 38*. London: HMSO.

Ostapiuk, E. B. & Westwood, S. (1986) Glenthorne Youth Treatment Centre: Working with adolescents in graduations of security. In C. R. Hollin & K. Howells (Eds), *Clinical Approaches to Criminal Behaviour*; Issues in criminological and legal psychology, No. 9. Leicester: British Psychological Society.

Patton, M. & Quinn, E. (1986) *Utilisation Focussed Evaluation*. London: Sage.

Prochaska, J. O. & DiClemente, C. C. (1986). Towards a comprehensive model of change. In W. R. Miller & N. Heather (Eds). *Treating Addictive Behaviours : Processes of Change*, pp. 3–73. New York: Plenum Press.

Ryle, A. (1985). Cognitive theory, object relations and the self. *British Journal of Medical Psychology* **58**, 1–7.

Sapsford, R. J. & Fairhead, S. (1980). Reconviction, alcohol and mental disorder. *British Journal of Criminology* **20**(2), 157–165.

Shamblin, W. J. (1986). Inpatient treatment of antisocial youth. In H. R., Reid, D. Dorr, D., J. I. Walker, & J. W. Bonner III (Eds). *Unmasking the Psychopath. Antisocial Personality and Related Syndromes*. New York: Norton.

Stark, M. J. (1992). Dropping out of substance abuse treatment: a clinically oriented review. *Clinical Psychology Review* **12**, 93–116.

Strasburger, L. H. (1986). Treatment of antisocial syndromes: the therapists feelings. In, H. R. Reid, D. Dorr, J. I. Walker & J. W. Bonner III (Eds). *Unmasking the Psychopath. Antisocial Personality and Related Syndromes*. New York: Norton.

Thornton, D. (1988). A measure of self esteem: S.E.0 (Unpublished).

Van Bilsen, H. & Van Emst, A. (1989). Motivating heroin users for change. In G. Bennett (Ed) *Treating Drug Abusers*. London: Routledge.

Walters, G. D. & Chulmsky M. A. (1993). The lifestyle criminality screening form and antisocial personality disorder: predicting release outcome in a state prison sample. *Behavioural Sciences and the Law*, **11**, 111–115.

Wishnie, H. (1977). *The Impulsive Personality*. New York: Plenum.

Woods, P. (1979) *The Divided School*. London: Routledge & Kegan Paul.

Young, J. (1990) *Cognitive Therapy of Personality Disorders: A Schema Focussed Approach*. Sarasota, FL: Professional Resource Exchange.

Young, J. & Swift, W. (1987). Schema focussed cognitive therapy for personality disorders: Part I. *International Cognitive Therapy Newsletter* **4**(5), 13–14.

PART III

International Perspectives

CHAPTER 7

Therapeutic Communities in American Prisons

Harry Wexler

Center for Therapeutic Community Research at
National Development and Research Institutes, Inc., New York

Therapeutic communities (TCs) have recently become the treatment of choice in American prisons. Today most criminal justice professionals and correctional administrators are aware of the demonstrated effectiveness of the TC model in both the community and prison (Wexler, 1994; 1995). This chapter will provide a brief history of the modern prison TC movement, including the landmark studies that established the effectiveness of prison TCs and their capability to reduce recidivism rates. The American self-help movement and community TC roots of the modern prison TC will be described. Adaptations of the classic TC for prison environments will be described, followed by a discussion of several major challenges facing modern prison TCs; and suggestions for meeting these challenges will be offered. Finally, a new direction will be suggested for expanding the prison TC to treat the large number of psychiatric problems that often co-occur with substance abuse.

HISTORY

The Stay 'n Out Prison TC

For many years the slogan 'nothing works' was accepted as an accurate appraisal of the effectiveness of prison rehabilitation

Therapeutic Communities for Offenders.
Edited by E. Cullen, L. Jones and R. Woodward. © 1997 John Wiley & Sons Ltd.

programs. Some optimism began to emerge during the mid-1980s when the evidence of positive prison TC outcomes data appeared. The pivotal evaluation study was conducted with the Stay 'n Out TC designed for inmates with substance abuse histories.

In 1977 the Stay 'n Out prison TC program was established on Staten Island, New York as a joint venture of New York Therapeutic Communities (a private not-for-profit TC organization operated by recovering addicts), the single State substance abuse agency, and the New York State Departments of Corrections and Parole (Wexler & Williams, 1986). The joint sponsorship was needed to establish a program capable of effectively treating criminal justice clients who fall under multiple government agencies.

The use of recovering program operators was a response to the recognized failure of traditional medical and mental health approaches to provide effective interventions for substance abusers in the criminal justice system. The establishment of close working relationships between related government agencies was an important response to the typical fragmentation found in treatment efforts as criminal justice clients move from one jurisdiction to another. The joint approach of having recovering persons with TC experience implement and operate the prison TC supported by related government agencies has become a model for other state efforts during the ensuing years. The development of synergistic partnerships has been an ongoing theme in the historical shift in corrections away from the singular emphasis on punishment to include prison drug treatment during the last ten years.

Acceptance and Expansion of Prison TC Programs

An important change in American corrections policy occurred with the 'Anti-Drug Abuse Act of 1986' that included substantial funding for correctional drug treatment. Based, in part, on the positive outcome findings for prison TCs, two sequential major technical assistance projects were funded which focused on developing effective substance abuse treatment in State departments of corrections. The TC model was accepted as the most effective type of prison drug treatment intervention and was widely utilized in many states. The two national technical assistance projects are summarized that provided critical impetus and guidance for the growth of prison drug treatment in America. (See Wexler et al., 1991; Wexler & Lipton, 1993; Wexler, 1994, for a detailed description of these historical developments.)

The national technical assistance projects included Project REFORM ('Comprehensive State Department of Corrections Treatment Strategy for Drug Abuse' project), which was funded by the Bureau of Justice Assistance (BJA) from 1987 to 1991, and Project RECOVERY (Technical Assistance and Training Services to Demonstration Prison Drug Treatment Programs) funded by the Center for Substance Abuse Treatment (CSAT) from 1991 to 1992. About 20 states participated in these projects and set up prison substance abuse programmes. Many of the treatment efforts included prison TCs.

The technical assistance projects provided leadership and support for the acceptance and expansion of prison substance abuse treatment. The technical assistance providers included program operators, researchers and correctional administrators who had been recognized as leaders in their respective fields. Technical assistance efforts included semi-annual workshops, development of a resource center, dissemination of information on prison drug treatment, and on-site consultation. A strong feature of these projects was the fostering of a sense of community and support for networking and mutual assistance among participants.

Participants in Projects REFORM and RECOVERY believed that a primary goal for correction is the reduction of recidivism, that is, to intervene in the lives of offenders so that they do not return to prior patterns of criminal behavior (Wexler & Lipton, 1993). In 1993 CSAT funded another 11 correctional drug treatment projects along with a technical assistance effort to support these programs following the model established by projects REFORM and RECOVERY. Nine of the 11 new CSAT programs are TCs and all 11 projects have an evaluation component which will provide information on program implementation and outcomes.

The important shift in correctional policy emphasis from deterrence to rehabilitation is dramatically demonstrated in Texas, although some of the impetus for the Texas prison drug treatment initiative has been decreased due to a change in state government administrations. As a direct outgrowth of the REFORM and RECOVERY initiatives and of the growing body of evidence supporting the effectiveness of prison therapeutic community drug treatment, Texas criminal justice treatment agencies have made correctional drug treatment a major goal. In 1991, a comprehensive treatment system for chemically dependent offenders that utilized TCs as the primary treatment modality was initiated in Texas. The approach has provided prison inmates with 12 months of TC treatment followed by another 12 months of transitionary services in the community.

Outcome Research

The Stay 'n Out prison TC was the focus of the first large-scale federally funded evaluation of prison drug treatment in the US (Wexler et al., 1990). The study included both a large-scale review of over 2000 criminal records and a smaller follow-up component.

The major Stay 'n Out finding for the male and female TC residents was a significant lowering of recidivism rates for the TC as contrasted with several comparison groups. The research also found a significant relationship between time in program and treatment outcomes for both male and female residents. Therapeutic community residents who participated in the program for greater lengths of time demonstrated significantly better outcomes (lower recidivism rates). The Stay 'n Out overall findings and the time in program results were essentially replicated by Field in his study of the Cornerstone Program (1989).

In 1991, NIDA funded a five-year evaluation of the Amity TC at RJ Donovan prison in California that was designed with the intention of attempting to replicate the Stay 'n Out findings 10 years later, with another TC and a different prison population in another region of the country. In addition, the Amity study included an evaluation of an aftercare TC component to explore possible additive effects of combining prison TC and aftercare community TC treatment.

The evaluations of the Stay 'n Out and Amity prison TCs are large federally funded studies which were funded by the National Institute on Drug Addiction (NIDA) and conducted by the National Development and Research Institutes, Inc. (NDRI). The Donovan evaluation is being conducted by the Center for Therapeutic Community Research (CTCR) which is housed at NDRI in New York City. Both programs are about 12 months in duration and inmates enter the TCs toward the end of their prison sentence. The Stay 'n Out TC has 150 beds and the Amity TC has 200 beds. Both programs have aftercare TCs in the community but the Stay 'n Out evaluation excluded the aftercare TC because it was not in operation at the time of the study. The Stay 'n Out data were collected and analyzed in the mid-1980s and the Amity evaluation is currently underway.

The main outcome findings of both studies are reductions in recidivism (e.g. rearrest and reincarceration). In addition, both studies found that the amount of recidivism reduction positively related to the amount of time in program. Generally, the inmates who spend a year in the prison TC followed by their participation in a community aftercare TC achieved the best results.

Table 7.1 shows that male inmates who participated in the Stay 'n Out program were arrested less frequently than a no-treatment

Table 7.1. Stay 'n Out therapeutic community (TC) evaluation at Arthur Kill New York State Prison: Rearrest status three years after release from prison (prison TC versus no treatment).

Rearrested	No treatment		Prison TC		Difference	% change
	n	(%)	n	(%)		
Yes	65	(40.9)	117	(26.9)	14.0	34.2
No	94	(59.1)	318	(73.1)		
Total	159		435			

Differences between the groups were significant at $p < 0.01$.

group (Wexler et al., 1990). Prison inmates who had attended the Stay 'n Out TC had an arrest rate of 26.9% vs. 40.9% for the no-treatment group three years after release to the community (while under parole supervision).

The Amity study was designed to replicate the Stay 'n Out study and to explore the added advantage of adding a community TC component. The Amity prison TC outcome data in Tables 7.2 and 7.3 show the reincarceration rates of inmates who participated in the program one year after release from prison, while under parole supervision (Wexler et al., 1995). Table 7.2 includes a randomly selected no-treatment group and a group that completed the prison TC and was released directly into the community. The difference between the groups was a significant 20.4% and the percentage decrease in recidivism shown by the treatment group was 32.4%.

Table 7.3 shows a comparison between the Amity no-treatment group and a treatment group that completed both the prison TC and went directly into an aftercare TC when released from prison. The

Table 7.2. Amity therapeutic community (TC) evaluation at RJ Donovan California State Prison: Reincarceration status one year after release from prison (prison TC versus no treatment).

Reincarceration	No treatment		Prison TC		Difference	% change
	n	(%)	n	(%)		
Yes	46	(63.0)	46	(42.6)	20.4	32.4
No	27	(37.0)	62	(57.4)		
Total	73		108			

Differences between the groups were significant at $p < 0.01$.

Table 7.3. Amity therapeutic community (TC) evaluation at RJ Donovan California State Prison: Reincarceration status one year after release from prison (prison TC plus aftercare TC versus no treatment).

Reincarceration	No treatment		Prison TC+ aftercare TC		Difference	% change
	n	(%)	n	(%)		
Yes	46	(63.0)	16	(26.2)	36.8	58.4
No	27	(37.0)	45	(73.8)		
Total	73		61			

Differences between the groups were significant at $p < 0.01$.

difference between these groups was a significant 36.8% and the percentage decrease in recidivism shown by the group who participated in both prison and aftercare TC treatment was 58.4%.

The preliminary Amity findings replicate the Stay 'n Out results, demonstrating that participation in prison TC treatment can significantly reduce recidivism rates. A comparison of overall recidivism rates in Table 7.1 versus 7.2 and 7.3 shows higher rates for Amity than Stay 'n Out. These overall differences are probably related to differences in the New York and California law enforcement practices and /or the 10-year difference in when the data were collected. In addition, the greatest recidivism reductions are obtained when inmates participate in both a prison TC and community aftercare TC. Preliminary analyses of the Amity substance abuse outcome data show a similar pattern of positive outcome results. Upon completion in 1996, the Amity study will include a variety of information for over 700 participants.

The finding of the far superior outcomes for California inmates who attend both the prison TC and aftercare TC is consistent with the well known finding in TC literature that longer time spent in TC programs is related to better outcomes. These findings provide support for a comprehensive approach that includes prison TC drug treatment along with integrated community TC aftercare facilities for prison inmates with histories of substance abuse.

The positive outcome results found for the Stay 'n Out and Amity prison TCs are being replicated and extended by the CREST project in Delaware, which is testing the efficacy of a new work release TC model (Inciardi & Lockwood, 1995). The CREST work release model is designed for inmates who are permitted to work in the community while living in a prison TC.

The ongoing evaluation of the CREST project includes four groups: participants in a prison TC (The Key) only, a work release TC

(CREST) only, both the Key and CREST, and a quasi-random comparison group. Preliminary findings are similar to the Amity study. At 18 months post prison 70% of the comparison group was arrested as compared with 52% of prison TC participants who did not attend CREST, 35% who attended the CREST only, and 29% who attended both the Key prison TC and the CREST work release TC (Inciardi & Lockwood, 1995).

Although the Stay 'n Out, Amity and Key prison TCs are somewhat different expressions of the TC model (See Wexler, 1995, for a description of some of their differences) the following discussion of the self-help TC description focuses on the general model and on what TC characteristics all three programs share in common.

SELF-HELP, COMMUNITY TCs AND PRISON TCs

Self-help

The community TC movement has grown out of the American self-help tradition (See Wexler, 1995 for an interview discussion of self-help and TCs in America). Historically, the self-help approach has been embraced by a variety of disenfranchised groups that were distressed by the failure of traditional health systems to meet their needs. The incarcerated substance abusers form an especially disenfranchised group who have pervasive problems that include early abuse, poverty, gang membership and a variety of psychiatric co-morbidities.

As contrasted with traditional medical and social welfare approaches, self-help programs are not 'services' which foster client dependence on providers. Rather, they are based on a philosophy of self-responsibility and empowerment. The self-help philosophy elicits strong individual commitment to one's own healing.

Compared with traditional social services programs that provide help for specific problems, the major goal of self-help is changing fundamental antisocial beliefs and unhealthy life-styles. Self-help and TC programs teach members that by taking responsibility for their own problems, participants can gain some control over their situation and improve self-respect and competence. Advanced members who have experienced healthy changes provide support and guidance and serve as credible role models for newer members. In summary, the self-help tradition offers a reasonable and hopeful approach for this population because it accepts them, provides credible opportunities for change, addresses values and emotional issues while providing them with community support.

Community TCs

The modern community substance abuse TC began as an offshoot of AA. In 1958 Charles Dederich founded Synanon in California. He was a recovering alcoholic who broke away from AA because of his dislike of their rigid alcohol focus and their rejection of substance abusers, who were more likely to be poor and members of minority groups. Synanon became a prototype of the concept-based TC (Kennard, 1983).

The early substance abuse community and prison TCs were based on a hierarchical model that was referred to as the 'concept based TC model' (Wexler, 1995). While the early TC model has been modified and expanded, many of the essential characteristics have remained constant and are found in most prison TCs. (See De Leon (1994a) for a description of how the American TC has evolved in recent years). The brief summary below of the main characteristics of the classic concept-based TC sets the context for understanding modern prison TCs.

A typical community TC staff primarily consists of ex-addicts and a limited number of professionals. Nine to 18 months is the usual length of stay and a very high dropout rate in the first 90 days is common. Meaningful work is a core TC characteristic. Residents are involved in all aspects of the community's operations including administration, maintenance, and food preparation. Community TCs rarely utilize outside contractors for facility maintenance to contain costs, provide training opportunities and to foster a greater sense of self-reliance within the community.

The TC approach views drug addictions as a symptom of immaturity. The immature addicted individual is seen as unable to postpone gratification or tolerate frustration, has difficulty maintaining stable relationships, and fails to take responsibility for his/her own life. The concept-based TC seeks to address these problems by setting therapeutic goals that include: abstinence from substance abuse, termination of criminal behavior, employment and/or school enrolment, and successful social adjustment (e.g. establishment of positive, stable relationships).

There is a hierarchical structure to the organization of concept-based TCs. At the top of the hierarchy, a charismatic leader commands the respect of staff and residents. As former addicts, these leaders have a special credibility and are important role models for all participants. The concept of the credible role model who has demonstrated the efficacy of the treatment by his/her own personal achievement is a major program component.

Staff and resident roles are aligned in an hierarchical manner with a clear chain of command. New residents are assigned to work teams with the lowest status (e.g. cleaning toilets). Residents move up the hierarchy as they demonstrate increased competency and emotional growth. Over time residents earn positions with improved status and associated privileges. Therapeutic communities usually have program phases that coincide with 'orientation', 'treatment' and 're-entry'. Success within the TC requires the acceptance of healthy authority and developing acceptable prosocial values. As residents advance through the program they develop expectations and skills for moving into positions of increasing responsibility and status.

There are several basic requirements for successful outcomes within the concept-based TC. A primary condition is the acceptance of the 'act as if' concept, which requires that new residents suspend judgment and make believe that they accept the basic TC values and rules of conduct. The resident continues to 'act as if' until the positive community values and attitudes become internalized. Maturity develops as specific roles and responsibilities are undertaken. The hierarchical character of the TC facilitates the working through of authority problems, which prepares residents to accept appropriate authority and to assume responsible roles within society.

The intense TC atmosphere provides a blend of confrontation and support that enables residents to undergo the arduous changes necessary for successful rehabilitation. Open discussion and the sharing of intimate experiences help develop the skills necessary for positive and stable relationships. Since many residents have experienced early physical and/or sexual abuse, the opportunities to share painful memories often lessens related underlying emotional upsets that can erupt in violent and criminal behavior. Finally, efforts are made to connect residents to the external community during the latter phases of treatment. Many of the relationships formed with peers in the TC extend into the community and provide ongoing support after program completion.

Empirical work has begun to identify TC components that are common to most modern community TCs (Melnick et al., 1993). Twenty-seven essential elements common to all TCs were identified in six areas: TC Perspective; The Agency: Treatment Approach and Structure; Community as Therapeutic Agent; Educational and Work Activities; Formal Therapeutic Elements; and Process. De Leon (1994b) gives excellent clinical descriptions of modern TC structure and program components.

TCs Modified for Prisons

Prison TCs utilize most of the community TC components described above. Many of the ways TCs are modified to operate within prisons are in response to the prison organization and the inmates' lack of access to the outside community. However, a basic similarity that provides common ground for communication and understanding between prison and program staff is their common highly structured work environments that assert considerable control over staff and participants.

A fundamental reason for the growing acceptance of TCs in American prisons is the willingness of TC operators to acknowledge the priority of security over treatment. The first requirement for the successful implementation of a credible TC is the understanding and full acceptance by program management that the TC is a 'guest' of corrections, and that while treatment is highly important it is secondary to security. The acceptance of a secondary position for the role and goals of treatment is often a difficult process for community TC personnel who are accustomed to unchallenged control of program environments. On the other hand, the effectiveness of a prison TC is partially related to the degree to which the program can maintain reasonable autonomy and commitment to supporting the growth of its members as contrasted with the usual coercive nature of prisons with their limited emphasis on 'doing time' and simple custody concerns.

A growing number of studies provide suggestions for the conditions needed for effective correctional treatment (Lipton, 1983; Wexler, 1986; Wexler et al., 1988). Among the most important conditions are: (1) an isolated treatment unit, (2) motivated participants, (3) a committed and competent staff, (4) adequate treatment duration, (5) an array of treatment options, (6) cooperative and supportive relationships with correctional staff and administration, and (7) continuity of care that extends into the community. The above guidelines for successful correctional treatment are only suggestive, since very little research has been done that links the nature of treatment that clients receive to treatment outcomes (Hubbard et al., 1988).

Prison TC programs can be arrayed along a dimension anchored at one end by traditional mental health and at the other end by self-help. The type of TC implemented depends, in part, on the kinds of treatment resources available and preferences of funding agencies. For example, heavily populated urban areas such as New York and California have a number of well established community TCs and pools of recovering addicts with TC experience. In contrast, more rural areas have few recovering addicts and must recruit staff from more traditional mental health sources. One of the essential challenges facing the prison TC movement in America is how to integrate mental health assessment and treatment approaches into the TC structure while maintaining the essential self-help and community orientation.

Restraints on inmates' freedom, and the working within the many rules and limitations of corrections, provide a number of problems that TC staff must cope with by modifying the program. These problems include:

- Program activities must be scheduled to conform to the prison general schedule (e.g. meals, and count (i.e. all inmates must be located and counted by security staff several times each day)).
- Permission for special groups that conflict with prison schedules must be negotiated.
- Many prisons require all inmates to hold prison jobs that reduce the time they can participate in the program.
- Recovering staff with prison records are not allowed into many prisons.
- Rewards for good program behavior and demonstrations of personal growth are limited.

The difficult work of gaining acceptance of TCs in American prisons has been accomplished. However, important challenges to increase prison TC effectiveness need to be addressed.

CHALLENGES FOR PRISON TCs

Prison TCs that treat inmates with substance abuse problems have been shown to be effective and capable of reducing recidivism. The next challenge is to reduce the recidivism rates further by improving the effectiveness of TC treatment. The main areas where prison substance abuse treatment needs improvement include training of counselors, incorporating meaningful and productive work into the TCs, provision of TC aftercare, vocational training along with job placement, and drug-free housing.

Training

As prison TCs receive greater acceptance and more programs are funded, the shortage of trained TC staff becomes more critical. A major problem for many TC programs is that most states have mandatory educational and 'traditional' experience requirements, that recovering counselors cannot meet. Many of the more experienced TC counselors received their early training as TC residents instead of at professional schools. Their training continued when they became junior staff as they struggled to demonstrate healthy drug-free life-styles. The TC requires an experienced core staff that has a comprehensive understanding of the TC approach to maintain a healthy TC community, as well as more traditionally trained staff with mental health and organizational skills.

Several state correctional departments have been active in developing academic training programs that welcome non-traditional counseling staff and give credits for job experience that are designed for recovering staff. The growing number of prison TCs are creating a market for skilled TC counselors that may interest some clinical programs in colleges and universities. There is a growing need for the formation of partnerships between recognized TCs (that have programs in prison and the community) and academic institutions. Working together, training curriculums need to be developed with strong academic and experiential components designed to meet the needs of the modern prison TC.

Role of Work in Prison TCs

Prisons TCs usually have an isolated unit where resident jobs often include facility maintenance (e.g. cleaning), community operations and assisting counselors with group management and equipment. However, while community TCs often require a considerable amount of construction and maintenance work that trains residents in marketable skills, the main work tasks in prisons are carried out by paid personnel. In most prison programs resident work is primarily comprised of 'make do' work. A production facility that is operated as an integral part of the TC is sorely needed.

Work is an essential ingredient for TCs. Meaningful demanding work is needed to challenge residents so they can use their energy constructively while learning both work and social skills that are needed to obtain and maintain employment. Work-related social skills include knowing how to interact with supervisors and sub-ordinates in a respectful and productive manner. Other skills include time management, making and keeping agreements, setting appropriate boundaries (knowing when and how to say no) and finding acceptable expressions of frustration. Program participants need meaningful work experiences when in prison and after release to the community. The ultimate goal is for participants to become self-sufficient, with a steady job and adequate income.

Prison TCs need 'production facilities' to maximize their impact upon residents. A production facility would produce or manufacture a product that has value in the community. The product can include physical activities or services. For example, an excellent TC model that includes a production facility can be found at the 'The Crossroads to Freedom House' TC operated by the Colorado Department of Corrections. The TC operates a flower business that includes a large nursery. The nursery is an essential part of the program and residents must respond to realistic demands of the business to ensure its success. During the planting and harvest seasons most regular TC activities are halted or modified so that all residents can dedicate themselves to the essential nursery tasks that must be done for the business to be a success. The demanding work necessary to operate a for-profit nursery inspires residents and staff and adds a critical element to the program. Thus, the greenhouse both engages the TC residents in meaningful work and trains them in marketable skills they can apply upon release.

TC Aftercare

The significant improvements in recidivism reduction related to participation in a work release TC (Inciardi & Lockwood 1995) and TC aftercare during parole (Wexler, 1995) provide important support for the expansion of prison TC treatment into work release and aftercare.

Two major challenges facing aftercare are jobs and drug-free housing.

Community Vocational Training and Jobs

Specific training in marketable job skills and the securing of decent employment are critical for successful aftercare. Although traditional community TCs provide many opportunities for work related to maintenance of the program they generally fail to provide strong vocational training or significant help in securing jobs. One exception is the Delancy Street TC in San Francisco, which has created businesses that promote the program, offer training opportunities for residents, and make a profit. Cooperative relationships between the government, treatment, and business communities create meaningful training programs and successful job placement. A promising cooperative venture is 'Project Re-enterprise', a program started by the Crime Prevention Institute, which teaches inmates the skills necessary to find employment and sponsors 'job fairs' in Texas prisons.

Drug-free Housing

Many of the people who participate in prison TCs are homeless when they are released to the community. Others have nowhere to go except to return to the communities where they lived and participated in criminal activities prior to entering prison. Housing is often overlooked when planning transitionary resources because it is viewed as outside the scope of treatment. However, return to 'the old neighborhood' exposes recovering individuals to very harmful influences.

An excellent model for drug-free housing for ex-felons is the Oxford House Network (Malloy, 1992). Oxford Houses are typically located in low crime and drug neighborhoods where they provide recovering addicts and alcoholics the opportunity to live in a safe and supportive environment. Oxford Houses are self-governing residences based on the Alcoholic Anonymous 12-step philosophy. While these houses do not provide drug treatment, they do have a self-help recovery atmosphere that reinforces positive behavior changes. Participants in Oxford Houses often take pride in maintaining an independent recovery house without dependency on outside authorities. Although an individual can stay as long as they pay rent and obey house rules of sobriety and responsibility, the average length of stay is about a year.

Since 1988, a federal law requires every State to make available a $100 000 revolving fund to encourage recovering individuals to establish self-run, self-supported recovery houses that utilize no paid staff, operate democratically, and expel residents who relapse into using alcohol or drugs. Currently, there are more than 400 Oxford houses for men and women throughout the country.

TREATMENT OF PSYCHIATRIC DISORDERS: A NEW DIRECTION FOR AMERICAN PRISON TCs

The increasing number of inmates with histories of substance abuse and other psychiatric comorbidities presents an important challenge for the American prison TC movement. The recognized success of prison TCs provides an excellent opportunity to build upon an established technology by enhancing and expanding it to meet the psychiatric needs associated with substance abuse. It is reasonable to entertain the possibility that an enhanced prison TC model that also treats comorbid psychiatric problems may significantly increase the effectiveness of the modality.

A major epidemiological study conducted by the National Institute of Mental Health (Reiger et al., 1990) found very high base rates of mental disorders in prison populations that were coupled with addictive disorders. Comorbidity of alcohol and/or substance abuse was found in about 90% of prisoners with schizophrenia, bipolar disorder, and antisocial personality disorder. Other prison research has indicated that approximately 26% of alcohol and drug abusers had a lifetime history of major depression, bipolar disorder, or atypical bipolar disorder, and 9% had a history of schizophrenia (Cote & Hodgins, 1990).

An important distinction needs to be drawn between inmates who have been identified as substance abusers in the general prison population and are also psychologically disturbed, and inmates who have been segregated with psychiatric diagnoses and also abuse substances. Although the TC approach is being used with increasing frequency for psychiatric patients with comorbid substance abuse problems in the community (Sacks & De Leon, 1994; Sack et al., in press), there are only a few prison TC programs for dual diagnosed prison inmates. The remainder of this chapter will discuss issues related to providing treatment for substance abusers with associated psychological problems who participate in regular prison TCs.

Most community and prison TCs do not utilize mental health diagnostic and treatment methods. The TC approach, which is designed for antisocial personalities, usually does not directly recognize and treat other major psychological problem constellations. The TC programs prefer to view participants more homogeneously as addicts with criminal life-styles who need to undergo psychological growth, learn to accept prosocial values such as honesty and responsibility and how to be productive members of a community.

Recent information on the incidence of comorbidity in prison TCs has been reported as part of the Amity prison TC evaluation study. Wexler and Graham (1993) reported the presence of four major diagnostic groups, including 52% antisocial personality disorder (APD), 27% depressive disorders, 18% phobic disorders, and 16% post-traumatic stress syndrome (PTSD). In addition, Wexler (1994) reported a 42% incidence of attention deficit hyperactivity disorder (ADHD) among inmates. The finding of a high incidence of ADHD is especially important, since it has been considered a disorder limited to childhood and has been identified as a precursor to substance abuse and criminality. Several recent literature reviews have indicated strong linkages between ADHD, substance abuse and criminality as well as ADHD and APD (Satterfield et al. 1982; Faraone et al., 1991; Ahadpour et al. 1993; Biederman et al. 1993; Patterson & Yoeger, 1993).

If concurring disorders are addressed as part of in-prison and post-prison TC treatment, it is likely that greater reductions in recidivism can be achieved. It is recommended that cognitive/behavioral treatments which have been identified by the mental health community as effective should be adopted and integrated into the prison and aftercare TC curriculum to reduce recidivism rates further. However, the integration must be done carefully so that the proven effectiveness of the TC is not inadvertently compromised by changing it into a mental health clinic.

The primary reason for the limited acceptance of psychiatric diagnoses and the direct treatment of diagnosed problems among TC clinical staff is the concern that program participants will seize upon the opportunity to 'blame' their addiction on 'labeled' mental conditions and avoid confronting their negative attitudes and lifestyles. Since working through denial is an important aspect of substance abuse treatment, the direct use of diagnostic language could interfere with this process. A related problem is that TC staff often have a strong discomfort with mental health approaches that use psychoactive medication which substance abuse clients can easily incorporate into an addictive pattern.

Another concern is that the use of diagnoses, derived from the medical tradition, is an objective and relatively sterile approach that contributes to the impersonal atmosphere often found in mental health clinics. Since a key aspect of effective TCs is a cohesive and caring community environment it is difficult to accept anything that diminishes the sense of community. A final consideration worth noting is that most TC clinical staff, who are primarily recovering addicts, find diagnostic concepts foreign because they have not had traditional mental health training.

Clinical sensitivity is needed when introducing mental health approaches into prison TCs. Mental health strategies can be presented as program enhancements capable of empowering staff and residents by increasing their knowledge of psychological problems and as methods of increasing self-awareness and coping mechanisms. The concepts 'making the problem into the solution' and of adding 'tools' that will assist residents help themselves and each other are consistent with the self-help/TC tradition. Successful integration of TC and mental health approaches will require the formation of partnerships between mental health and TC staff based upon mutual understanding and respect. It would probably be a mistake if a mental health orientation became dominant in any joint venture with the TC, because the effectiveness demonstrated by the TC approach might be compromised.

The prison TC movement has made great strides during the past 10 years and it is poised for the next major step. The next generation of prison TCs needs to respond to the significant psychological problems of residents that accompany their substance abuse. While there is a growing recognition of the need to treat the large numbers of inmates with multiple psychiatric disorders, the idea of enhancing the TC approach that has demonstrated significant levels of effectiveness to treat disorders that accompany substance abuse is only starting to be introduced (Wexler, 1995). The next major breakthrough in correctional rehabilitation is possible if it builds on the successes of prison TCs by addressing the problems of comorbidities.

REFERENCES

Ahadpour, M., Horton, A.M. Jr & Vaeth, J.M. (1993). Attention deficit disorder and drug abuse. *International Journal of Neuroscience*, **723**, 89–93.

Biederman, J., Faraone, S. V., Spencer, T., Wilens, T., Norman, D., Lapey, K. A. Mick, E., Lehman, B. K. & Doyle, A. (1993). Patterns of psychiatric comorbidity, cognition, and psychological functioning in adults with attention deficit hyperactivity disorder. *American Journal of Psychiatry*, **150**, 1792–1798.

Cote, G. & Hodgins, S. (1990). Co-occurring mental disorders among criminal offenders. *Bulletin of the American Academy of Psychiatry and Law*, **18**(3), 271–281.

De Leon, G. (1994a). The therapeutic community: toward a general theory and model. In F. M. Tims, G. De Leon & N. Jainchill (Eds). *Therapeutic Community: Advances in Research and Application*. NIDA Monograph 144, Rockville, MD.

De Leon, G. (1994b). Therapeutic communities. In M. Galanter & H. Kleber (Eds). *Textbook of Substance Abuse Treatment*. Washington, DC: American Psychiatric Press.

Faraone, S. V., Biederman, J., Keenan, K. & Tsuang, M. T. (1991). Separation of DSM-III attention deficit disorder and conduct disorder: Evidence from a family-genetic study of American child psychiatric patients. *Psychological Medicine*, **21**, 109–121.

Field, G. (1989). A study of the effects of intensive treatment on reducing the criminal recidivism of addicted offenders. *Federal Probation*, **53**(10), 51–56.

Hubbard, R. L., Collins, J. J., Rachal, J. V. & Cavanaugh, E. R. (1988). The criminal justice client in drug abuse treatment. In C. G. Leukefeld & F. M. Tims. *Compulsory Treatment of Drug Abuse: Research and Clinical Practice*. National Institute on Drug Abuse Research Monograph 86. Washington DC: US Government Printing Office, pp. 57–80.

Inciardi, J. A. & Lockwood, D. (1995). When worlds collide: Establishing CREST Outreach Center. In F. M. Tims, F. W. Bennett, J. A. Inciardi & M. A. Horton (Eds). *Innovative Approaches to Drug Abuse Treatment: Implementation Issues and Problems*. Westport, CT: Greenwood Press.

Kennard, D. (1983). *An Introduction to Therapeutic Communities*. London: Routledge & Kegan Paul.

Lipton, D. (1983). Important conditions for successful rehabilitation. Paper presented at the Bellevue Forensic Psychiatry Conference, New York City.

Malloy, J. P. (1992). *Self-run. Self-supported Houses for More Effective Recovery from Alcohol and Drug Addiction* (Technical Assistance Publication Series No. 5). Rockville, MD: US Department of Health and Human Services.

Melnick, G., De Leon, G. & Zingaro, M. (1993). Essential elements of therapeutic community treatment for drug abuse. Poster presented at the American Psychological Association Annual Convention, Toronto, August.

Patterson, G. R. & Yoeger, K. (1993). Differentiating outcomes and histories for early and late onset arrests. OSLC, Eugene, Oregon. Annual Conference for the American Society of Criminology, Phoenix, AZ.

Peters, R. H. & Hills, H. A. (1993). Inmates with co-occurring substance abuse and mental health disorders. In H. J. Steadman & J. J. Cocozza (Eds). *Providing Services for Offenders with Mental Illness and Related Disorders in Prisons*. Washington, DC: The National Coalition for the Mentally Ill in the Criminal Justice System.

Reiger, D. A., Farmer, M. E., Rae, D. A., Locke, B. Z., Keith, S. J., Judd, L. L. & Goodwin, F. K. (1990). Comorbidity of mental disorders with alcohol and other drug abuse: Results from the Epidemiologic Catchment Area (ECA) study. *Journal of the American Medical Association*, **264**(19), 2511–2518.

Satterfield, J. H., Hoppe, C. M. & Schell, A. M. (1982). A prospective study of the delinquency in 110 adolescent boys with attention deficit disorder and 88 normal adolescent boys. *American Journal of Psychiatry*, **139**(6), 795–798.

Sacks, S. & De Leon, G. (1994). Modified therapeutic communities for dual disorders: Evaluation overview. *Proceedings of the Second Therapeutic Communities of America Planning Conference: Paradigms: Past, Present, and Future*. Chantilly, VA: 6–9 December 1992.

Sacks, S., De Leon, G., Bernhardt, A. I. & Sacks, J. (in press). *Modified Therapeutic Community for Homeless People with Mental Illness and Chemical Abuse Disorders: A Treatment Manual*. The Center for Substance Abuse Treatment and The Center for Mental Health Services.

Wexler, H. K. (1994). Progress in prison substance abuse treatment: A 5 year report. *Journal of Drug Issues*, **24**(2), 361–372.

Wexler, H. K. (1995). The success of therapeutic communities for substance abusers in American prisons. *Journal of Psychoactive Drugs*, **27**(1), 57–66.

Wexler, H. K. & Lipton, D. S. (1993). From REFORM to RECOVERY: Advances in Prison Drug Treatment. In J. Inciardi (Ed.). *Drug Treatment and Criminal Justice*. Sage Criminal Justice System Annuals, Vol. 29.

Wexler, H. K. & Williams, R. (1986). The Stay'n Out therapeutic community: Prison treatment for substance abusers. *Journal of Psychoactive Drugs*, **18**(3), 221–230.

Wexler, H. K., Falkin, G. P. & Lipton, D. S. (1988). A model prison rehabilitation program: An evaluation of the Stay'n Out therapeutic community. *A Final Report to the National Institute on Drug Abuse*.

Wexler, H. K., Falkin, G. P. & Lipton, D. S. (1990). Outcome evaluation of a prison therapeutic community for substance abuse treatment. *Criminal Justice and Behavior*, **17**(1), 71–92.

Wexler, H. K., Blackmore, J. & Lipton, D. S. (1991). Project REFORM: Developing a drug abuse treatment strategy for corrections. *Journal of Drug Issues*, **21**(2), 473–495.

Wexler, H. K. & Graham, W. F. (1993). Prison-based therapeutic community for substance abusers: Six month evaluation findings. Toronto, Canada: American Psychological Association.
Wexler, H., Graham, W., Koronkowski, R. & Lowe, L. (1995). Amity therapeutic community substance abuse program preliminary return to custody data: May 1995. Report by the Office of Substance Abuse Programs, California Department of Corrections.

CHAPTER 8

Social-therapeutic Institutions in Germany: Description and Evaluation

Friedrich Lösel

Institute of Psychology, University of Erlangen–Nürnberg, Germany

and

Rudolf Egg

Center for Criminology, Wiesbaden, Germany

INTRODUCTION

Over the past 20 years, two differing trends can be observed in the crime policies of many Western countries. On the one hand, attempts were made to reduce punishment, particularly for first offenders or less severe offences. More importance was placed on dismissal, of charges, diversion, victim–offender mediation, community service and other non-custodial measures alongside traditional fines and probation orders. On the other hand—particularly in the USA— there was a trend toward increased punitiveness, and toward general or individual deterrence and incapacitation. Regardless of how these two trends may relate to the development of crime rates (e.g. Farrington et al., 1994), the *rehabilitative* ideal of imprisonment largely disappeared (Allen, 1981; McGuire & Priestley, 1992). Prisons

Therapeutic Communities for Offenders.
Edited by E. Cullen, L. Jones and R. Woodward. © 1997 John Wiley & Sons Ltd.

were viewed as a necessary evil, and educational or therapeutic possibilities were broadly denied under the doctrine 'nothing works.'

However, in recent years, attention has turned again toward the demand for correctional treatment (e.g. Gendreau & Ross, 1987; Hood, 1995; Lösel, 1993; Palmer, 1992; McGuire, 1995). Although alternative measures expanded, in many countries prison populations have grown and probably become more difficult. Under these circumstances treatment-oriented regimes may at least help in reducing violence, suicide, negative effects of imprisonment, or stress for inmates and staff (e.g. Cooke, 1991; Genders & Player, 1995; Liebling, 1992; Peat & Wirfree, 1992). Furthermore, recent meta-analyses of offender-treatment programmes have shown that outcomes are more promising than the 'nothing works' doctrine suggested (e.g. Andrews et al., 1990; Antonowicz & Ross, 1994; Garrett, 1985; Lipsey, 1992). However, most of the available research refers to specific programs for juvenile offenders, frequently also in non-custodial settings. The treatment of persistent adult offenders in prisons is clearly under-represented in the meta-analyses (Lösel, 1995a,c). None the less, this particularly difficult and complex field also exhibits promising approaches (e.g. Cooke, 1989; Cullen, 1993; Genders & Player, 1995; Wexler et al., 1990).

Complex institutional treatment concepts are partially subsumed under the heading of 'therapeutic communities' (Kennard, 1983). They emphasize a positive inmate and staff culture, and a structure that includes the formation of relationships and resources for treatment as well as discipline and security (e.g. Agee, 1986). Although some outcome results are not very impressive, institutional therapeutic communities represent a central paradigm of prison management (Gunn & Robertson, 1987). In international discussions about this treatment concept there should be recognition of one type of institution that has already been in practice and researched for more than two decades: the social-therapeutic prisons in the Federal Republic of Germany. This chapter contains a short overview of the development of these institutions and gives examples of their practices. Findings on treatment evaluation, as well as some of the problems that this involves, are also reported. Finally, conclusions are drawn regarding future work.

When dealing with social-therapeutic prisons, it has to be remembered that only a small number of incarcerated offenders in Germany are to be found in these institutions (831 inmates from figures collected in December 1994). This compares with 20,203 incarcerated remand prisoners, 32,454 sentenced prisoners are in regular prisons for adult offenders and 4265 in prisons for young offenders. About

2500 are in high-security departments at psychiatric hospitals or special hospitals for mentally disordered offenders, and approximately 1200 are in special institutions for drug-dependent offenders (data from 1991).

The social-therapeutic prisons represent Germany's prototype of a rehabilitative approach. They are the closest counterparts of the therapeutic prisons or communities in other countries. They also are evaluated more systematically than the other German institutions mentioned above. However, types of institutions are not homogeneous: there are differences not only *between* but also *within* them. For example, regular prisons vary widely regarding the degree of openness, offender population, personnel resources, and so forth. On the other hand, social-therapeutic prisons also share many of the problems of regular prisons or hospitals for mentally ill offenders. For reasons of space, this chapter will have to ignore these similarities and differences.

THE DEVELOPMENT OF THE SOCIAL-THERAPEUTIC PRISONS

The first discussion about social therapy in the German criminal justice system can be traced back to 1966. At that time, 14 German and Swiss experts wrote an alternative draft of the Penal Code in which they proposed for the first time 'admission to a social-therapeutic institution' (see Baumann et al., 1966). This idea of a new treatment-oriented institution within the criminal justice system was guided in part by examples from other countries, particularly the Netherlands and Scandinavia (see Lösel et al., 1987). However, in Germany, it was not associated with an indeterminate sentence. The social-therapeutic institution entered into § 65 of the German Penal Code (Strafgesetzbuch, (StGB), passed by parliament in 1969, to be enforced in 1973. Thereafter, various model institutions were established in several federal states. As there was a lack of clarity regarding the selection criteria and treatment methods, as well as a lack of resources, the implementation of § 65 StGB was postponed for a testing period during which prisoners were not sentenced to social therapy by the court but transferred at their own request.

As would be expected, there was criticism of the social-therapeutic concept from the very beginning. At first, primarily by representatives of 'conservative' crime policy positions, it was argued that social therapy is (a) not an appropriate retribution for guilt, (b) too insecure in protecting the public, (c) insufficiently oriented toward general deterrence, and, particularly, (d) too costly. Somewhat later, objections arose from the 'critical' views on crime policy in the 1970s, such as (a) the danger of individualization of social problems, (b) the inappropriateness of a medical model of treatment, (c) the insufficient legal control of social services' decisions, and (d) the unresolvable conflict between treatment and punishment. This political reasoning has been supported by references to primarily American evaluation studies that seemed to confirm the failure of therapeutic efforts in the penal system (e.g. Lipton et al., 1975; Sechrest et al., 1979).

Economic factors have been particularly influential on the further development of social therapy. The staff–prisoner ratio and the daily costs in normal prisons are about one half those in social-therapeutic institutions. Since the early 1970s, various recessions reduced the former expansion of criminal justice budgets. In addition, issues such as terrorism, drug criminality, and (recently) organized crime as well as measures of deterrence, decarceration, and diversion became more central in crime policy. After almost 20 years of controversy surrounding its legal basis, in 1984 social therapy as an individual sanction by the court was rejected. Instead of implementing § 65 StGB, the transfer to a social-therapeutic setting was decided according to § 9 of the Prison Law (StVollzG). This so-called 'prison solution' is:

> § 9 – Placement in a social-therapeutic prison.
> (1) A prisoner can, if he or she agrees, be transferred to a social-therapeutic prison if the particular resources and social assistance in the prison are indicated for his or her resocialization. He or she can be returned to a normal prison if it becomes apparent that these resources and assistance are not successful.
> (2) Transfer to a social-therapeutic prison requires the consent of the governor of the social-therapeutic prison.

In contrast to the original estimate by which nearly one-quarter of all prisoners were expected to need social therapy, the current population is only about 2%. Treatment is not mandatory, and it is up to the justice system to introduce, expand or even not to plan such institutions. This legal situation led to restrictions upon but not to the end of social-therapeutic settings. The early model institutions still remain and social therapy even expanded, if only hesitantly. At the present time, there are a total of 15 social-therapeutic settings and departments (Table 8.1; for further details see Egg & Schmitt, 1993).

Overall, social-therapeutic prisons are a consolidated part of the criminal justice system in the 'old' West German states. However,

Table 8.1. Social-therapeutic institutions or departments in Germany.

Social-therapeutic institutions/departments	Year of opening	Number of places	Particular features
Asperg	1969	66	Oldest social-therapeutic institution, independent since 1975
Crailsheim	1982	24	Only for drug-dependent juvenile offenders
Bad Gandersheim	1973	24	With a new separate section
– Department Alfeld	1994	11	only for women
Berlin – Tegel	1970	160	Two treatment fields: Social training, social therapy
Berlin – prison for women	1988	15	Social-therapeutic institution for women
Düren – Transit house Köln	1971	32 22	Transit house for prisoners with outside jobs (not only from Düren)
Erlangen	1972	41	Independent since 1983
Gelsenkirchen	1974	54	Focus on vocational training
Hamburg – Altengamme	1984	60	Open institution for men and women (co-educational)
Hamburg – Bergedorf	1969	31	Diagnosis and therapy carried out by members of staff from the university hospital at Eppendorf
Kassel – Open department	1980	140 25	Located directly beside the juvenile detention center Kassel I, partly joint administration
Ludwigshafen	1972	68	Also accept juveniles
Lübeck	1974	35	Relocation to another institution in Neumünster planned
München	1972	23	Department within remand prison; only for sexual offenders
Total		831	

conceptual and structural problems have remained. The future of the social-therapeutic setting may well depend on how these issues are handled. In the following section, the characteristics and problems of social therapy will be explained in more detail, good practice will be illustrated by taking a closer look at one of these institutions.

CHARACTERISTICS AND PROBLEMS OF SOCIAL-THERAPEUTIC PRISONS

Therapeutic Concept

When the concept of the social-therapeutic prisons originated, the content of treatment was obviously a very important issue. The early concept was based mainly on traditional psychotherapeutic methods. Although the whole interactional, organizational, and material setting was thought to be relevant, individual or group psychotherapeutic, and particularly psychoanalytic, methods played a central role. Further provisions such as school and vocational training, or contacts with the outside world, were seen as additional parts of the intervention (Mauch & Mauch, 1971). The main aim of therapy was the treatment of those personality disorders that were regarded as 'causes' of criminality. An additional idea was to shape and support those characteristics that are considered necessary for a life without offending.

One of the orientations in psychoanalytical treatment was the concept of the dissocial syndrome (e.g. Böllinger, 1983). This posits a severe disturbance of the mother–child relationship between the ages of 8 and 24 months. It is assumed that the defense structure of the client and the social reactions of the environment engender a cumulative process that leads to delinquent development. The social-therapeutic institute should provide a santuary in which the inmate can develop emotional bonds and commitment to someone who acts as a social reference. On this basis he/she should catch up on maturation through supportive educational measures.

As classical psychoanalysts had already emphasized (e.g. Eissler, 1949), the treatment of delinquents proved to be particularly difficult. There were also only a few psychoanalytically trained therapists who were active in the social-therapeutic model institutions. When they came into the institutions from the outside, problems of inconsistency with the permanent staff inside sometimes arose. For these and other reasons, most social-therapeutic institutions soon integrated other therapeutic concepts (e.g. behavior modification, cognitive-behavioral approaches, client-centered therapy, communication and systems therapy). This also meant that most therapeutic work was not done by medical psychotherapists but by psychologists, special educators, and social workers. Originally, these were not specialized in offender treatment and acquired their knowledge and skills through further education. Similarly, different forms of community life were developed in the institutions. The participation of inmates and staff in daily procedures and decisions became important parts of the social-therapeutic programs (see Egg, 1984).

In none of the institutions has it proven to be useful to adopt specific modes or schools of psychotherapy in a schematic way. Modifications and mixtures of the 'pure' therapies arose everywhere (Schmitt, 1980). Parallel to this, the status of psychotherapeutic methods in the programme changed: today, they mostly do not count as the center piece of social therapy but as one of several provisions. Work in housing groups, social-educational measures (e.g. social training courses), as well as the inclusion of the social surroundings (family, work) have gained increasingly in importance. This development was not explicitly planned but has taken place more or less naturally. Thus, social therapy in the penal system appears in a colorful variety. The therapists who work in the different institutions determine the specific program according to their special competencies, knowledge, and (more or less implicit) attitudes. A uniform and systematic concept of the social-therapeutic institution does not exist. This heterogeneous approach may be in line with the more general or eclectic concepts emphasized in modern psychotherapy (e.g. Garfield & Bergin, 1994). However, there is also the danger that such work is not always oriented toward the empirical knowledge that is now available on specific characteristics of appropriate offender treatment (e.g. Andrews, 1995; Hollin, 1993; Lösel, 1995a).

Clients

Treatment in a social-therapeutic institution was planned originally for the following groups of offenders: (a) recidivists with serious personality disorders; (b) dangerous sexual offenders; (c) young adult criminals who have been assessed as especially crime-prone; and (d) criminally non-responsible offenders or those of reduced responsibility, if placement in a social-therapeutic prison would appear to provide a better opportunity for resocialization than transfer to a psychiatric clinic. In practice, the first category was predominant. Over the years, various admission criteria and methods have been developed in different social therapeutic prisons, which altogether have led to a quite heterogeneous clientele. This applies to the formal admission criteria (e.g. age, offense type, sentence remainder) as well as motivational and other personality criteria. The criteria particularly differ with respect to sexual, violent, and drug offenders. They often are subsumed under the three concepts 'treatment willingness,' 'treatment ability,' and 'treatment necessity.' There is no common assessment scheme applying, for example, the categories of ICD-10, DSM-IV, or more specific assessments of antisocial personality/ psychopathy (see Blackburn, 1993; Hare et al., 1991).

Notable differences between the institutions also become visible in terms of the number of clients who are moved back to a normal prison after a temporary admission (drop-outs). For example, violations against the house regulations (e.g. alcohol use) or lack of cooperation in the treatment program can result in such a return. The relevant proportions vary between 20 and 60%. The apparently wide scope of the institutions regarding admission and rejection of prisoners raises the important question of to what extent a clientele of 'medium difficulty' is selected in order to guarantee successful work. As limits of space and staff are unavoidable, it is plausible that, at least implicitly, a positive selection may take place. On the other hand, social-therapeutic institutions also claim that recently more and more offenders are being transferred because they are not able to cope with the situation in normal prisons.

Preparation for Release and After-care

Social therapeutic treatment can be viewed as a complex provision for the preparation of life in freedom. Prisoners should learn to act autonomously step by step; existing social bonds should be stabilized and new ones built. Especially in the last phase of their stay, relaxations of the penal system such as permission to work outside as well as vacations from the prison are of great importance. Contact between prisoners and the outside world is reinforced at an early stage, for instance, by visits or the inclusion of relatives in counseling and therapy, although major variations arise here because family relationships are, at times, very desolate. Opportunities are also restricted when the social-therapeutic institution is situated in a rural area far from the clients' homes.

The legal rules for release preparation are the same as those in regular prisons. However, in social therapy, individual measures are used more frequently and, to some extent, also differently. There are also special rules applying to social-therapeutic institutions designed to permit particularly intensive release preparation as well as after-care. One of these is a special leave of up to six months (§ 124 StVollzG), which is used very frequently. Another regulation (§ 125 StVollzG) permits the readmission of previous prisoners of their own free will. This should make crisis intervention possible. However, this option has been used very unevenly up to now, and some institutions have not used it at all. One problem here is the lack of adequate accommodation facilities for released clients. There are also insufficient staff or financial resources for after-care treatment. Most cases are referred to the usual probation service that, in Germany, is totally separate from the prison system. Probation officers have a heavy case load. They also do not have the same level of knowledge or commitment to their clients that a stable staff structure for through- and after-care could provide.

Organization of the Institution

The original concepts of social therapy in the penal system always emphasized that they must be independent institutions separated from the rest of the penal system. This would be the only form of organization that could guarantee that restrictive regulations would not hinder the special tasks of treatment. However, Prison Law also permits the development of social-therapeutic *departments* in normal prisons. This solution has been chosen occasionally in more recent times. It makes it possible to test special therapeutic approaches or the treatment of special offender groups without having to set up totally new institutions. This is not only more flexible but may, for example, reduce problems of selection and drop-out. The department solution can also save money.

However, the law does not specify 'the special reasons' for the foundation of departments instead of independent institutions. This raises the danger that the exception rule will be applied too frequently and that social therapy will be reduced to a 'penal system inclusive of treatment' (Rehn, 1990). It is crucial for social-therapeutic work that a climate marked by closeness to reality, frankness, and the adoption of self-responsibility is created (e.g. Egg, 1984). If it is at all possible to establish such a therapeutic milieu, it is far more likely in a separate institution. In departments of normal prisons, however, too many aspects of daily life may be dominated by the influence of the normal penal system (particularly with respect to control and safety). For these reasons, the development of social-therapeutic departments is viewed critically by various experts and should be evaluated carefully.

Institution Management

The original plans for social-therapeutic prisons favored medical governors and management. This was to ensure the dominance of therapeutic aspects in important decisions. In reality, however, most social-therapeutic institutions are not governed by physicians but by

psychologists, special educators, or lawyers. While this last qualification prevails among governors of regular prisons, leading positions
in social-therapeutic prisons are more open to social scientists. This
seems to be a good decision, although neither legal, medical nor any
other training provides particular qualifications for managing such a
complex organization. The prison management has to be able to
develop and monitor a relatively independent intervention program.
It should promote a treatment-oriented climate and decentralization
of decision processes. Successful cooperation with various other
institutions is also very important (e.g. the court, probation service,
social services, community administration, private business). For
these and many other tasks, there is no a priori preference in favor of
a certain academic training, but practical experience and further
education in the specific field are expected.

Social-therapeutic prisons not only became models for the introduction of treatment measures in prisons but also for interdisciplinary
management. Originally, the promotion of social science professionals
to management positions was not just accompanied by skepticism
from lawyers (who are more dominant in the German prison system
than in many other countries). Sometimes psychologists were also
hesitant about applying for administrative positions because of their
apprehensions about giving up specific characteristics of their own
professional role (e.g. Braune et al., 1983). The need to integrate
competencies from fields such as clinical psychology and psychiatry,
organizational psychology and sociology, law, economics, and so forth
is still one of the main challenges for the development of a successful
management system.

AN EXAMPLE OF A SOCIAL-THERAPEUTIC PRISON

The social-therapeutic prison at Erlangen (Bavaria) lies in the center
of the city. It has 41 therapy places for males: 35 are closed prison
places and six are open. All cells are for single occupation. The
inmates are accommodated in five relatively stable residential
groups. Each residential group has its own common room; every two
share a small kitchen. The staff consists of a governor (a psychologist), two psychologists, two teachers, two social workers, 20 prison
officers, and two administrative staff.

Prisoners in regular Bavarian prisons receive information on the
possibility of being transferred to Erlangen through a pamphlet and
talks with local staff. After making a written application, they are
interviewed by one of the team at Erlangen. The assessment

procedure also draws on the applicant's records and test data in order to estimate their motivation, competence, and need for therapy. The prisoner must still have at least 24 months to serve, because social therapy is planned for this length of time. Although there are no clear formal selection criteria, it is mostly offenders with personality disorders who are selected. Unlike most other social-therapeutic prisons, Erlangen does not take in sex offenders, because there is a special department for this group at Munich. Acutely drug- or alcohol-dependent prisoners are also excluded. If admitted, prisoners have to commit themselves to participate in the following regular provisions: individual therapy sessions (at least once a week), group therapy with a specific reference therapist, social competence training, antiviolence training, self-control training, and basic school education (for offenders with specific deficits in this area). As in normal prisons, inmates are also obliged to work.

Social therapy at Erlangen is structured into three phases (see Schöner, 1995):

1. *Access phase.* This lasts three months and serves as a 'probation' phase. In the first three weeks, inmates are not assigned to a residential group. Intensive interviews are carried out in order to become more familiar with their personality, motivation, life conditions, and specific problems. These examinations lead to a treatment and sentence plan. After three weeks, subjects can decide whether they want to remain in social therapy. After this, they are assigned to a residential group with a set therapy team. A final decision on admission is made after three months. During the trial phase as well as in the subsequent therapy phase, subjects work in an institution business or do domestic work.

2. *Therapy phase.* This lasts until the end of the 15th month. The goals of the therapeutic and educational provisions mentioned above as well as further measures are to promote: social responsibility and self-responsibility; the ability to make bonds and cooperate; the enhancement of relationships with relatives and friends; confrontation with the offense and possibilities of reparation; and the settlement of debts. The therapeutic measures differ in their theoretical conception. They include cognitive-behavioral, client-centered, and Gestalt therapy approaches; parts of the program have been modified in comparison with the earlier approach. When needed, additional therapeutic provisions are called in from outside; for example, local drug therapy or Alcoholics Anonymous. There are also various sports and leisure-time groups, a cookery course, and

contact groups with voluntary helpers from outside. After the fourth month, the inmates can go shopping outside under supervision. From the ninth month onward, they can leave the prison by themselves. If they comply with the rules for this, individual outings can be extended up to a maximum of 32 hours per month. This permits them to engage in activities with sports associations, hobby groups, and in academic or vocational further training. From the 10th month onward, the inmates can apply for a vacation. Through increasing contacts with the outside world, the focus of therapy shifts to everyday life situations. These include not only the family, partner, and peer reference groups but also how to deal with public administration and money.

3. *Preparation for release.* This phase begins after 15 months at the earliest and lasts up until release. The main concern is that inmates should take what they have learned within a protected environment and try it out for themselves in the outside world. They have to look for jobs outside the prison. The institution has little to do with this as possible in order to promote independence. The clients can also start a professional training or enter an employment office scheme. After three months of this phase, they can be allowed to enter a so-called free employment relationship (with normal pay). This is accompanied by transfer to the open prison department and a change in the therapy team. Individual and group therapy as well as, when necessary, drug therapy are continued. In addition, a special open prison group is available. This group focuses on problems in working life, in relationships with relatives, living together in the group, and, in particular, coping with money problems. For the latter, an individual household plan is drawn up covering, for example, living costs, travel costs, maintenance, paying off debts, contribution to the costs of prison accommodation, and savings. As in regular incarceration, inmates can be released on probation after serving two-thirds of their sentence. As a rule, clients have steady jobs when they are released, they can pay off debts regularly, and they have their own accommodation.

EVALUATION RESEARCH

The social-therapeutic prison is one of those rare cases in Germany in which the plan was to base crime policy directly on empirical research. The final legal ruling should depend on practical experiences and the outcomes of evaluation research. However, unlike the

USA, no set percentage of the program costs was reserved for evaluation. The empirical findings were only used to a small extent in political decision making. This state of affairs can be observed frequently in program evaluation (see Cronbach et al., 1980; Lösel & Skowronek, 1988). None the less, alongside the direct instrumental use of evaluation outcomes, one should not overlook the longer-term conceptual benefit of what the criminal justice system learned about itself.

Although a comprehensive evaluation program was lacking, empirical studies were carried out a few years after the establishment of social therapy (e.g. Dolde, 1982; Dünkel, 1980; Egg, 1979; Rasch & Kühl, 1978; Rehn, 1979; for an overview, see Lösel et al., 1987), and evaluation still continues (e.g. Dünkel & Geng, 1993; Egg, 1990; Ortmann, 1994). Most of the research was done by independent research institutes or took the form of doctoral dissertations. Some of the studies were more qualitatively oriented and designed as *formative evaluation*. These included documentation of strategies and problems of program implementation, organizational structures and regulations (e.g. Driebold, 1981; Schmitt, 1980). Researchers monitored programs in individual institutes, and there were also evaluations based on fundamental criticism of social therapy (e.g. Lamott, 1984).

Alongside these formative studies, various quantitative *outcome evaluations* have been carried out. Inmates released from social therapy were compared with more or less equivalent groups from normal prisons in terms of their recidivism rates or other effect criteria (e.g. personality measures). A problem with such evaluations is that the content of the evaluated treatment is not very clear (see Lösel et al., 1987; Kury 1986). The individual social-therapeutic prisons not only follow different treatment concepts, but even these concepts are not homogeneous. Over the course of time, original concepts have been modified according to experience, in line with changes in personnel and so forth, without this being documented in systematic process evaluations. As a result, the program integrity of the object of each evaluation is not very clear. However, this is not due just to deficits in the process evaluation, but also depends on the complexity of 'social therapy.' Individual therapy, group therapy, or social training measures are embedded within a context of informal group processes, education, work training, leisure-time provisions, organizational climate, contacts with the outside world, and so forth. It is difficult to distinguish these conditions from the impact of specific programs. Thus, unlike most studies in the USA, evaluations of German social therapy do not deal with separate program packages (like cognitive-behavioral training), but with the institution 'as a whole.' Because of the lack of evaluation of individual components, it is not possible to specify the particular reasons for success or failure.

A similar problem to that of treatment evaluation in complex institutional settings also occurs for comparison groups. If one compares social-therapeutic prisons with normal prisons, this is not an evaluation of 'treatment' versus 'nothing' or 'placebo.' For instance, the basic aim of Germany's regular prisons is also rehabilitation. They also have regulations for holidays and day passes. After a while, non-dangerous and reliable offenders can work outside if employment is available. Normal prisons are also partially structured in wings or sub-departments that can trigger educational group processes. They offer some psychological counseling, social training, special education, crisis intervention, preparation for release, and so forth. However, social-therapeutic prisons do not just have more general and therapeutic staff, there are also process data that validate conceptual differences compared with regular prisons. For example, Lösel and Bliesener (1989) undertook a time-budget analysis of a sample of German prison psychologists. The duties could be grouped according to three dimensions: (1) security, order, and smooth day-to-day running; (2) treatment, counseling, and resocialization; and (3) organization management and development. The results showed that psychologists from social-therapeutic prisons were clearly more involved in the second and third areas than psychologists from regular prisons. In the first area, these differences were reversed. Ortmann (1994) was able to show that inmates from two social-therapeutic institutions received more measures with social-therapeutic goals than a group from regular prisons (e.g. day outings, vacations, outside work, etc.). Also, in line with the concept, there was a slightly more favorable situation on release (accommodation, job, partner, etc.). Corresponding findings from Dünkel and Geng (1993) showed that inmates from social therapy at Berlin were released more frequently before serving all their time and also were assigned a probation officer more frequently than subjects in regular prisons. These and other data suggest that although social therapy may have various similarities with regular prisons (particularly in the general legal and institutional conditions), it differs at least in the *degree* of therapeutically relevant variables and processes. Thus, outcome comparisons are meaningful.

Lösel et al. (1987) and Lösel and Köferl (1989) have performed a meta-analysis of 16 outcome comparisons between social-therapeutic and normal prisons, and Lösel (1995b) has integrated more recent studies. In some institutions, several studies have been carried out, so that individual evaluations are not independent. They also differ widely in methodological quality. Most are quasi-experiments with non-equivalent control groups. Randomized experiments are rare (Ortmann, 1994; Rasch & Kühl, 1978). Some studies used matching procedures or descriptive data to improve comparability (e.g. Dünkel & Geng, 1993; Ortmann, 1987; Rehn & Jürgensen, 1983). Although the lack of true experiments is regrettable, this point should not be emphasized in isolation. Subject drop-out frequently reduces randomized designs to the quasi-experimental level, and even in the case of random subject assignment, there can be many other threats to validity, such as experimental rivalry, unreliability of outcome measures, regression, treatment diffusion, and so forth (Cook & Campbell, 1979). Thus, it is not surprising that Lipsey (1992) and others have found no important differences in the outcome of randomized versus non-randomized offender treatment evaluations. Our detailed analysis of methodological quality has shown that it is not just threats to internal and statistical validity that are relevant but particularly those to construct validity (Lösel & Köferl, 1989).

Our research synthesis also indicated that drop-outs (who have been referred back to regular prisons) had the worst outcomes. In most studies, they had even higher recidivism rates than control groups. This clearly shows the importance of sound offender assessment and differentiated sentence planning. Trial and error should be reduced as much as possible. On the one hand, drop-outs may already be the most difficult group, with low motivation for treatment and behavioral change. On the other hand, it can be assumed that they are additionally demotivated and stigmatized by the experience of failure.

Table 8.2 shows selected results of two evaluations with recidivism outcome criteria. Both studies had long follow-up periods. They illustrate the positive (Dünkel & Geng, 1993) versus the negative (Egg, 1990) poles of the range of outcomes.

In our meta-analysis, we computed one mean effect estimation for each primary study. We did not only compute means across the different outcome criteria, but also used comparisons both with and without drop-outs to the disadvantage of the treatment group. For the data from Dünkel & Geng (1993) this mean study effect size was $r = 0.16$, for the results from Egg (1990) it was -0.04. An effect size of about 0.16 can be interpreted as the difference in percentage points of recidivism (or other negative outcome) between treatment and control group. If, for example, 58% of a group from normal prisons are recidivists, there is a recidivism rate of 42% for offenders released from social-therapeutic institutions. A negative effect size indicates

Table 8.2. Examples of outcomes in two evaluations of social-therapeutic prisons (STP).

	STP	Normal prison (control)	Drop-outs	STP + drop-outs
*Dünkel & Geng (1993)**				
Sample size	160	323	27	187
All kinds of recidivism (%)				
(Federal Central Register)	79.4	87.6	100.0	82.4
Severe recidivism (%)				
(Prison sentence)	46.9	59.8	63.0	49.4
Egg (1990)†				
Sample size	28	73	22	50
All kinds of recidivism (%)				
(Federal Central Register)	78.6	75.3	90.9	84.0
Severe recidivism (%)				
(Prison sentence)	46.4	49.3	77.3	60.0

* STP Berlin – Tegel; follow-up period 10 years.
† STP Erlangen; follow-up period 8 years.

that the control group did better than the treated group. As can be seen from Table 8.2, the different outcomes from the two studies also depend on differences in the dropout rates and in the recidivism of the control-groups.

When we added these two studies to our meta-analysis of 16 earlier comparisons, the main results remained very similar (Lösel, 1995b): with one exception, all mean effects were positive. However, they were only small. The mean correlation coefficient was 0.11 (95% confidence limit: 0.07–0.14). In the most recent primary study, Ortmann (1994) evaluated samples from the social-therapeutic prisons at Düren and Gelsenkirchen. For recidivism data, his study effect size was 0.01 (follow-up period: 2 years). If one integrates this outcome in our meta-analysis, the mean effect is about 0.10. Thus, we may expect a 10 percentage point difference in favor of the treatment.

The results of the various evaluation studies did not differ significantly with respect to outcome criteria, characteristics of the offenders, and institutions. There was only a tendency towards better results in institutions using more structured treatments. Probably this relative similarity in outcome is due to the small number of studies and the lack of detailed process characteristics. However, studies with good construct validity (i.e., results that are more generalizable) showed significantly lower effects (Lösel & Köferl, 1989).

If the methodological limitations mentioned above (as well as others) are taken into account, our mean of approximately 0.10 is unlikely to be an underestimation of the current 'real effect' of social-therapeutic prisons. Its size is very similar to the overall effects found in Anglo-American meta-analysis of offender treatment that are mostly integrations of studies on juveniles (Lösel, 1993, 1995a). Stronger effects were reported for specific programs such as those with a multimodal and cognitive-behavioral design that addressed the criminogenic needs and learning styles of offenders (e.g. Andrews et al., 1990; Antonowicz & Ross, 1994; Lipsey, 1992). However, such comparisons cannot be made for German social therapy, because an insufficient number of homogeneous treatments is available.

CONCLUSIONS AND PERSPECTIVES FOR THE FUTURE

In the 25 years since the opening of the first model institutions, social therapy has become established and consolidated as a permanent element of the German criminal justice system. A recent survey indicates that the Ministries of Justice in the federal states continue to view social-therapeutic institutions as both necessary and desirable (Egg, 1993). Thus, in practice, no drastic political change can be noted. Occasionally there are plans to reduce independent institutions in favor of social-therapeutic departments in regular prisons.

As before, there continues to be criticism, and sometimes the possibility of successful treatment in custodial settings is categorically denied (e.g. Ortmann, 1994). However, although there are some discouraging results, overall the evaluations do not support such sweeping generalizations. Evaluators should not so much strive for an 'experimentum crucis' but use the whole variety of information (Cronbach et al., 1980). Most studies on social therapy show positive effects, although not larger than approximately 10 percentage points difference in recidivism rates compared to regular prisons. In regard to this small effect size, the following facts should not be overlooked.

(a) Offenders in social therapy are a particularly difficult group of clients with long criminal careers.

(b) Even in evaluations that show no long-term positive effects, there are initial differences that are possibly lost through insufficient aftercare (e.g. Egg, 1990).

(c) Official recidivism—like other outcome criteria—show a number of weaknesses (see Lloyd et al., 1994; Lösel et al., 1987).

(d) Even in regular prisons, it is not all but 'only' about 50–60% of released offenders who fall back into serious crime. This means that for statistical reasons a realistic treatment effect cannot be higher than approximately 0.30 (see Lösel, 1996a).

(e) The available evaluations are still insufficiently differentiated with regard to clients, individual program elements, and various outcome criteria.

(f) Because of long follow-up intervals, most available findings are based on older treatment concepts that have been revised in the meantime.

(g) Methodological deficits in the available studies make further research essential.

However, the need is not only for stronger efforts in the area of research. As reported above, there is no comprehensive concept of social therapy. To some extent, individual institutions have taken highly different paths of development with no clear empirical foundations. The composition of therapeutic programs, the diagnosis and selection of clients, the practice of retransfer, and so forth follow local experiences and preferences, without these being subjected to systematic evaluation. Some psychodynamic or non-directive counseling concepts do not seem to be well based from the perspective of international research into relatively successful forms of correctional treatment (see Andrews, 1995; Lipsey, 1995; Lösel, 1995a). Similar to the situation in the Anglo-American world, there is a lack of sound practice and research to ensure treatment integrity, positive organizational factors, and the optimization of personnel influences (Hollin, 1995; Lösel, 1993; 1996b). Assessment strategies and the decision criteria used in selecting clients are also insufficiently based on empirical research. Standardized assessments of antisocial personality or psychopathy (e.g. Hare et al., 1991) as well as instruments for the diagnosis of offender risks and needs (Bonta & Motiuk, 1992) are rarely applied. This certainly has something to do with the rejection of a traditional medical model and the fear of stigmatizing prognoses by many experts in the criminal justice system. The utility of classifications for treatment decisions is also not generally established (e.g. Blackburn, 1993; Sechrest, 1987). However, it should not be overlooked that a differentiated treatment implementation and preparation for discharge require a reliable diagnosis. Measures for the assessment of individual risks and disorders can help to avoid misplacements and negative treatment outcomes (e.g. Andrews & Bonta, 1994; Rice et al., 1992). Even if no general set of instruments is introduced, social-therapeutic institutions should at least implement and evaluate local documentation systems.

Within the context of the revived international discussion on 'what works,' German social therapy presents one of the few multi-center examples that refers to serious criminal offenders in custodial settings. Despite some encouraging signs, it is not sufficient to simply continue as before. A careful discussion on framing concepts and (yet again) increased efforts in research and practice are needed. The goal of these considerations should not be the creation of a uniform institution, but a differentiated, well adapted provision based on a professionally justified treatment concept. Experience and findings from other countries should be taken more into account when considering such reforms.

The scientific knowledge and the practical experience necessary for successful work in social-therapeutic prisons are more sound today than during the period of rapid growth. On the basis of recent international evaluations, there are principles that may be helpful for developing successful treatment concepts (e.g., Andrews, 1995; Lösel, 1995b). Guidelines are also available for the planning of more adequate evaluations (Lösel et al., 1987; Palmer, 1992). However, the further development of social therapy must take account of current problems in German prisons. These include (a) the introduction of treatment-oriented incarceration in the new federal states (there was no social therapy in the German Democratic Republic); (b) the maintenance of treatment elements despite increasingly overcrowded prisons and further serious problems such as AIDS or drug dependence; and (c) the development of concepts for the rapidly increasing numbers of foreign prisoners from a wide range of ethnic and cultural backgrounds. In view of these problems, it is not surprising when sometimes resignation can be heard in criticisms of unfavorable circumstances. However, emphasis on the basic idea of an effective and humane treatment in prisons should not just be limited to periods of 'fine weather,' but—with realistically adjusted goals—should be maintained in difficult times.

REFERENCES

Agee, V. L. (1986). Institutional treatment programs for the violent juvenile. In S. J. Apter & A. P. Goldstein (Eds), *Youth violence: Programs and prospects* (pp. 75–88). Elmsford, NY: Pergamon Press.

Allen, F. A. (1981). *The decline of the rehabilitative ideal: Penal policy and social purpose*. New Haven: Yale University Press.

Andrews, D. (1995). The psychology of criminal conduct and effective treatment. In J. McGuire (Ed.). *What works: Reducing reoffending*, (pp. 35–62). Chichester: Wiley.

Andrews, D. A., & Bonta, J. (1994). *The psychology of criminal conduct*. Cincinnati, OH: Anderson.

Andrews, D. A., Zinger, I., Hoge, R. D., Bonta, J., Gendreau, P. & Cullen, F. T. (1990). Does correctional treatment work? A clinically relevant and psychologically informed meta-analysis. *Criminology*, 28, 369–404.

Antonowicz, D. & Ross, R. R. (1994). Essential components of successful rehabilitation programs for offenders. *International Journal of Offender Therapy and Comparative Criminology*, 38, 97–104.

Baumann, J. et al. (1966). *Alternativentwurf eines Strafgesetzbuches.* Tübingen: Mohr.

Blackburn, R. (1993). *The psychology of criminal conduct.* Chichester: Wiley.

Böllinger, L. (1983). Psychoanalytisch orientierte Sozialtherapie. In F. Lösel (Ed.), *Kriminalpsychologie* (pp. 239–247). Weinheim: Beltz.

Bonta, J. & Motiuk, L. L. (1992). Inmate classification. *Journal of Criminal Justice*, 20, 343–353.

Braune, P., Klapprott, J., Linz, P., Lösel, F. & Runkel, T. (1983). Psychologische Organisantionsentwicklung im Strafvollzug. In F. Lösel (Ed.), *Kriminalpsychologie* (pp. 228–238). Weinheim: Beltz.

Cook, T. D. & Campbell, D. T. (1979). *Quasi-experimentation. Design and analysis issues for field settings.* Chicago: Rand-McNally.

Cooke, D. J. (1989). Containing violent prisoners: An analysis of the Barlinnie Special Unit. *British Journal of Criminology*, 29, 129–143.

Cooke, D. J. (1991). Violence in prisons: The influence of regime factors. *The Howard Journal of Criminal Justice*, 30, 95–109.

Cronbach, L. J., Ambron, S. R., Dornbusch, S. M., Hess, R. D., Hornik, R. C., Philips, D. C., Walker, D. F. & Weiner, S. S. (1980). *Toward reform of program evaluation.* San Francisco: Jossey Bass.

Cullen, E. (1993). The Grendon Reconviction Study, Part 1. *Prison Service Journal*, 90, 35–37.

Dolde, G. (1982). Effizienzkontrolle sozialtherapeutischer Behandlung im Vollzug. In H. Göppinger & P. Bresser (Eds), *Sozialtherapie* (pp. 47–64). Stuttgart: Enke.

Driebold, R. (1981). *Sozialtherapie im Strafvollzug.* Weinheim: Beltz.

Dünkel, F. (1980). *Sozialtherapeutische Behandlung und Rückfälligkeit in Berlin-Tegel.* Berlin: Duncker & Humblot.

Dünkel, F. & Geng, B. (1993). *Zur Rückfälligkeit von Karrieretätern nach unterschiedlichen Strafvollzugs- und Entlassungsformen. In G. Kaiser & H. Kury (Eds.), Kriminologische Forschung in den 90er Jahren* (pp. 193–257). Freiburg i.Br.: Max-Planck-Institut für ausländisches und internationales Strafrecht.

Egg, R. (1979). *Sozialtherapie und Strafvollzug.* Frankfurt a.M.: Haag & Herchen.

Egg, R. (1984). *Straffälligkeit und Sozialtherapie.* Köln: Heymanns.

Egg, R. (1990). Sozialtherapeutische Behandlung und Rückfälligkeit im längerfristigen Vergleich. *Monatsschrift für Kriminologie und Strafrechtsreform*, 73, 358–368.

Egg, R. (1993). Sozialtherapie aus der Sicht der Bundesländer—eine Umfrage. In R. Egg (Ed.), *Sozialtherapie in den 90er Jahren* (pp. 107–111). Wiesbaden: Kriminologische Zentralstelle.

Egg, R. & Schmitt, G. (1993). Sozialtherapie im Justizvollzug. In R. Egg (Ed.), *Sozialtherapie in den 90er Jahren* (pp. 113–189). Wiesbaden: Kriminologische Zentralstelle.

Eissler, K. R (1949). Some problems of delinquency. In K. R. Eissler (Ed.), *Searchlights on delinquency* (pp. 3–25). New York: International Universities Press.

Farrington, D. P., Langan, P. A. & Wikström, P. O. (1994). Changes in crime and punishment in America, England and Sweden between the 1980s and the 1990s. *Studies in Crime and Crime Prevention*, 3, 104–131.

Garfield, S. L. & Bergin, A. E. (1994). Introduction and historical overview. In A. E. Bergin & S. L. Garfield (Eds), *Handbook of psychotherapy and behavior change, 4th ed.* (pp. 3–18). New York: Wiley.

Garrett, P. (1985). Effects of residential treatment of adjudicated delinquents: A meta-analysis. *Journal of Research in Crime and Delinquency*, 22, 287–308.

Genders, E. & Player, E. (1995). *Grendon. A study of a therapeutic prison.* Oxford: Clarendon Press.

Gendreau, P. & Ross, R. R. (1987). Revivication of rehabilitation: Evidence from the 1980s. *Justice Quarterly*, 4, 349–407.

Gunn, J. & Robertson, G. (1987). A ten year follow-up of men discharged from Grendon Prison. *British Journal of Psychiatry*, 151, 674–678.

Hare, R. D., Hart, S. D. & Harpur, T. J. (1991). Psychopathy and the DSM-IV criteria for antisocial personality disorder. *Journal of Abnormal Psychology*, 100, 391–398.

Hollin, C. R. (1993). Advances in the psychological treatment of delinquent behaviour. *Criminal Behaviour and Mental Health*, 3, 142–157.

Hollin, C. R. (1995). The meaning and implications of programme integrity. In J. McGuire (Ed.), *What works: Reducing reoffending* (pp. 195–208). Chichester: Wiley.

Hood, R. (1995). Introductory report. In European Committee on Crime Problems (Ed.), *Psychosocial interventions in the criminal justice system* (pp. 11–21). Strasbourg: Council of Europe.

Kennard, D. (1983). *An introduction to therapeutic communities.* London: Routledge & Kegan Paul.

Kury, H. (1986). *Die Behandlung Straffälliger, vol. 1.* Berlin: Duncker & Humblot.

Lamott, F. (1984). *Die erzwungene Beichte.* München: Profil.

Liebling, A. (1992). *Suicides in prison.* London: Routledge.

Lipsey, M. W. (1992). Juvenile delinquency treatment: A meta-analytic inquiry into variability of effects. In T. D. Cook, H. Cooper, D. S. Cordray, H. Hartmann, L. V. Hedges, R. L. Light, T. A. Louis & F. Mosteller (Eds), *Meta-analysis for explanation* (pp. 83–127). New York: Russell Sage Foundation.

Lipsey, M. W. (1995). What do we learn from 400 research studies on the effectiveness of treatment with juvenile delinquents? In J. McGuire (Ed.), *What works: Reducing reoffending* (pp. 63–78). Chichester: Wiley.

Lipton, D., Martinson, R. & Wilks, J. (1975). *The effectiveness of correctional treatment.* New York: Praeger.

Lloyd, C., Mair, G. & Hough, M. (1994). *Explaining reconviction rates: a critical analysis.* London: Home Office.

Lösel, F. (1993). The effectiveness of treatment in institutional and community settings. *Criminal Behaviour and Mental Health*, 3, 416–437.

Lösel, F. (1995a). The efficacy of correctional treatment: A review and synthesis of meta-evaluations. In J. McGuire (Ed.), *What works: Reducing reoffending* (pp. 79–111). Chichester, UK: Wiley.

Lösel, F. (1995b). Increasing consensus in the evaluation of offender rehabilitation? Lessons from recent research syntheses. *Psychology, Crime & Law*, **2**, 19–39.

Lösel, F. (1995c). Evaluating psychosocial interventions in prison and other penal contexts. In European Committee on Crime Problems (Ed.), *Psychological interventions in the criminal justice system* (pp. 79–114). Strasbourg: Council of Europe.

Lösel, F. (1996a). Changing patterns in the use of prisons: An evidence-based perspective. *European Journal on Criminal Policy and Research*, **4.3**, 108–127.

Lösel, F. (1996b). Working with young offenders: The impact of meta-analyses. In C. Hollin & K. Howells (Eds), *Clinical approaches to young offenders* (pp. 57–82). Chichester, UK: Wiley.

Lösel, F. & Bliesener, T. (1989). Psychology in prison: Role assessment and testing of an organizational model. In H. Wegener, F. Lösel, & J. Haisch (Eds), *Criminal behavior and the justice system: Psychological perspectives* (pp. 419–439). New York: Springer.

Lösel, F. & Köferl, P. (1989). Evaluation research on correctional treatment in West Germany. In H. Wegener, F. Lösel & J. Haisch (Eds), *Criminal behavior and the justice system: Psychological perspectives* (pp. 334–355). New York: Springer.

Lösel, F., Köferl, P. & Weber, F. (1987). *Meta-Evaluation der Sozialtherapie*. Stuttgart: Enke.

Lösel, F. & Skowronek, H. (Eds) (1988). *Beiträge der Psychologie zu politischen Planungs- und Entscheidungsprozessen*. Weinheim: Deutscher Studien Verlag.

Logan, C. (1972). Evaluation research in crime and delinquency: A reappraisal. *Journal of Criminal Law, Criminology and Police Science*, **63**, 378–387.

Mauch, G. & Mauch, R. (1971). *Sozialtherapie und die sozialtherapeutische Anstalt*. Stuttgart: Enke.

McGuire, J. (Ed.) (1995). *What works: Reducing reoffending—guidelines from research and practice*. Chichester: Wiley.

McGuire, J. & Priestley, P. (1992). Some things do work: Psychological interventions with offenders and the effectiveness debate. In F. Lösel, D. Bender & T. Bliesener (Eds), *Psychology and law: International perspectives* (pp. 163–174). Berlin: de Gruyter.

Ortmann, R. (1987). *Resozialisierung im Strafvollzug*. Freiburg i.Br.: Max-Planck-Institut für ausländisches und internationales Strafrecht.

Ortmann, R. (1994). Zur Evaluation der Sozialtherapie. Ergebnisse einer experimentellen Längsschnittstudie zu Justizvollzugsanstalten in Nordrhein-Westfalen. *Zeitschrift für die gesamte Strafrechtswissenschaft*, **106**, 782–821.

Palmer, T. (1992). *The re-emergence of correctional intervention*. Newbury Park, CA: Sage.

Peat, B. J. & Winfree, L. T. Jr (1992). Reducing the intra-institutional effects of 'prisonization'. A study of a therapeutic community for drug-using inmates. *Criminal Justice and Behavior*, **19**, 206–225.

Rasch, W. & Kühl, K. P. (1978). Psychologische Befunde und Rückfälligkeit nach Aufenthalt in der sozialtherapeutischen Modellanstalt Düren. *Bewährungshilfe*, **25**, 44–57.

Rehn, G. (1979). *Behandlung im Strafvollzug.* Weinheim: Beltz.

Rehn, G. & Jürgensen, P. (1983). Rückfall nach Sozialtherapie: Wiederholung einer im Jahr 1979 vorgelegten Untersuchung. In H.-J. Kerner, H. Kury & K. Sessar (Eds), *Deutsche Forschungen zur Kriminalitätsentstehung und Kriminalitätskontrolle, vol. 3* (pp. 1910–1948). Köln: Heymanns.

Rehn, G. (1990). Sozialtherapie: Strafvollzug plus Behandlung? *Kriminalpädagogische Praxis*, **18**, 7–13.

Rice, M. E., Harris, G. T. & Cormier, C. A. (1992). An evaluation of a maximum security therapeutic community for psychopaths and other mentally disordered offenders. *Law and Human Behavior*, **16**, 399–412.

Sechrest, L. B. (1987). Classification for treatment. In D. M. Gottfredson & M. Tonry (Eds), *Prediction and classification: Criminal justice decision making*. Chicago: University of Chicago Press.

Sechrest, L. B., White, S. O. & Brown, E. D. (Eds) (1979). *The rehabilitation of criminal offenders: Problems and prospects*. Washington, DC: National Academy of Sciences.

Schmitt, G. (1980). *Sozialtherapie. Eine Gratwanderung im Strafvollzug*. Frankfurt a.M.: Haag & Herchen.

Schöner, E. (Ed.) (1995). *Das Behandlungsangebot der Justizvollzugsanstalt Erlangen*. Erlangen: Sozialtherapeutische Anstalt.

Wexler, H. K, Falkin, G. P. & Lipton, D. S. (1990). Outcome evaluation of a prison therapeutic community for substance abuse treatment. *Criminal Justice and Behavior*, **17**, 71–92.

PART IV

Staff Issues: Aptitude, Antipathy and Training

Context for Change (whilst Consigned and Confined): A Challenge for Systemic Thinking

Peter Lewis

HMP Grendon, Aylesbury, UK

Most therapeutic units within the Prison Service are small, isolated and fragile systems set within larger establishments, small sub-systems of a a larger institutional system, each however part of the larger prison estate. These configurations create problematic dynamics. A small unit can be likened to a foreign body or transplant in the human body and is subject to the same process of 'rejection' (Lewis, 1988). The wider system seems to have complex, subtle and frequently unconscious forces of a powerful annihilitative nature which constantly threaten the well-being of such enterprises. Their very existence is a tribute to the dedication of staff who are prepared to work in ways which are seen as antithetical to conventional prison management and mores; consequently this work can be excessively demanding and stressful.

The promotion and maintenance of a culture which gives to inmates a voice to discuss their concerns with each other and an opportunity to show increased individual responsibility for the welfare and well-being of each other, are difficult tasks. Developing a therapeutic milieu is not

Therapeutic Communities for Offenders.
Edited by E. Cullen, L. Jones and R. Woodward. © 1997 John Wiley & Sons Ltd.

dissimilar to growing an orchid—considerable time and care has to be given to creating the right conditions for development and growth but even an accidental cold draught or even a big boot can destroy the atmosphere and the plant in a trice (cf. instruction of staff and education/training therapy later).

Similar dynamics beset even the bigger therapeutic communities (TCs) like Grendon which has been in existence for over 30 years. Grendon is a collection of five TCs contained in one establishment orientated by the therapeutic community approach. It, like all therapeutic communities, is subject to external stresses as outlined earlier, and is inevitably subject to its own internal ones because all such systems are in a state of flux and are potentially unstable, since their dynamic equilibrium and efficient working are determined by many factors both intrinsic and extrinsic.

As well as the external factors inherent in the prison establishment the fact that the Prison Service is part of the Home Office indicates a further higher level of external pressures. The Home Office, like any government department, is subject to fiscal policy and current political beliefs on law and order and the place and priority of sentencing policies. This can have an effect upon the numbers in custody generally. A severe sentencing policy increases the prison population significantly. With a rise in the number of people in custody a larger proportion of the increased prison population must be absorbed. Thus the TC function may be compromised by increased numbers in now overcrowded accommodation, stretching the therapeutic resources beyond the critical level of efficiency with the risk of producing a dysfunctional system.

The transfer of inmates across the boundary from one establishment to another, between a therapeutic system and the custodial system, has to be effectively managed. A resistance by the custodial system to accept back those individuals unable and unwilling to cooperate with the therapeutic ethos and therefore requiring transfer, leads to a weakening of the ethos of the community. This undermines its therapeutic potential, which requires significant effort from most if not all its members to maintain its therapeutic efficacy. This is achieved through repetitive 'working through' of the re-enactments of conflict which highlights progressively each individual's personality deviation or disorder. The capacity of the community to absorb these difficulties through interaction, exploration and experimentation embodies the therapeutic health of the community (Whiteley (Foulkes Lecture, 1994)).

In a response to Whiteley's Foulkes Lecture, Kennard (1994) expands the idea of the 'holding' action of therapeutic communities turning the Latin verb *tenere* (to hold) into a series of functions of a therapeutic community:

Contain
Sustain
Maintain
Entertain

To this should be added for prison TCs *retain*, which is a pre-eminent prison priority.

The vital functions of containing, sustaining, maintaining and entertaining require continuing attention, which implies that fresh thought has to be brought to bear upon the therapeutic input. Thus the therapeutic ethos is not static. It depends on the capacity of staff and residents to continue to work appropriately and systematically. Staff and residents change, indicating the need for the ethos to be continuingly evolving and self-renewing. Staff and inmates require to be re-enacting the therapeutic work principles continuously, thereby enabling new residents to become familiar with 'therapeutic ethos or 'tradition'. However, as Ramon Pajares, general manager of the Savoy Hotel, said in a recent interview (Pajares, 1995). 'tradition has to be kept fresh or it doesn't work'. This brief statement about a very different institution, The Savoy Hotel, is a reminder of the words of Roberts (1995)

> The therapeutic community requires commitment from staff and inmates and has lost credibility in units where the name 'therapeutic community' has been applied to organisations which never reach the level of a containing and healthy social environment, or, subject to destructive processes had become irretrievably damaged.

The key word here is *commitment* to therapeutic principles. This immediately creates a problem. Apart from professional civilian staff (only some of whom have undergone therapeutic training) the main group of staff who are required and expected to interact with inmates/residents of prison therapeutic communities are prison officers, most of whom have no previous experience in the caring professions. Their basic training does not have any input that prepares them for a 'caring' role, only a 'custodial' one which involves procedural training about locks, bolts and bars and searching. These staff members are required to re-enact the therapeutic community principles continuously. While many of these officers show significant aptitude for a caring concerned approach, this requires supplementation by education for their therapeutic role. Unless systematic and supportive training is introduced to increase the competence and confidence of staff, the process outlined by Roberts will inevitably occur. If significant effort is expended on therapeutic education then the destructive processes can be averted and a containing healthy social environment will be maintained. Thus enabled, the prison officer can more confidently tread the complex tightrope between care, containment, therapy, security and safety of significantly deviant, dangerous and difficult inmates.

Cell searching is a necessary and complementary staff function to the inmates/residents intended function of self-searching. The hidden dangerous implements in a resident's possession require revelation, recognition and recovery so as to maintain an environment where an individual's innermost, retained, as yet unrecognized dangerous thoughts and intentions can be progressively examined, explored and evaluated, and changed in therapy.

THE INTERACTIVE MATRIX—A MILIEU FOR ENACTMENT, EXPLORATION AND EXPERIMENTATION

The predominant experiences in men who come to Grendon are of having been in receipt of hurtful experiences, aggressive, abusive, unreliability of early relationships, inconsistency of care, even abandonment. These leave the individual lacking in trust and self-confidence while having an interactive style of behaviour of an aggressive and suspicious kind. This makes the development of a therapeutic relationship difficult. Inevitably, therefore, the inmate will tend to transfer into most, if not all, current relationships a tendency to re-enact these feelings. These feelings may have been exacerbated through the repetitious re-enactment of such emotions in establishments prior to Grendon where staff easily become embroiled in a reactive way, contributing to a repetitious reactivation of earlier unhelpful relationships.

At Grendon, therefore, the significant therapeutic task for staff is to try to understand the subtle danger of repeating such a destructive interpersonal re-enactment. It is all too easy in everyday interaction for inmate and officer to become engaged in such a non-productive repetition of unhelpful ingrained behaviour.

The context of a therapeutic community lends itself to re-examining these repetitive phenomena through the process of supervision, discussion and review of events in groups, community meetings and ongoing everyday living experiences in the therapeutic milieu. This day-to-day work is an important source of learning for both inmates and staff. For staff to enhance their cognitive and emotional awareness of these experiential issues, theoretically based sessions should be available which help to link established knowledge with what is experienced and learned in practice.

The greater confidence and competence that each member of staff acquires through practice complemented by review, continuing development and education, the more effectively the therapeutic milieu can promote the important interaction and exploration which allows each individual to experiment with new, more functional interpersonal behaviour of a kind which shows respect for others. Staff and inmates are inevitably locked in behaviour which is 'grist to the therapeutic mill'. Understanding and not reacting to the different components of behaviour and making it available for analysis are very important parts of the therapeutic activity.

An important task for the experienced group therapist/group analyst is to help, advise and support staff who are unconsciously caught up in these interactions and enable them to examine critically the unconscious subtle part that they may be playing in this process. The presence of an experienced group therapist/group analyst as a supervisor is an important part of the coherent strategy and the supportive infrastructure which is necessary for the ongoing support, education and training of staff.

Inputs which clarify and reduce abrasive 'unconscious' interactions allow the development of a working alliance between staff and inmates that facilitates the continuing dialogue leading to understanding and acceptance. This in itself is an important experience, 'the corrective emotional experience' which differs from the 'defective emotional experience' which existed in the early years of rejection and inconsistency of care. The consistency, continuity of contact, and the caring context of the developing alliance between staff and inmate form an important foundation for the exploration and interaction that unfolds and enables the individual to experiment with new styles of thought, feeling and behaviour in his psychological journey to personality reformation.

Resolution of these complex transferential issues is an important part of the staff group discussions in the ongoing everyday review of the dynamic interactions in communities. 'Working through' these issues in the staff group parallels the 'working through' of issues in inmate groups. While transferential issues are of significant import- ance in the interactive milieu of the therapeutic community, there are other important mechanisms which impede the process of therapeutic change. Projective mechanisms which attribute responsibility to another rather than accept it oneself, are a significant impediment to progress in therapy where the owning of responsibility for damaging acts towards other persons is important.

This mechanism, allied to denial, is a considerable hurdle to therapeutic progress in the early stages of therapy. Increasing acceptance of the individual by the staff group coupled with continuing concern, models the increasing acceptance by the individual of those characteristics he was previously impelled to deny. The creation of an accepting milieu, as described, is not easy, it does not happen naturally even though there may have been a tradition of it occurring for many years—'tradition has to be kept fresh or it doesn't work'. Tradition is the adherence to therapeutic principles as set out by Roberts earlier. These ideas have to be restated continually, establishing them for new members of staff and refreshing them for others, maintaining the infrastructure for therapy alluded to previously. How can this be accomplished?

THERAPY, CUSTODY AND TRAINING—
A RECONCILIATION: RATIONALE AND REALIZATION
(DESPITE RESTRICTION AND RESISTANCE)

We have to reconcile issues of therapy, custody and training for a therapeutic community to be maintained in a prison setting. This is a task being addressed at Grendon and the following examines these complex issues and implications for action.

Unfortunately, learning about therapy does not obey the rule of three steps for a procedure which can be:

1. See one.
2. Do one.
3. Teach one.

Learning about therapy requires an understanding of personal development and the factors which may be formative or deformative in an individual's development (this is the study of psychopathology).

It is important, then, to understand something of the complex ways in which individuals deal with these life stresses, the compensatory ways in which they may protect themselves by adopting actions and postures which serve only in the short term to make themselves feel 'better', but tend to be detrimental to other persons and to the individual's long-term interest. These are called 'defence mechanisms' or 'adaptive psychological styles'.   Understanding of these principles is helpful in giving staff a map of how it is possible to understand an individual whose cumulative responses have ended in antisocial and offensive actions towards persons in particular, leading to alienation from society, significant breakdown of personal relationships and unacceptable behavioural patterns and reactions. If it is possible to formulate an understanding of how an individual has developed into what he now is, the next task is to help him to correct the maladaptive learning that has taken place and put in its place new, more acceptable ways of 'seeing', thinking, feeling and reacting to present and past life stresses, i.e. re-adapt in response to new 'learning'. In effect he is being asked to experiment with new ways of thinking about and re-evaluating patterns of behaviour, as well as taking on board newer, different values and different patterns of decision-making, as well as having his belief systems questioned. This can be done through a process which begins to effect change, that is, living in a community where there is a greater capacity to speak what one thinks, where over-rigid rules are relaxed while distinct rules of conduct and expectation are retained, but giving opportunities for negotiations through appropriate communication. This is a way of everyday living which leads to increasing degrees of honesty, accountability, responsibility and, moreover, an understanding of interdependence and trust that had previously been lacking. There is, in addition, an expectation of decreased aggressivity in interpersonal relationships achieved through 'modelling' a conversational means of resolving interpersonal and interactional difficulties.

This milieu effect is very important and may be responsible for the change which Grendon produces, because it allows for understanding and an acceptance that other persons require to be related to with respect and concern. This type of therapy is important but does need to be augmented by personal change and adjustment which re-forms the individual's internal resources and problem-solving capacity.

Personal change involves *psycho*therapy, which is more complex than milieu therapy and involves more personal commitment by the individual, coupled with the willingness to face up to the aspects of psychological distress which will be involved, like accessing painful buried memories which, by virtue of being suppressed or repressed, had led to important altered mechanisms of thought, feeling and action that have been detrimental to the individual and to others. Psychotherapy is effected through a relationship, sometimes referred to as the therapeutic alliance, which supports and enables, in a caring, concerned, consistent way, the individual to express and re-think many aspects of his life history—'His Story'.

The relationship is conventionally with *the* therapist, a trained individual with an understanding of psychopathology and psychodynamics, as well as an understanding of ways of helping the individual to examine and link his complex life experiences through language and metaphor. At Grendon we have chosen to make the *group* the therapeutic agent or 'Therapist'. Group therapy requires a complex set of skills but does have the benefit of many useful therapeutic factors, which have been well researched (Yalom, 1985). The group has, however, to remain a group rather than a mob and, consequently, its milieu needs to be supported by definitive guidelines with a group conductor/therapist/facilitator, adopting a complex role in promoting and maintaining the milieu. This role requires specific training.

McKenzie, subsequently President of the American Group Psychotherapy Association, said 'The effective use of the group format requires specialised training in the modality. Management of the group context calls for skills beyond those learned in the course of individual therapy. Without experience and leadership, groups may become ineffectual, resulting in a sense of demoralisation, or harmful because of the mismanagement of group conflict' (McKenzie, 1992). Similarly Aveline (1993), a British psychiatrist/psychotherapist, 'All applications of group psychotherapy require special expertise if they are to be beneficial in their impact'. These authors restate an important prerequisite of group work: specialized training. One should therefore ask 'If group work is an important aspect of what is provided at Grendon, how does the discipline officer become conversant with, confident about and competent at this modality of treatment?' Should the discipline staff be asked to take responsibility for understanding a role as a group therapist? Can the discipline officer be expected to take responsibility as a therapist to a group?

If an officer fulfils some duties in a role as 'Therapist' in the group he/she requires, and should expect, a comprehensive familiarization with aspects of group treatment. It should be noted that the word 'training' is omitted. Training requires a more complex process to be followed which many officers would not have the basic credentials to embark upon.

Since psychotherapeutic expertise cannot be acquired in the way that procedural learning can be acquired (see one, do one, teach one) it must be considered how this process of 'familiarisation' can be achieved. Until the present, there has been an initial introduction to the concepts of therapy, after which it tended to be left to chance and anecdote. This method is inherently flawed and has seemed to have promulgated a vocabulary for therapy and a style of therapy which is combative rather than *psychotherapeutic*. Many words used in therapy prevent the process of therapy because they may activate and maintain resistance to progressive revelation of painful memories and conflicts by being confrontative, challenging and critical in aggressive ways rather than being encouraging, enabling and inviting the curiosity so necessary in therapeutic endeavours.

It should further be stressed that therapy is a process that stretches over a period of time and links *apparently* unrelated events, feelings, thoughts and beliefs. Consequently, those individuals responsible for therapy need to maintain a long-term perspective on any events that occur in an isolated episode of therapy. Any therapy session is incomplete in itself and could be deemed to be merely a still shot in a film. This implies that judgement should not be made on one episode in therapy but 'held' and put in the context of the evolving picture. If staff have only intermittent involvement in groups an incomplete picture of the process and progress of the individual group members may be obtained. Interventions of designated 'leaders' may be flawed by virtue of their feeling that a contribution has to be made on business transacted *now* rather than reflecting on the part those disclosures or communications play in the whole life of the individual or his life in the group. Therapy requires the retention of a longitudinal perspective on the task. The task of psychotherapy could be described as making what is unconscious become conscious, what is 'unknown' known. This process is hindered by many phenomena which can be briefly described as resistances or defences against awareness.

Psychotherapy is defined in a number of different ways by different authorities. Pre-eminent in these definitions is the importance of the therapeutic alliance. This assumes that the patient (client/inmate) wishes to expose himself to therapy. All too often this is not the case since the individual is in a setting in which he is consigned and confined by a process of law. It is unlikely that he would have submitted himself to a voluntary relationship with a therapeutic agency if the behaviour which he has exhibited had not been censured by society. In other words, a behaviour for which he is being 'treated' has afforded him some 'advantage' and reinforcement which has been psychologically rewarding to him. One must ask therefore: 'Might he be seeking help? Why might he be seeking help in the prevention of repetition of this behaviour if it is rewarding to him?'

Thus there is likely to be significant reticence in becoming involved in this process of therapy. It is inevitably undertaken under some duress, often because someone thinks he will benefit from treatment or because it seems to others that he *requires* treatment. All this does not mean that he *wants* treatment. The motivation for treatment may be complex and involvement in treatment may be merely a token effort to create the least uncomfortable management of a period of life whilst confined and incarcerated. This means that the process of therapy becomes more complex, not merely a process of movement from unconscious thinking to conscious thinking but a process of conscious withholding (deliberate) designed to avoid disclosure of known parts of the self, wishing these to be retained because of the pleasure that that affords the self, as opposed to the displeasure or pain that is created for others if that behaviour is retained.

It has to be considered therefore that, given these complex antecedents of an individual's arrival at Grendon, one must suspect that his treatment is going to be difficult. Indeed, it might be considered that inmates at Grendon would not normally be regarded as likely candidates for therapy. In normal circumstances, those persons commonly regarded as suitable psychotherapy candidates correspond to the attributes of the YAVIS criteria. This is a mnemonic which summarizes those people who are most suitable for psychotherapy, i.e. those who are **Y**oung, **A**ttractive, **V**erbal, **I**ntelligent and **S**ocially adjusted. By definition, therefore, most, if not all, Grendon inmates might be regarded as unsuitable. Should we not therefore be bringing significant expertise to bear upon this group of individuals whose behaviour has been deceptive, deceitful, damaging, destructive and frequently dishonest? It seems unfair to ask a workforce of untrained personnel to undertake a task assessed as impossible by experienced psychotherapists, without an extensive well developed programme to provide the complex educative structure, supervision and review of recorded experience that enhances and develops what is learned by 'experiential exposure', i.e. on the job 'doing', sitting in on groups.

As a form of learning, this type of experience is essential. In learning about therapy, acting and observing with an experienced therapist is a useful mode of exposure—'testing out the water'. Questions about what happened in the group and how the subject matter discussed in the group is relevant to the individuals in the group can be reviewed in supervision in post group discussion. This allows for increased confidence and more ease at sitting in on therapy sessions. Progressive ease in sitting in on groups is an important prerequisite to learning about groups. It is doubtful, however, whether officers ever experience a group consistently session after session, nor necessarily with an experienced therapist. They may, however, be accompanied by other members of staff, more familiar with groups—this is previously referred to as 'learning by anecdote'. Currently, the content of the group is reviewed by a procedure called 'feedback' on some wings. The amount of time allocated to this process is limited by the pressures of other duties. While the content of what has transpired and what has been discussed in the group is important and relevant, it is not sufficient to understand the more complex transactions that take place which require greater demands of analysis in order for psychotherapy to proceed. Many authors point out that 'hands on clinical experience' is the necessary but intimidating training tool in group therapy. Enhancement of time available for post group discussions is essential and a continuing development of the quality of such discussion is vital.

Group therapy will provide the useful microcosm in which to observe, assess and treat various types of maladaptive behaviour (Yalom, 1985). This approach assumes that group members bring their interpersonal issues to the group setting and proceed to manifest them in a number of ways. Much of the group work then involves attending to this interpersonal material and using it as a springboard for therapy. Learning to harness the inter-personal processes within the group in a skilful manner is generally a difficult endeavour, even more so for the neophyte or learning therapist. Indeed, group therapy training is particularly stressful for the learner on a number of counts. There is simply an overabundance of stimuli and tasks with which to contend. The therapist must monitor various interactive subgroups, pay attention to the individual patients and their psychopathologies, keep an eye on a group process, model interventions and perform managing and gate keeping functions while following and participating in the flow of the group.

This experience for the trainee may render the trainee fearful, useless or vilified in relation to other group members. To make matters even more stressful, all of these stimuli must be confronted and managed in the group, i.e. 'a goldfish bowl'. There are anxieties about how the group members experience the trainee as a therapist. There needs to be a supervisor evaluating the proceedings directly, as a co-therapist as outlined above or in spirit, i.e. in supervision sessions.

Various writers on learning about therapy stress the need for the trainee (learner therapist) to construct modest but fundamental goals for the group: how to engage and value the therapeutic process, re-establishing of interpersonal boundaries and connections, clarifying and modulating the anxieties that stem from actual events and processes which occur in the institutional setting. Writers view the small therapy group as embedded in the larger organizational context of the institution and underscore the need for appropriate management of the boundary that separates the two, lest the group be inundated or isolated from its surroundings. They stress the idea of matching specific levels of group structure with levels of psychopathology or the functional capacity of the recipients of treatment.

Some authors point out that the leadership role entails activity, structuring, direction; the group therapist is likened to a 'shepherd' who is continually heading off strays—strays into 'outside material'—directing them towards discussion of past events of the patient/inmate/clients lives, not into abstract intellectualization. Authors differ as to the sort of approach that might be made. One author (Yalom, 1983) points out that a slow patient reflective non-directive approach has no place in institutional work. Others (Rice & Rutan, 1987) address the development of empathic listening, of sensitivity and receptivity to a wide range of clinical data, emanating from the encompassing social context of the institutional ward/wing, from the history, development and ongoing processes of the group as a whole, from the inner worlds of the individual patients and from the affective-cognitive reactions of the therapist. Rice & Rutan (1987) warn that *'hearing and understanding* must always take precedence over the blind application of guidelines' and point out that the actioning and directing of interventions may be related to the therapist's defensive counter-transferential dynamics (by which they mean that all too often the therapist's intervention may be directed towards protecting himself or contain many feelings which are aroused in him/her by the context of the group). They point out that the therapist may need to be respectful of, and keenly attentive to, the natural intrinsic processes of the group, and patiently and currently hold lower expectations—more realistic and less illusion-ary, more enabling and eliciting rather than confrontational and directive, with the expectation of instant results. In psychodynamic models the ideas are derived from psychoanalytic, object relations and social systems theories.

The overwhelmed fledgling therapist may ask: 'What am I supposed to do?' and 'How am I supposed to do it?' This is the issue that must be addressed. The amount of work required to reach a level of competence is considerable and requires allocation of time and resources in a structured form and continuing regular and critical review. Currently, whilst there are difficulties about the progression from 'novice' to 'competence', it should not be assumed that compet-ence will imply proficiency in practice without further specialized training.

At present selection of officers for Grendon is random, so that 'all comers' are expected to function in a therapeutic context. Given the expectation of the therapy task outlined previously, in fairness to the officers and the inmates, these issues must be comprehensively addressed.

Officers are expected to fulfil a dual role. They are expected to function as custodian and as therapeutic aide. They receive compre-hensive teaching and instruction in the custody role, and learn progressively by experience and exposure to custody procedural matters by practice and from the support and advice by colleagues.

The secondary role as a therapeutic aide has not received enough appropriate adjunctive attention. As stated previously, the task of learning about therapy is complex and requires, not only experience, but continuing practice accompanied by regular review, revision and supervision through discussion, complemented by relevant reading about therapy matters. This is the course followed by trainee therapists in all training establishments for psychotherapy, and it should not be overlooked when expecting members of staff to function as aides in a therapy group. Failure to provide this structure is going to expose staff to significant *stress and tension*. Without, this supportive structure and continuing education it is like dropping someone in a minefield without giving them a map of a path to safety. As in a minefield, explosions are disruptive and harmful, and certainly do not allow therapy to proceed constructively.

Most writers on education maintain that *much* experience is required to produce a *small* change in competence. The present system, which provides some early instruction followed by intermittent exposure and experience, prevents an individual member of staff from moving to a higher level of competence. Experience when 'extracted' in this way is often likely to contain many 'contaminants' by way of the development of therapeutic styles unhelpful to the therapeutic process.

An educational process should recognize the starting point and the learning potential of the learner and should promote confidence in response to changing and increasing demands. Most educational processes indicate that whatever is being done must help individuals to move from a state of 'not knowing' to 'knowing', it should enable staff to be more capable of coping and being competent in a milieu which is new and for which staff may be ill-equipped by their education or training. Naturally an emphasis must be placed on everyday experience. This experience, however, has to be augmented by a process of *development* which connects experience and competence by promotion of self-directed, learning using the systematic application of four principles: learning media, reading, reflection and audit. It may be difficult to ask staff to engage extensively in reading to learn about therapy, although many have sought courses which help them learn. There is no doubt, however, that reflection, audit, revision and supervision are processes which could be integrated into staff training. Information which would normally be acquired through self-directed reading may be distilled by trainers into important theoretical principles for dissemination at appropriate times as they arise in the experiential sphere. The key task of continuing education is to help individuals find in their professional experience not just the learning agenda required for competence but also ways to focus learning activity.

One should not automatically assume that anyone or everyone has an aptitude for therapeutic work, nor indeed could proceed to a specific level of competence. Competence is the capacity of an individual to act in a given situation at the required level. It has been outlined previously how difficult the task of therapy is. It frequently activates complex emotional responses which are difficult to handle if there is no subsequent discussion to elucidate and understand the origins of these responses in both the patient/inmate and therapist.

Because therapy is often unstructured the therapist requires the capacity to hold many threads together, which is often confusing and uncomfortable, especially since resolution is not always achieved in each therapeutic session. When this is contaminated by complex emotional responses which occur when an individual group member describes real life situations it can be a difficult situation to cope with for the learning therapist. This is a significant difficulty because therapy is a demanding issue even for those persons who are competent. It is also a fallacy to assume that the competent, however defined, will always perform competently given the complex interactions which take place in therapy. These complex interactions are referred to as transference and countertransference issues and require extensive discussion.

Competence should not be confused with expertise and it is unlikely that a training in the work situation can confer 'expertise', this is only acquired by lengthy complex training. Competence is based on aptitude brought out by the process of selection, exercised by experience and elaborated by organization and interpretation. It is applied through continued experiential learning. It also requires the processes of reflection, reading and acquisition of new information accompanied by audit of the task.

Further aids to competence could be participation in outside courses, as well as appropriate mentorship, facilitation and containment in a planned educational structure, which could also minimize the continuing stresses which arise in relation to therapy. This requires specialized input. It will not be developed unless some structure is created which allocates time and priority to this process. It should be borne in mind that in the transition from dependency to competence individuals require significant levels of motivation together with willingness and capacity to learn. Thus it may require the system to examine aptitudes prior to selection for work in this sort of sphere, as well as promising continuing education in order to enhance competence and confidence in carrying out the task of therapy.

What seems to be required is a commitment by management to support building and maintaining a comprehensive system by means of which newcomers, once selected and adopted, would be given, on a regular basis, opportunities to experience, review and revise happenings that occur in therapy, thereby learning increasingly competent ways of facilitating the process of therapy. This requires compromise with custodial care and appropriate allocation of time to the process of therapy for those who are required to work in an environment where a therapeutic approach is allied to a custodial approach.

An outline of this process could be:

1. An orientation to therapy.
2. An initiation to therapy with the allocation of a therapeutic mentor.
3. Progressive exposure to therapy and a review of the practices in therapy.
4. Practice at recording the therapeutic process, not so much in content (what was talked about) but *how* it was talked about and *by whom*.
5. An examination of the process of therapy.
6. Detailed discussion about techniques and analysis of therapy sessions, perhaps in a group with other staff.

This could be done at a wing level, by ensuring that officers are regularly exposed to the same groups and have some continuing discussion with the principal therapist on that group. Each group could be supervised and the process outlined could be reviewed by the wing therapist. The wing therapist himself or herself could then join with other wing therapists in another setting to review the situation with the intention of processing groups and group events in ways which would be mutually helpful, i.e. the therapists would in fact learn from each other and from each others' groups.

The experienced wing therapists themselves could also expose themselves to new ideas and revision of the general principles of group therapy through a journal club as well as a group supervision which they would offer themselves. The wing therapists might be expected to go on outside courses which would enhance and maintain their competence, confidence and up to date understanding of groups. It should be recognized that there are definitive connections between experienced learning and competence and performance and that much experience is required to produce a small change in competence.

These proposals require appropriate allocation of funds, time, effort and motivation to practise more effectively. Currently the continuity and budgetary constraints may have their own restricting effect creating a stranglehold which may destroy such therapeutic enterprises in prisons.

The implications of this are important. All therapeutic systems should expose themselves to clinical audit and examine themselves critically. This critical evaluation should support its efficacy in producing change in high service users significantly unchanged by any other procedure within the prison system.

ADAPTATION LEADS TO SURVIVAL

The ideas and concerns expressed in this chapter are now being progressively implemented so that a more extensive, involved post group supervision takes place. There are dedicated, regular, weekly theoretical seminar sessions held with wing staff, medical/psychiatric, probation, psychology and discipline staff involved constructively together helping to widen their theoretical and experiential horizons.

REFERENCES

Aveline, M. (1993). Principles of leadership in brief training groups for mental health care professionals. *International Journal of Group Psychotherapy*, **43**, 107–129.

Kennard, D. (1994). Response to Whiteley, S., 18th S. H. Foulkes Lecture. *Group Analysis*, **27**, 383–387.'

Lewis, P. S. (1988). Therapeutic use of an ethogram in a drug addiction unit. In M. R. A. Chance (Ed.). *Social Fabrics of the Unit*, Chapter 9. Hove: Lawrence Erlbaum Associates

McKenzie, R. (1992). Newsletter report on group therapy. New York: American Group Psychotherapy Association.'

Pajares, R. (1995). Savoy Savvy—Interview between Ramon Pajares, Savoy General Manager, and Iain Murray. *Money Observer* **December**. 27–28.

Rice, C. & Rutan, J. S. (1987). *Inpatient Group Psychotherapy* New York: Macmillan, pp. 105–106.

Roberts, J.P. (1995). Reading about group psychotherapy, (therapeutic communities). *British Journal of Psychiatry*, **166**, 124–129.

Whiteley, S.(1994). Attachment and loss, the space between (18th S. H. Foulkes Lecture). *Group Analysis*, **27**, 359–381.

Yalom, I. (1983). *Inpatient Group Psychotherapy, Strategies and Techniques of Leadership*, New York: Basic Books, pp. 105–172.

Yalom, I. (1985). *Theory and Practice of Group Psychotherapy*, new York: Basic Books, 3–18.

CHAPTER 10

Selection and Training of Staff for the Therapeutic Role in the Prison Setting

Roland Woodward

HMP Gartree, Leicestershire, UK

> Because, like many others, I was naive and innocent when I started work in a community, I was very often affronted in the early days by how uncomfortable the work was. It seemed wrong for a form of therapy which I had thought promised satisfaction for everyone. The first impact the community makes on the newcomer is usually to do with the way it makes him feel.
>
> R. D. Hinshelwood (1987)

This chapter is probably best approached as if the reader is in the happy position of being in the process of establishing a therapeutic community. Only after that process has been explored will the issues surrounding the training of new staff joining and existing team be addressed. This will include a look at Continuing Professional Development for all staff working in a therapeutic community team.

THE STARTING POINT: PHILOSOPHY AND THEMES

Beginning at the End: An Introductory Thought

At the end of the selection and the training of a staff team what have you got? The answer to this depends on how you view the task of

Therapeutic Communities for Offenders.
Edited by E. Cullen, L. Jones and R. Woodward. © 1997 John Wiley & Sons Ltd.

creating a staff team for a therapeutic community (TC). If you are going to have responsibility for the TC that is being created then you are more likely to be aware of the issues of continuing work and development. If you are a consultant/trainer going into a situation for a fixed period of time then you are likely to be focused on the delivery of your contract and be less concerned with the longer-term issues. This is not to imply that consultants or trainers are insensitive beings, but reflects the fact of life that they move on and away from the team that they have helped to create. The team remains to evolve as best it can. Of course, consultants and trainers will know that their input will need to be congruent with the overall philosophy or ethos of the TC that is being created or enhanced; however, it is difficult to take into account the way the staff team is likely to develop. This is always difficult to predict as teams develop differently because of the way in which their own TC presents them with new experiences to be understood and worked with. As Douglas (1983) noted, 'they (TCs) are self-generating problems'.

Anyone selecting and training staff for a new or established TC needs to be very clear about the theoretical and research framework that will underpin the work of the staff team. This is crucial because the team will need to have a framework that is understood by them all and that can be used in a pragmatic way, and within which to work in order to make meaning of what is happening in the community and to them as a staff team. It is much easier for the manager of that team to help and support them if they can use a familiar framework within the supervision and support sessions. In Atherton's (1989) terms this may be seen as providing the team with a Shell into which they can retreat when their collective Skeletons are faced with a challenge that they find difficult to make sense of.

This is particularly true in the custodial setting, where the training of prison staff has to take into account the role for which they are originally trained. Certainly at the time of writing the priorities of the British Prison Service are keenly focused on the issues of security in the wake of the recent escapes from maximum security prisons. Even before this the Genders & Player (1995) study of Grendon, possibly the oldest therapeutic community-based prison in the world, quoted a recently recruited members of staff as saying, 'I feel like I've been trained as a plumber and given a job as an electrician'. This sense of being ill prepared for the task in hand is echoed by Jeff Pearce (1994), a founder staff team member of TC for life sentence prisoners that opened at Gartree prison in November 1993: 'What a job this proved to be! We had prepared ourselves fully for the unit opening, but no matter how trained you felt, there's no comparison to the real thing'.

So before selecting and training staff, ask the question, 'How am I or someone else going to supervise and support this staff team once they are working?' This means being clear about why you are setting up or continuing your community and what you want the staff to actually do. What is your understanding of a TC and how it works? How are they going to enact the TC goals? What are the goals of your TC? What is the role of the staff going to be? At the end of the day you and perhaps others are going to be responsible for placing staff in what is likely to be one of the most challenging yet intimate experiences of their lives, so it is incumbent on you to know how you are going to enable your staff to continue to develop and to fulfil their role. As Kaplan & Shaddock (1971) point out, 'The group is a powerful vehicle; but just as it has the power to heal, it also has the power to harm, as does any therapeutic tool'.

When working with prison staff one must also ask how the legitimate role of the prison officer is to be integrated into the fabric of the community. The very real role of being a prison officer is important in that it constitutes a set of boundary holding obligations that the staff have to perform. As Hodkin & Woodward (1996) point out in a recent article, much of the existing professionalism of prison staff is related to the maintenance of these boundaries, and this must be acknowledged. Staff are often made to feel that the prison officer role is incompatible with the TC ethos, as the perception is that it is less caring than the 'therapy' role. This, of course, is not true. Winnicott's 'Good enough' parents who hold the boundaries within a family are being parents, not giving their children therapy. In the prison setting the 'good enough' officer is providing the boundaries for a safe environment, the role within the TC setting adds the extra tasks related to therapy but this is built upon the reality of being in prison and all that that means. As 'recapitulation of the family' is one of the therapeutic factors that comes into play in the TC setting, the prison officer is faced with both the adult and childhood dynamic behaviours of the prisoner.

A Quick Word about Frameworks

However hard they try, not everyone can get excited or make psychodynamic explanations fit the world with which they are confronted. This is especially true of TCs in the prison setting. It is understandable that so much written about TCs is set in psychodynamic terms. All the early TCs come into being under the medical umbrella with its associated psychiatric links. The influential papers by Main (1966), Jones (1959), Bion (1961) and Foulkes

(1948, 1964) were set in psychodynamic frameworks and established a way of thinking about communities for some time to come. For those interested in the history of the TC both Kennard (1983) and Manning (1989) provide good commentaries. There is often a desire to bring staff into the world of group dynamics in all its psychodynamic complexity, with the danger that the pragmatic needs of staff working in the prison setting are overlooked or trivialized. What is required is a way of explaining and exploring what is going on in both the community and the staff team which enables all staff to use a common language. My experience has been that prison staff initially given Bion (1961) and Foulkes (1948, 1964) find it difficult to relate them to their experience in the groups, and that frustration can ensue. My own preference has been to use Yalom (1985) and Bloch & Crouch (1985) as the basic framework for the groupwork that the TC entails. This model focuses on those factors that can be demonstarted to have a therapeutic effect regardless of the theoretical orientation within which group therapy is conducted. As Yalom (1985) puts it, 'the core consists of those aspects of the experience that are intrinsic to the therapeutic process—that is, the bare-boned mechanisms of change.' The staff that I have trained found the material well written, extremely accessible and easy to relate to their own experience. Once staff have got used to using this as a framework it is easier to move to more 'dynamic' material if desired.

If such a framework of group work is coupled with the work of Kennard (1983), Atherton (1989), Hinshelwood (1987) and Manning (1989) as explanations for the processes of a TC, staff are able to work as TC staff very quickly. All of the above writers explore the way in which TCs function by examining the behaviours and processes commonly experienced in them. Each of the writers suggests frameworks and techniques by which TCs can be understood and worked with. It is, of course, for each TC's manager (although 'manager' may not be the acceptable term to some within the TC school) to ask themselves what their staff are going to need in their TC. The manager might need to suspend his or her own favoured approach, not to mention his or her own years of personal positive experience with one approach, and carefully consider the skills and needs of the staff. In many cases those who have spent years working in TCs forget how long it took then to grasp the concepts and the ways of working, and forget where the staff start from. The temptation is to assume that they will 'pick it up all right' and in some unclear way come to the same level of understanding as the managers. We start with our clients from where they are, we should also do the same for new staff. Salvendy (1985) noted, 'Training is the heraldry of group therapy. One shows one's colours according to the type of training one has received. Trainees are remarkably faithful to their alma mater ...'

The Parallel Experience Concept

One of the themes of this chapter is that it is not possible, or fair to staff, to exclude them from the experience of the TC resident. Wherever possible the staff team of a TC should be given the opportunity to experience as many of the residents' experiences as is practicable. This might be an argument for not using an assessment centre and for modelling the selection process for staff as closely as possible on that intended for community members. If the selection of staff is for a new TC then this presents a rather 'chicken and egg' situation, because in a new TC the new staff team would be devising the admission process for community members. One solution to this is to provide a selection process that the new staff team can use as an experience to build on when they are faced with constructing the procedure for residents.

It is important to draw a link between the parallel experience of staff and the 'parallel process' of supervision. Once the TC team is trained and in place the supervision of the team will often focus on 'who is leading who' in the TC dynamics. Is the staff team 'responding to' or 'creating it is often the question posed in supervision as the team tries to understand what is going on in the community. The same parallel process that Page & Wolsket (1994) and Hawkins & Shohet (1989) discuss in supervising counsellors is apparent in the workings of the staff team. They too must be aware that they can often unconsciously begin to mirror the resident group of the TC. The more experiences that the staff team can parallel, the better able they are to analyse and understand situations in relation to the interaction between the two groups. The staff team is also better able to understand the need to look at 'parallel process' and more equipped to do so.

The opportunity for the staff to internalize the process that the TC members go through in their journey into the TC and through it gives them a basic understanding of the residents' experience. This basic map can be referred to when they are asking themselves, or being prompted to ask themselves, 'what is going on for this person now, where are they in the process and what are they experiencing? The paralleling of the staff's experiences through selection and training provides a basic safety net for staff and a tool within themselves that is always available to them. This process enables the 'Skeleton' within each of them to develop and grow. It also provides a common underpinning for the staff team to which they can all relate and which also helps bind them together as a team. What can strengthen an individual 'Skeleton' can also strengthen a group 'Shell'. Team building through this process seems to be more effective than through activities whose aim is to team build. Common involvement in a group activity that has as its aim something outside of its self would appear to be more lasting than self-directed attempts to bond!

A Word About Power

Power is often written about in the TC arena because of the nature of TCs and their underlying philosophy. The urge to 'Democratize' is strong in those who work in TCs but the reality for those of us working in the prison setting is that POWER is not an issue that will go away, and it has to be grasped openly and honestly. The staff team of a prison TC and the manager or managers of that team work in an hierarchical organization that has as its priority the protection of the public. Every staff member of the TC team will have a 'discipline' role to play which is linked to the security aspects of the wider establishment that their TC is in. Even if the entire establishment is operated as a TC the same constraints regarding security exist. The implication for this in the training of staff in the prison setting is large. Very many of the staff to be trained will come from the prison officer grades, and for them the security nature of their role cannot be ignored or lessened in importance. Consideration must be given to how the boundary setting demanded by the role of the prison officer as part of the 'discipline and security' needs of the prison can contribute to the overall boundaries that the TC residents must observe for the TC to function within the prison setting. The balance of these requirements needs to be analysed in each establishment that decides to open a TC so that the staff selected to work in the TC know that they will be given clear guidance as to how to fulfil what can actually be contradictory roles.

Men and Women

When I first considered putting a TC staff team together in HMP Gartree I thought it would be nice if the team could be an even balance of men and women. This seemed very reasonable in terms of the staff team modelling the way in which a group could meet and overcome all the issues that such a team would experience. It also seemed very sensible that in an all-male resident group the therapeutic processes would be helped by a mixed sex staff group of equal balance. A mixed sex staff team allows the full range of transference phenomena to occur and the related recapitulation of the family to take place. For practical reasons, it was not possible to have an evenly balanced gender staff team; for example, because of the then current practice a shift could not comprise only women because of the searching requirements. Each person having his cell searched was also strip searched. Women officers cannot strip search a male prisoner. The staff team could not meet its security requirement of so many searches per month without a majority of men in the team. It was not possible to remedy this through the shift system even though the staff team are extremely flexible in their working arrangements. Even such issues as to whether or not separate toilet facilities are available may have a bearing on the way in which men and women can be recruited into a team. As all prisons are subject to Health and Safety regulations it is likely that these issues will also need to be considered.

Genders & Player (1995) devote some time in their investigation of Grendon to the role of women staff and suggest that women have the added difficulty of coming under pressure to fulfil the prisoners idealized expectations of them. This needs to be considered when considering the training needs of the whole team, especially when examining the roles that the team will take and have thrust upon them.

Not only do the staff team members have to deal with the relationships that are formed with the community members, but also with the relations between themselves. In a mixed sex team this means confronting the issues of sexism within the team. The experience of women staff members in a prison TC is extremely demanding and it requires the men in the team to be open to being taught about this experience and examine themselves and the working of the team in the light of this.

As already said, the individual circumstances and parameters of the TC will dictate some of the constraints. It is the staff team themselves who will be able best to discover the problems that are going to be relevant to them. The sooner some or all of them are drawn into the design and planning stages the better.

Who Should Be in the Therapeutic Community Staff Team?

Within the prison setting the major part of the team is likely to be drawn from uniformed prison staff. The nature of the prison environment is going to demand that the TC works within a security framework which in itself will be governed by the demands of the prison system as a whole. Because of this the expectation would normally be for uniformed staff to constitute the majority of the team in order to maintain security and also to fulfil the day-to-day maintenance functions of the community within the prison organization which cannot be done by community members themselves.

In all the TCs in the British Prison Service the model used to date has been one of the multidisciplinary team. The specific make up of the team will depend on the resources available, the interest of specific departments, the underlying philosophy of the community and the stated goals and objectives of the team. To the core multidisciplinary team must be added a Therapy Manager who can take responsibility for the integrity of the therapeutic process and undertake the routine therapy supervision of the team in its daily work. Who this is depends on the individual situation. It is important that this person is experienced in the work of TCs and can help the team maintain its role, promote the continuing professional development of the team and take responsibility for the continued examination of the work of the TC in terms of its effectiveness and response to new knowledge.

The community will also require a residential manager to manage the interface between the wider organization and the TC. This person has responsibility for the attendance system and the requirements of the prison as a whole. They must be committed to the TC and yet be clear that the TC remains part of the prison organization and about the responsibilities of staff which ensue from this. This needs to be somebody of Governor grade or a person with enough experience of the prison system to be able to appreciate the demands required and yet be able to balance the tension between therapeutic need and prison requirements.

If a TC is to be set up in a prison establishment or as an entire prison then either the host prison or the prison authorities have requirements that the TC must recognize as legitimate. No host establishment or prison authority is going to give carte blanche permission for a TC to be set up. There are serious issues of how such a TC can be integrated and what effect it will have on the rest of the system in which it will be embedded. It is important to educate the administrators within the organization about the nature of a TC and to involve them as soon as possible in the planning process.

All TCs in the prison setting should consider having an independent consultant/advisor. There needs to be someone who can enter the community at any time, participate in any of the community activities and observe the community in action. It is this person's role to ask the community, and in particular the staff team, why things are happening the way they are. They should check that the staff team is continuing to interrogate themselves about the processes in action and their part in it. Such a safeguard is crucial and helps to ensure that the staff team continue to act in the best interests of the community members through appropriate action and interaction with them. The consultant/advisor must be experienced in the area of TCs and if possible in the prison system. It is possible that someone who has a role in a community elsewhere in the prison system can be invited to fulfil this role. Currently there is a slow movement towards greater cooperation between the existing TCs in the British Prison Service with managers exchanging time to support each other as independent consultants/advisors.

SELECTION

What Do We Want in Staff of a TC?

What we want from staff of a TC is at least what we expect of TC residents. There have been several studies in recent years of TCs in the British prison system (Genders & Player, 1995; Gunn & Robertson, 1978) that demonstrate that there are some basic requirements which enable residents to be successful. These factors apply equally well to the staff of a TC.

At Least Average Intelligence

The process of the TC through the medium of therapy is a complex one that focuses on the 'here and now' experience in the community. It takes a certain amount of intelligence to understand the experience and be able to generate new behaviours that can then be generalized to other situations.

Residents of TCs who are not of average intelligence tend to struggle to survive in the group therapy setting. They have problems in grasping the processes and can become very frustrated at what they experience as games and manipulation. Very often they feel that they are picked on or singled out for criticism by the rest of the community. Within the prison culture this can lead to extreme acting out and a reversion to the violent defence of image. This preservation of image should not be underestimated as it is one of the major ways that prisoners maintain their safety in an unpredictable interpersonal environment. (Woodward, 1989).

There are exceptions: occasionally someone comes along who appears not to be of the level of intelligence to cope with the demands of the TC but who has extremely high levels of motivation. In some cases this carries the resident through to the point where change is possible. Such residents are always difficult to assess and create a lot of discussion in the staff team. Often it is the current state of the TC that determines whether the applicant is offered a trial period in the community.

If the above is true for the residents of a TC then clearly staff of the TC must be able to understand what is going on in the community and the staff group in order to analyse the parallel processes and the shifts of emotion in the community/staff team interactions. The staff team needs to be capable of understanding what the residents are talking about and how the themes of the community are driven at any one time. Unlike the prisoner applicant who is less intelligent and extremely motivated, it seems to me that no such allowance should be given to a staff member. Staff teams tend to be small and very interdependent in what can be an exceedingly difficult interpersonal environment. To introduce someone into the team who will have to be watched over will not help the team, the community or the staff member. In the same way that therapy is not neutral and is for better or worse, so is being a member of a staff team in a TC. There is no point in taking a member of staff who cannot cope with the issues as this will only embitter them and affect their self esteem. It is much better to be open with a staff member from the start and tell them that they would not perform well in this role than either ask them to leave a team or wait until they move on themselves, the worse for the experience.

Psychological Mindedness

In order to change or cooperate so as to change one's behaviour there must be an understanding that what 'goes on in the head' affects behaviour, or to be 'psychologically minded'. There is, however, very little agreement about the exact nature of psychological mindedness. Appelbaum (1973) noted that, 'Different people mean different things by 'psychological mindedness'. Such words as insightfulness, reflectiveness, introspectiveness, capacity for self observation, self appraisal and self awareness are often used synonymously'. Macallum & Piper's (1990) definition comes from a psychodynamic orientation and states psychological mindedness to be, 'The ability to identify dynamic (intrapsychic) components and to relate them to a person's difficulties'.

Despite this lack of agreement about the exact nature of the concept it is clear that it plays an important part in the process of therapy. In the TC environment it enables those in a TC to understand that what they do today informs what they do tomorrow.

Motivation

It goes without saying that staff must be motivated to do the work. For many of the staff who apply it is an opportunity to perform a new role within the prison setting. Staff need to be motivated to try to help prisoners change but not by doing everything for them. The nature of institutional life is that staff begin to do many things for the prisoners that the prisoners are capable of themselves. This tendency is highlighted in the TC environment. Staff motivation needs to be focused on allowing prisoners in the TC to be able to organize things for themselves and to make their own mistakes. For many prison staff this is difficult to do and their motivation in applying for a post in a TC is that they want to do even more in the way of helping in a personal sense. (Graham-Davies, 1994). In one TC team that was being trained a team member decided it was not what they wanted to do as they thought that it would mean 'getting to know them better and to help them on a more one to one level'. The member of staff decided to leave the team whilst still in training. Another member of staff who was active in his church applied to join the team as he felt it would help him resolve his dilemma of how best to serve others. In these situations there appeared to be a need to be helping others that was at least in part motivated by the need to resolve personal needs and to clarify a life position.

The author's experience is that staff who apply for TC teams and are successful members have a combination of motivations most commonly characterized by the desire to be actively involved in some form of rehabilitative work with prisoners and have in the past enjoyed the opportunities to get to know prisoners in other locations. There are also those who want to try working with prisoners in a different way that allows them more time to understand them and make sense of what prisoners do, with a view to helping.

In dynamic terms much of what has been said could be seen as falling into the four hypotheses generated by Khaleelee (1994) in her study of staff selection for the Cotswold Community. She hypothesized from the interview material she collected the four following reasons for joining a TC team:

1. The staff member identifies unconsciously with a 'damaged' mother and tries to 'repair' her to do a better job.

2. The staff member identifies unconsciously with an 'impoverished/ damaged' child and wants to make the child 'better'.
3. The staff member is unconsciously trying to repair their relationship with a lost, damaged, or 'damaging' father.
4. The staff member consciously sees their employment in the TC team as a career development before moving on to something else.

Whatever the motivation, conscious or unconscious, there is a need to consider the overall psychological integration of the person.

Psychological Integration

It is clear that people can be intelligent, take responsibility for themselves and be motivated to help others and still not be suitable for a TC team for a number of reasons. It is possible for someone to be extremely rigidly defended who may be able to survive the rigours of a TC, but by cutting off from the residents and colleagues, i.e. 'tough isolator' (Khaleelee, 1994).

Some people apply to join a TC team carrying a great deal of free-floating anxiety which, if allowed, will flood into the community as a whole and generate crises which are nothing to do with the community residents. Clearly when one of the prime tasks of the staff team is to help contain the anxieties of the community it is not helpful to exacerbate the situation. Staff suffering from bouts of recurring destructive drinking or other debilitating behaviour are also likely to experience problems coping with the pressures of a TC and are best not included.

There are without doubt some staff in any large organization who could be characterized as being 'psychopathic'. They may apply and use the TC experience as an opportunity to fulfil their own dysfunctional needs. Such staff tend to create havoc by using the community to involve residents and colleagues in destructive relationships and create fractures in the structure of the TC. Once this situation has arisen this person then leaves the team and moves on to another group to start the process again. The author was involved in one situation where a member of staff enmeshed several residents in relationships that acted against them and was only stopped when he was found to be entering into criminal dealings with some of them. The damage caused to the community in this case was great and required much work to restore trust with and between residents and staff.

Interactive Skills

We have all met intelligent, motivated and psychologically minded people who seem to be psychologically 'good enough' but do not manage to get on with people. There are people who appear to be devoid of listening skills, who are short in empathy and seem not to notice that their responses to people are punitive or at the least aversive. The question here is, can this be assessed? A panel interview may be the only opportunity to assess this unless an assessment centre model of selection is adopted. References from past employers or managers can be asked for specifically to assist a panel in making its assessment. Ideally there should be enough indication that applicants have available to them a degree of interactive skills which can form the foundation on which to build during training.

So How Do We Assess Intelligence, Psychological Mindedness, Motivation, Psychological Suitability and Interactive Skills?

'We may not have to', is one possible answer to the above. One option is to use a consultancy with the skills to devise an assessment centre for the selection of the staff team. There are consultancies that specialize in the design of assessment centres for clients, analysing the requirements of the client and devising a structured experience that maximizes the possibility of surfacing and assessing the presence or absence of core competencies. As Fincham & Rhodes (1994) point out, 'Assessment centres typically last two days. They are gruelling, intense experiences which normally provide both the applicant and the assessors with valuable insights into suitability.' Feltham (1988) considers that the critical feature of assessment centres are that they make use of work simulation and are repeatedly shown to be the most powerful and robust of selection procedures. Fincham & Rhodes (1994), however, say, 'Assessment centres represent the Rolls-Royce of selection techniques. They are expensive to build, usually involving consultants developing custom made exercises. They are also expensive to run.'

The response to assessment centres by applicants appears to be good but there is some work by Fletcher (1991) that suggests that unsuccessful candidates may in the long term suffer a drop in self-esteem, competitiveness and work ethic. This is not dissimilar from the findings of Jefferson (1991) in his study of prisoners passing through the Grendon assessment unit. The use of an assessment centre obliges the sponsors to ensure adequate feedback and support of candidates after the event.

Given what has been said about assessment centres it is for those concerned to decide whether it is desirable and affordable to use this method of selection. If it is an option that is not to be taken up then the question remains of how selection of the staff team will be undertaken and by whom. The next section addresses this.

Intelligence, Psychological Mindedness and Motivation

Intelligence

'IQ is relatively easy to test'. This is clearly a contentious statement but for the pragmatic purposes of staff selection it is true. Although there is much argument about the nature of intelligence, in practice there are instruments that will provide a reasonable estimate of someone's capabilities. There are many IQ tests available, from the Alice Heim range to the Wechsler Adult Intelligence Scale (1981). Consideration must be given to the constraints placed upon you by the situation that you are in. How many candidates have you got to test? Have you got someone qualified to do it? How much time have you got? Have you got the money to buy the tests? Is this the test you use for selection of community members? The last a most important issue if you are trying to make the staff experience truly parallel that of the community member. If it is good enough for the community applicant, should it not also be good enough for your staff member? Perhaps there is a trap in this: right from the start it is possible to give the message that 'we are all the same except that staff do different IQ tests because we are not really like you'.

From research related to IQ tests Grendon has provided data in this area. Research by Genders & Player (1995) showed that the IQ test used there did in fact indicate those who were able to deal with the TC process. The earlier study by Gunn et al. (1978) also suggested this. The test used at Grendon is Raven's Progressive Matrices (1960). It has the advantage of being 'culture fair' in that it is not dependent on ability to read and write.

Psychological Mindedness

Psychological mindedness appears to be a factor associated with insight that facilitates good outcome in insight-based therapies. Bloch & Crouch (1985) in reviewing the literature suggest, '... the association between psychological mindedness and outcome in the insight oriented group echoes the common clinical observation that in the long-term group therapy psychological mindedness is an important criterion for selection.' They later state that, 'It is widely agreed, though with a large degree of vagueness, that psychological mindedness or conceptual ability is a requisite for insight oriented therapy.'

Recently Macallum & Piper (1990) have suggested a procedure for assessing psychological mindedness by asking people to rate a video recording of a therapy session between a therapist and a single client. This approach seems worth pursuing if time and resources allow. Shine (personal communication, 1996) is currently beginning to assess the usefulness of the technique in the British Prison environment at HMP Grendon.

The interview phase of the selection procedure is often used to test psychological mindedness. By presenting various interpersonal situations which may occur in the TC setting to the candidate and asking them to explore the relationship between the actions and the feelings of the main participants, an estimate of the candidate's ability can be made.

Motivation

The motivation of applicants can be difficult to test. The approach of Khaleelee (1994) assumes that the mostly unconscious motivation can be elicited by the Defence Mechanism Test in conjunction with an interview that focuses on a brief family sketch, formative experiences and what makes the applicant want to work in a community. This approach is interesting and may fit very well into the framework that is going to underpin the community. It would certainly have the advantage of monitoring the loss of staff from the onset of the staff team's life and provide information about criteria for future selection for that particular TC.

A structured interview in which the applicants are asked to account for their reasons for working in a TC and what they think motivates them seems to be the most usual way of testing this. There are, however, some things that can be added to this in order to test motivation. In advertising that posts are available it should be made clear what the process for selection is going to be. If the process is to include psychometric testing, interviews (either individual or group), group tasks or a presentation then this should be clearly stated. There will be some would-be applicants who will lack the motivation to put themselves through the selection process.

Asking applicants to provide the selection panel with a short presentation will also provide a guide to motivation. It will be clear how much effort has gone into the preparation of the presentation, either in the use of materials or the level of thought that has gone into it. If the presentation is specified as a brief life history with what are considered to the most important experiences of the person's life in relation to the work they think they will be doing in the TC team, then much may be gleaned about some of the unconscious motivations and provide many leads that the selection panel can follow up.

Who Should Select?

An assessment centre run by consultants is likely to include a panel interview. In a different situation an interview of some kind is very likely to be an important part of the selection process. In either case, someone has to conduct the interview.

Selection of staff should not be left to one person, even if that person is to have responsibility for the TC in the wider organization. A panel of individuals to whom the results of any psychometric or other testing available, who are able to represent the interests of the wider organization, the therapeutic integrity of the eventual therapeutic community and finally the interests of the yet unformed staff team, appears to be a rational choice. The Residential Manager is an obvious panel member as he or she is able to represent the interest of the wider organizations. It may be that this person also has access to information regarding the work performance and career of the applicant to date which if necessary can be discussed with the applicant. The Independent Consultant should also be a panel member. This person will be working with the team and can bring to the team selection experience of other relevant situations. The Therapy Manager should be included. The staff selected are going to be accountable to this person for the quality of the work delivered on a day-to-day basis and to a greater or lesser extent are going to be his or her team.

At least these three people need to be involved with any selection panel that sits. The circumstances and the above core of panel members may well decide to include others, depending on the individual circumstances of the situation. The above is summarized in the Appendix, An Action Plan for Selection.

TRAINING AND CONTINUING DEVELOPMENT

Training a New Therapeutic Community Staff Team

Tom Main (1966) in his address Knowledge, Learning, and Freedom of Thought, said: '...if the trainer is concerned not with thinking and choosing but only with knowledge and views then the trainee will be filled only with knowledge and views which he may later repeat and enlarge. But he will not think much. The form of the training is thus as important for the result as is the content.'

The task of training staff in the prison setting, many of whom will be prison officers used to a different role, demands creativity and flexibility. The following remarks are based on the experience of training a new staff team that opened the Gartree Therapeutic Community in 1993.

What can be achieved is constrained by time. Common sense dictates that it is not possible to equip staff adequately in a short time. Neither is it easy to stipulate how long training can go on before the urge to actually be 'doing it' becomes the primary motivation of the team. It is also unrealistic to expect an open timescale when the use of precious public resources is an issue. Every project in the public sector is expected to deliver an outcome in a relatively short time. In the English prison system at the time of writing the prison population is the highest it has ever been so the pressure to use all available space is great.

As a minimum, staff, need to be able to identify the boundaries that they will need to hold and those that they will need to relinquish. They will also need to know that there are structures in the community that recognize that the staff team has needs and that those needs are adequately met by the routine of the community. Finally the staff team must be aware that there is a framework of knowledge and experience which can be used to make sense of what is happening to them and the community, even if at that moment they do not fully understand it.

Any initial training programme should promote a sense of ownership in the staff team and a sense that they have an equal influence on the decisions made by them as a team. To this end the following components are suggested for a training programme. How much of each it is possible to include will depend on the time available and whether the staff team build it into their training.

The Nature of the Training

You will have noticed that the last section ended with 'whether the staff team build it into their training'. If in opening a TC you subscribe to the basic tenets that the residents must be allowed to democratize the community and to take responsibility for it, then the same must be true for the staff team wherever possible. The staff team needs to be encouraged to take control of their own learning experience as much as possible. They may say that they have no idea what they require because it is all new to them, and expect the trainers or the therapy manager to act as leader. The skill level of the individuals determines how much of the training is prescribed and how much the team discovers for itself. This process is similar for any group in this situation, initially input maybe more prescribed but as the team develops it will take control of things itself. It seems that providing the right balance is the key. It is likely that the constraints will once again come into play here: there may not be enough time for the team to develop their training programme and some input will be required so that all the possibilities are considered.

A Possible First Step: Saying Hello

There is a moment when the team come together for the first time. How people use this in training terms will vary according to their outlook. Some of the options are immediately to form a T group or a seminar group, or to do a general introduction and suggest a timetable for the immediate future. It may also depend on whether trainers are provided who are not part of the team from the very beginning. There is research that strongly supports the hypothesis that the most important therapeutic factor in group psychotherapy in the initial stages of a group is acceptance. For a good review of this research see Yalom (1985) and Bloch & Crouch (1985). The first coming together of a team is an anxious time for everyone, and people need time to find their way into the team. It seems presumptuous to start working with the new team as if they are entering therapy. They are not, their task is to form a team which will allow others to benefit from a TC and as such they need time to discover the task and their individual and collective role in it.

In that very first stage of meeting, remembering that some of the team may already be work colleagues, a simple introductory exercise with suffice that involves no more than who they are, what their work experience is and their expectations.

Providing the Tools to Plan with

After saying 'hello' to each other, the first task of the team can be undertaken. The new team is about to bring into being a new therapeutic community. This is no mean feat and is a major project. The number of people in the team who have project planning and management skills is likely to be small, so the first real step is to provide the team with the skills they require to actually design and manage the project. There are project planing training exercises available to do this. The one used by this author was designed by Human Synergistics-Verax (1989), a consultancy based in England. It teaches the team a framework for dealing with project planning by asking them as individuals to rate the priority of a list of planning activities. The team then has to agree a ranking of the same activities. This not only stimulates the team to think about the process of planning a project but also engages them in a team task in which they can begin to discover how each other works. The added bonus is that it also demonstrates that the team makes better decisions than the individuals.

Once the team has completed this first exercise they may be given as a project the design and creation of a therapeutic community using the framework that they have just learnt from the previous exercise. The first stage of this to design a project plan to be presented to the therapy manager, the organizational manager and, if possible, the independent consultant. In two days the team should be able to present a plan that lists all the issues that have to be considered, how the issues are to be tackled, the alternatives to the original project, a timetable, mechanisms for checking progress and of course the training required.

At the end of the two days, when the presentation is made, the plan can be agreed by all and then implemented. In two days, providing all goes well, the team has taken ownership of the project, begun to understand how they function as a team and begun to explore their needs in relation to the task they have in hand.

Important Elements in the Training Programme

Experiential Group

It is crucial that the team experience what it is like to be in a group in which process is examined. The team needs to know what happens when they as a team are asked to examine how they function but without being led. In this situation the team is given the following task: 'The task of this group is to examine the group', and provided with a process commentator. This is taken from the Tavistock model of group training and allows the team to experience the processes that groups go through and the associated dynamics. It is an opportunity to experience on an emotional level what residents will experience when they enter the community and teaches the team some of the things that they will need to help the residents make meaning of. The team members, of course, are first faced with their own feelings and how they make sense of their experience.

This experience can be over a short but intense period or on a regular basis during the training period. I believe it to be crucial that the team know what the boundaries of the group are, so that they know how many times they will meet in this format and when the last session will be. It is also important that the session takes a regular place in the day if it is to be over a period of time.

Therapeutic Factors in Group Psychotherapy

To give the team a framework and information to help them make sense of what they are doing and experiencing, there must be some formal input. The team needs to know about the fundamental therapeutic factors in group psychotherapy, some of the explanations for those factors and general group theory. This information can be presented in seminars or lectures. Either it can be delivered to the team or the team can be provided with the resources and research it for themselves and present it to each other. The way this is done is likely to depend on the resources and time available. It may be possible to mix the means of learning in this area.

Research on the Effectiveness of Therapy and TCs

The team needs to be aware of what work has been done and what the current thinking is. This is important because they are very likely to come under scrutiny by their peers and will be asked why they have joined the team. They will inevitably face colleagues who will challenge them as to whether 'it' works or not.

In the UK, a team's project plan should include joining the Association of Therapeutic Communities. In addition to the Association's journal, a number of books should be available: Kennard (1983), Atherton (1989), Hinshelwood (1987), Manning (1989), Rapoport (1960) and Douglas (1986) provide a good base from which to work. Of particular interest to any new TC in the prison setting will be the study by Genders & Players (1995) of HMP Grendon & Cullen's (1993) reconviction study. There is also a study of Barlinnie Special Unit by Cooke (1989). The Dolan & Coid (1993) book on the treatment and research of psychopathic and antisocial personality disorders is also a very useful resource. Once again the basic information in these can be delivered via a seminar format while the texts themselves can be circulated or made available in a TC library. In my experience the team became avid readers of anything to do with TCs and the role they, the staff team, had to play. Perhaps the most stimulating way to receive this work is from the authors themselves. Many of the authors named above were pleased to come and present their work and share their experiences of TCs with the new team. There seems to be something special, perhaps a sense of belonging and intimacy, that draws, people with experience of TCs together and makes them willing to share their knowledge and experience.

Training Placements and Visits to other TCs

If at all possible the new team should visit another TC for a period of at least one week, and visit as many TCs as possible. The experience gained from being involved with a working community is invaluable. It allows the team to see in operation the things that they have only read about. The new team inevitably begins to raise new issues about their role, group techniques and alternative ways to structure a TC. Importantly, it allows them to watch staff who, like themselves, started out as novices from within the prison setting working in the group and community setting. Talking to these staff allays some of the new team's fears and provides them with models of people like themselves fulfilling the role.

Diaries

Everyone should be encouraged to keep a diary of their experience over the training period and beyond if they wish. People who write such diaries are able to return to their experience at a later date and re-evaluate their experience. At the time of training it encourages an activity which helps to consolidate the day's learning and stimulate further thought. Quite often the result of writing the diary will come out in the experiential group, or team members will refer to events that they have recorded as examples of group behaviour that they become aware of at a later date.

A Group Work Course

In the training period there the group must be introduced to some of the group activities that can take place. The new team will probably have had some theoretical input about the functioning in group. In addition they require a new experience of being group members experimenting with new roles and tasks. For some years now Grendon has used a three-day group work course to train and refresh staff with good results. The crucial point is who facilitates the course. If the course is for a new staff team then there is great merit in bringing in a pair of facilitators to run the course for the team.

Such a course can use exercises to explore the various tasks of staff in the group setting. There are many training manuals and books on this topic but most of them contain a range of exercises to explore and enhance core skills. They range from manuals geared for the use of a specific user group, e.g. the Kingsley-Mills et al. (1992) manual designed for teachers, to general skills manuals, e.g. the Fewell & Woolfe (1991) manual designed as a general basic skills manual.

Alongside these is a range of books that provide ideas for exercises to explore. Many of these books are written with a specific philosophy or framework in mind. The range of these books is very wide and includes such titles as Gaie Houston's *The Red Book of Groups* (1987) and *The Red Book of Gestalt* (1982), and Earnst & Goodison (1981) *In Our Own Hands*. Once a group work trainer begins to research the area the richness and variety of the material soon becomes apparent. Given this, it is important that whoever commissions the work or designs the course for the new team is clear about which of the skills and roles need to be focused on.

Invited Staff Members of Other TCs

An opportunity should be provided to examine specifically the issues involved in being a staff member of a TC embedded in a host establishment. Staff experience a separation from their colleagues when they join a TC in a prison. Other staff often do not understand the role of the TC or are hostile to the concept of it. As a result new TC staff can find themselves having to deal with a range of unexpected responses from colleagues. Being able to meet other staff who have gone through the same experience is of immense value.

Basic Counselling Skills

A short course which highlights the basic counselling skills and enables the team to practise them is of great value. Many of these may be embedded in the groupwork course but a specific course to look at the individual skills helps to hone the appreciation of the skills required outside the formal group and community meeting settings. It is these skills that the staff team will be using for much of the time in the total immersion experience of the TC. Once again it is possible to bring in facilitators or trainers to run such a course, or to use the resources that are at hand to design and deliver an in-house course.

The above is probably not an exhaustive list of what should ideally be included in the training of a new TC staff team, but it is nevertheless demanding. In reality, the management teams or the new TC team itself may have to prioritize the training elements that can be included in the time that they have available to them for training. What cannot be included or has to be reduced needs to be considered for inclusion in the on-going professional development of the staff team.

Selection and Training of Staff who Join an Established TC Staff Team

Selection

Any new member of a TC staff team needs to have as much of the existing team's initial experience of selection as possible. All the reasons discussed earlier in the chapter apply equally well to an incoming member to a team as to the original team. There are some extra issues to consider by the time that this occurs.

Any established team is likely to support the experience of a new team member passing through a selection process that contains many if not all of the elements that they experienced. However, they are also likely to ask where they fit in to the process. Any team that has been working within a community will have ideas about who will fit in and who will not. This is particularly true within the prison setting. Staff are aware of colleagues and have views about their abilities and characteristics, some rational, some fantasy, and some wishful thinking.

To deny the existing staff team a say in who they are to work with seems insensitive and denies that they have anything to offer in the process. The staff team should have an input to the process, even if they do not make the decision. The latter is of course an option.

Having ascertained that someone has the right basic attributes of intelligence, motivation, psychological mindness and integration through whatever procedure is chosen, final selection can take several forms. The final form that staff selection will take for a particular TC will depend on the way in which that TC has evolved and the practical constraints that apply at a particular time.

It would be ideal if, like the residents, an initial adjustment period could be allowed after which the new staff member could decide whether or not to remain in the team. Of course, a new staff member could leave at any time but in reality in many situations this is not possible. When staffing levels are lean across the organisation and the establishment it may not be possible for a new member of staff to decide to leave, or to negotiate with the host establishment to hold a post open for a specific time. The TC is probably expected to be able to select new staff with a degree of efficiency that does not require the establishment to absorb the TCs' difficulties in this area. If a trial period is not possible, the TC must choose new staff in a way that gives them the best chance of retaining them.

At Grendon new staff would often arrive from the Officer Training School, having been posted to their first establishment untrained and ill-prepared for their new role. Many found this very difficult, some transferred as soon as possible but many became accustomed to the role and performed very well. If it is possible to recruit from a volunteer pool of staff, at least some of the problems experienced by 'posted' staff can be avoided. Like TC residents, staff should be volunteers.

The overall choices for selection of new staff to a TC team come down to a balance between formal selection procedures that can mirror selection procedures for a new team and the needs of the established staff team to be involved in the process. The team may vote as a group, or select representatives to be involved in the formal procedures, meet with the candidates in a group setting, take candidates into the community setting and observe them or leave it entirely to their therapy and residential managers. What is important is the process by which the TC team reaches its decision. Like so many things in a TC, it is the *process* by which the team decides to make decisions that is the strength of the staff team. Like the residents, a staff team has to face the consequences of its decisions and find a way forward regardless of the outcome.

Training Incoming Staff

The expectation of all new staff is that they will be trained to do what they need to do. The process seems to have three phases for the new staff member. First they need to be able to survive their initiation into the community—their first group, their first community meeting and all the other firsts that seem to come thick and fast when joining a TC staff team. Secondly, new staff need to be equipped quite quickly with some basic tools in order to begin to function with a degree of confidence. Thirdly, they need to become, and to perceive themselves as becoming, part of a continuing professional development programme.

The first phase is a very difficult one for prison staff. Prison officers are trained to control situations, to lead and to be decisive. It is therefore difficult for some new staff not to feel the need to 'lead' a group session or to 'put someone straight' in a community meeting. Clearly there is a need in this situation to provide some guidelines for new staff to help them work in the new environment. For new staff it is useful to explain to them that they need do nothing in a group until they feel ready and that they will initially sit alongside another member of the staff team in groups and community meetings. It is crucial to get the other team members to share with new staff their initial experiences of sitting on groups and community meetings and to reassure new staff that it is 'OK' to say nothing. An early explanation of the effect of being a staff member in a group and what that represents in dynamic terms can be very useful. All of this can be achieved through an introductory discussion with the staff team about the staff role and some initial reading prior to joining the team. The most crucial element of this phase is integrating the new member of staff into the supervision sessions of the staff team. Here the new staff member's experience of the community can be explored and valued. The new staff member can be encouraged to ask the team questions about what happened in the group and to say what they feel about the situation. It is through this process that the therapeutic factor of acceptance can be experienced by the new staff member with the attendant benefits to the team as a whole. As the new staff team member begins to feel accepted and orientates to the new environment and ideas it becomes possible to explore more and more complex ideas.

The second phase of training begins as soon as the new staff member joins the team. A series of experiences needs to be programmed over the first few months in order to provide some knowledge and tools that the new staff member can begin to apply. Like many new counsellors the need is to know 'what to do when...'. This is a reasonable expectation, as everyone needs efficacy as part of their meaning-making process. Tools and knowledge give a feeling to new staff that they are able to contribute to the team's work and that they have something to offer. Kennard (1983) has analysed what new staff said they wanted in terms of training. One of the important issues was this need for knowledge and tools. As he points out: 'what is being sought is the ability to stop, think and plan rather than get carried away by repeated demands for action'.

This phase needs to include as much opportunity as possible for the new member of staff to visit other TCs both in the prison setting and outside. The wider view of the world that includes experience of other TCs is important. Alongside visits to other TCs they need to learn about the mechanisms of group processes. This enables the staff member to begin to relate what is being experienced in the group and community setting to a framework that helps to make meaning of the experience. To this end the new staff member needs to attend a group work course. Whether this is 'in house' or external to the organization will depend on opportunity and finance. Generally speaking the more experiences that broaden the range of people, environments and experiences that the new staff member has, the richer the whole staff team becomes.

This phase is often one of intense reading. It is usually possible to provide enough material to keep even the most avid reader occupied until it becomes apparent to the person that it is what they take of themselves into the therapy situation that actually makes the difference between well read worker and therapist. It is important, however, that the new staff member is encouraged to bring their reading into the staff team situations. It is often the new member who reminds the team of forgotten research and views. New staff often spark off renewed interest in the literature in a staff team that feels too busy to be bothered with 'all that academic nonsense'.

Naturally any new member of staff should be included in any workshops or conferences in which the rest of the staff team are involved. To exclude them from consideration on the basis that they are 'under training' is to deny them their equal status in the staff team.

Continuing Professional Development

The third stage in the training process, and perhaps the most difficult to sustain, is that of continuing professional development. There should be continuing supervision. Either the 'therapy manager' or the 'independent consultant' should provide regular input to the team alongside the team's own peer group analysis and support. These sessions are crucial in reinforcing the team in their work and their exploration of the community dynamics. They also provide regular opportunities to expand knowledge, both practical and theoretical. Kennard (1983) points out that there are other options in terms of supervision. For example, sessions with individuals may be appropriate especially with new staff. It may be possible to organize meetings between staff teams from different TCs in order to exchange experiences and to examine the state of the individual TCs. The issue of continuing personal development is a crucial one, especially for prison staff. It is possible for prison TC staff to spend many years working in the TC and to have nothing to show for it. In the modern prison service, where people are looking to have a career, staff must be able to have something to show for the time that they have spent in a TC team. One possibility is to provide the opportunity to undertake accredited counselling courses. This will depend on finance, as it is not always possible to pay for staff to be away from the establishment to take courses. Correspondence courses are becoming increasingly available and allow a staff team to pursue further training as a group. It may be possible to organize regular seminars to provide support and input for those taking the course. The same method also allows some of the staff team to specialize once they reach a certain level, for example courses on bereavement or drugs counselling.

Some staff may also wish to train in psychotherapy or undertake personal therapy as a way forward. Once again finance will determine how much support can be provided for staff wishing to pursue this but professional and personal support can be provided for those who choose this route. Encouragement should be given to staff who wish to join professional associations.

Continuing professional development is for all staff, including the non-uniformed members of staff in the prison. It must be remembered that prison staff have to be able to maintain their training as prison staff. TC staff have to balance the training they need to be part of a TC team against the wider demands of the service and their careers in it. A realistic perspective must be kept on demands that can be made of staff, and it must be recognized that staff will leave the TC team, and they need to do so as competent prison staff as well as therapists. They will have experienced one of the most intimate working experiences of their lives and will need to enter into new work sufficiently well equipped to be able to leave the TC behind.

The therapy manager/leader/consultant who performs the focal role of maintaining the therapeutic integrity of the TC, also has to continue their development. Not only do they need to learn from the community and the staff team but they have to be able to maintain a learning culture amongst the staff team. It is perhaps a sobering thought that none of us can take those around us beyond our own level of development.

REFERENCES

Appelbaum, S. A. (1973). Psychological Mindedness: word, concept and essence. *International Journal of Psychoanalysist*, **54**, 35–46.

Atherton, J. S. (1989). *Interpreting Residential Life*. London: Tavistock/Routledge.

Bion, W. R. (1961). *Experiences in Groups*. London: Tavistock.

Bloch, S. & Crouch, E. (1985). *Therapeutic Factors in Group Psychotherapy*. Oxford: Oxford University Press.

Cooke, D. J. (1989). Containing violent prisoners: An analysis of Barlinnie special unit. *British Journal of Criminology*, **129**, 129–143.

Cullen, E. (1993). The Grendon Reconviction Study. *Prison Service Journal*, **90**, 35–37.

Dolan, B. & Coid, A. (1993). *Psychopaths and Antisocial Personality Disorders: Treatment and Research Issues*. London: Gaskell.

Douglas, T. (1983). *Groups. Understanding People Gathered Together*. London: Routledge.

Douglas, T. (1986) *Group Living*. London: Tavistock Press.

Earnst, S. & Goodison, L. (1981). *In Our Own Hands*. London: The Women's Press.

Feltham, R. (1988). Validity of a police assessment centre: a 1–19 year follow up. *Journal of Occupational Psychology* **61**: 129–144.

Fewell, J. & Woolfe, R. (1991). *Groupwork Skills, An Introduction. Edinburgh: Health Education Board for Scotland*.

Fincham, R. & Rhodes, P. S. (1994). The Individual and Work and Organisation, 2nd Edition. Oxford: Oxford University Press.

Fletcher, C. (1991). 'Candidates' reactions to assessment centres and their outcomes. *Journal of Occupational Psychology*, **64**, 117–27.

Foulkes, S. H. (1948). *Introduction to Group-analytic Psychiatry*. London: Heinemann.

Foulkes, S. H. (1964). *Therapeutic Group Analysis*. London: George Allen & Unwin.

Genders, E. & Player, E. (1995). *Grendon. A Study of a Therapeutic Prison*. Oxford: Clarendon Press.

Graham-Davies, S. (1994). *Results of staff responses to the GTC interviews*. HMP Gartree staff survey (unpublished).

Gunn, J. & Robertson, G. (1978). *Psychiatric Aspects of Imprisonment*. London: Academic Press.

Hawkins, P. & Shohet, R. (1989). *Supervision in the Helping Professions*. Milton Keynes: Open University Press.

Hinshelwood, R. D. (1987). *What Happens in Groups*. London: Free Association Press.

Hodkin, G. & Woodward, R. (1996). Another British first. *Prison Service Journal*, **103**, 47–50.

Houston, G. (1982). *The Red Book of Gestalt*. London: The Rochester Foundation.

Houston, G. (1987). *The Red Book of Groups*. London: The Rochester Foundation.

Human Synergistics-Verax (1989). *The Project Planning Situation*. Odiham: Human Synergistics-Verax.

Jefferson, A. (1991). An Evaluation of the Assessment Unit at HMP Grendon. Psychology Department, HMP Grendon (unpublished).

Jones, M. (1959). Towards clarification of the therapeutic community concept. *British Journal of Medical Psychology*, **32**, 200–235.

Kaplan, H. I. & Shaddock, B. J. (1971). *Comprehensive Group Psychotherapy*. Baltimore: The Williams & Wilkins Company.

Kennard, D. (1983). *An Introduction to Therapeutic Communities*. London: Routledge & Kegan Paul.

Khaleelee, O. (1994). The defence mechanism test as an aid for selection and development of staff. *Therapeutic communities*, **15**. 3–13.

Kingsley-Mills, C. McNamara, S. & Woodward, L. (1992). *Out From Behind the Desk*. Leicester: Leicestershire County Council.

Macallum, M. & Piper, W. E. (1990). The psychological mindedness Assessment procedure. *Psycholocal Assessment a Journal of Consulting and Clinical Psychology*, **2**, 412–418.

Main, T. (1966). Knowledge, Learning, and Freedom of Thought. Given at the Third Annual Congress of the Australian & New Zealand College of Psychiatrists in 1966. Psychoanalytic Psychotherapy 1990 Vol. 5 No. 1 59–78.

Manning, N. (1989). *The Therapeutic Community Movement*. London: Routledge.

Page, S. & Wolsket, V. (1994). *Supervising the Counsellor*. London: Routledge.

Pearce, J. (1994). Prison officer and therapeutic community worker. *Therapeutic Communities* **15**, 79–282.

Rapoport, R. N. (1960). *Community as Doctor*. London: Tavistock.

Raven, J. C. (1960). *Guide to the Standard Progressive Matrices*. London: H. K. Lewis.

Salvendy, J. T. (1985). Training, leadership and group composition. A review of the crucial variables. *Group Analysis* **xviii**, 132–141.

Shohet, R. & Wilmot, J. (1991). The key issues in the supervision of counsellors: The supervisory relationship. In Dryden W. & Thorne, B. *Training and Supervision for Counselling in Action*. London: Sage.

Wechsler, D. (1981). *Manual for the Wechsler Adult Intelligence Scale—Revised*. London and New York: The Psychological Corporation.

Woodward, R. (1989) Arts against machismo. Paper presented to the Arts and Crime conference, Birmingham, England.

Yalom, I. D. (1985). *The Theory and Practice of Group Psychotherapy*, 3rd Edn. New York: Basic Books.

APPENDIX

Action Plan for Selection

1. Determine the size and composition of the team. Most teams are mutidisciplinary.

2. Determine who is going to fill the roles of therapy manager, independent consultant, and organization/residential manager.

3. Identify the qualities and skills required in the staff. Create a Person Specification.

4. Determine the assessment process for staff, based loosely on what might be the assessment process for community applicants. Added to this might also be the requirement for applicants to provide a short presentation to the selection panel.

5. Advertise for staff in appropriate areas detailing the Person Specification and assessment process. If a TC is to be set up in a prison setting it may well be the case that staff in the first instance will come from the existing staff. If this is not the case

then a general trawl might take place across the prison service staff population. In the case where recruitment can be made outside the service then the appropriate journals and associations need to be considered.

6. The response to the advertisement will determine whether or not a sift of applicants is required.

7. Hold the selection process. Psychometric testing, panel interview with or without presentation, and assessment centre elements if required.

8. Select team plus a reserve list.

CHAPTER 11

Key Issues for the Future

Eric Cullen and Tim Newell
HMP Grendon and Springhill, Aylesbury, UK

Roland Woodward
HMP Gartree, Market Harborough, UK

There are many lessons to be learnt from this book about therapeutic communities for offenders. We have grouped them in six main categories for presentation and ease of reference: Management, Programme Integrity, Training, Finance, Research and Community Links. The first, and main, section of the chapter covers the management of TCs in secure, e.g. prison, settings and is from the perspective of a prison governor with both local and national management experience.

MANAGING A THERAPEUTIC COMMUNITY PRISON

Therapeutic communities are vulnerable in any setting and particularly within a prison environment as the values they represent bring them into conflict with the underlying assumptions of security, good order and control which dominate a prison system. The survival of TCs in prisons is partly dependent upon their ability to deliver results to other prisons. This entails taking prisoners with serious problems to do with offending and their inability to survive in traditional prisons without violence, self-injury or the need for

Therapeutic Communities for Offenders.
Edited by E. Cullen, L. Jones and R. Woodward. © 1997 John Wiley & Sons Ltd.

expensive isolation for the sake of Good order and discipline or self-preservation.

The requirements of a prison governor have remained constant for many years. The task is to manage the total prison environment so as to achieve and maintain the correct balance between security, control and care and to manage the dynamic of human relationships within a total institution to achieve that. What has changed dramatically is the environment in which the role is enacted, both internally and externally. The effect of these changes has been to make the job of Governor more exacting and stressful when, for example, they are obliged to create an environment which reduces risks to security to a minimum but foster one where TC dynamics maximize opportunities for taking risks within more trusting relationships.

External changes include changing attitudes to authority, sharper accountability in public service organizations, technical changes and alterations in the nature of work and peoples' attitudes towards work. Internally the environment is more susceptible to what is happening externally. Governors cannot operate 'behind the walls' any more. Expectations of staff and prisoners have changed to require more consultation and involvement. The impact of devolution of responsibilities and accountabilities and the increased emphasis on effective resource management are additional pressures which are proving particularly painful and lead to reduction of staffing and activities.

The pain and challenge but also the fascination of being a prison governor lies in how to reconcile and blend the general management aspects of the role with the highly specialist element. To perform effectively a proper analysis and understanding of the components, demands and skills of the job are essential. Personal and organizational strategies to respond can then be developed. These factors include a management and organizational structure which will be effective in achieving the functions of the prison, a rigorous management of personal time, and support mechanisms which are right for the individual. Much of this is relevant to all governors. Governing a TC prison includes all those elements with bells on! The increasing demands on senior managers in the prison service are important to recognize before examining the particular nature of governing a TC prison. The sensitivity within TC prisons is that personal feelings of staff and prisoners are so much nearer the surface and are readily expressed. Although the culture of enquiry is encouraged in order to achieve good therapy, it also impacts on the organization of those aspects of the prison which are not excused the standards and procedures which apply to prisons of its security category. The need to maintain *balance* is critical in maintaining the primary task: to be a therapeutic community prison!

A number of *core* and *specialized* management functions, each with appropriate skills needed of a governor, are discussed below.

Core Functions

Planning and Resourcing

With the trend in all organizations towards the devolution of functions from the centre closer to the point of service delivery, the demand on governors calls for a set of skills which were not present through selection or training until lately. Financial and human resource management are delegated areas of planning which are critical to the smooth running of prisons now, as well the need to plan and manage activity strategically within a long-term vision.

Planning and resourcing for UK TCs has involved a rigorous examination of the environment in which we operate. It is clear that TCs 'work' in achieving the main political aims of helping dangerous offenders to become less so within a demanding environment. It is necessary for managers continually to stress with the media, visiting dignitaries and service officials the pressures on prisoners to address the most painful parts of their past and present experiences in order to counter the possible assumption that being in therapy may involve sitting around all day within a stress-free environment. Thus there is a presentational problem which has to be regularly addressed by the governor. It is therefore vital that there is good evidence to present in order to justify the way of working and to prove to sceptics that the well behaved, socially adjusted, positive people that generally visitors meet have been very dangerous and disturbed offenders and are in the process of painful change.

Resourcing for TCs is proving difficult at a time of reducing expenditure in the service. The evidence from planning shows that if the resources made available to staff the communities are reduced, the quality of dialogue and the opportunities for therapeutic contact would be eroded to such an extent that the work would not be possible with the current population, and a far less risky group would have to be recruited. Demonstrating this to line managers at Headquarters is very dependent on them appreciating the dynamics of the Community concept, and calls for developed communicating skills from the governor and senior staff. Inevitably quality regimes will be affected by the reduction in resource provision. Strategic planning has to face this threat and demonstrate through effective management that all possible economies have been made without threatening the core therapeutic environment. Therapeutic community staff should be able to manage change through their experience of helping others. There is an increasingly hard-nosed approach towards protecting what are seen as expensive luxuries—'If they are so effective, let them hard charge sending prisons and see how much they are wanted'.

Organizing/Directing/Communicating

This essentially involves turning plans into action and delivery. Skills required in this area include communicating, briefing, team leading and team building. Visible leadership emerges as a requirement for this function particularly, but is a thread throughout the governor's role.

Organising/directing/communicating are totally different experiences for a governor in a therapeutic community prison, particularly when communities are well established with their own decision-making structures and as many matters as possible are dealt with at that level. Communicating is particularly sensitive and often involves having to account for a particular decision made by management. With the dominance of therapy staff in the determination of activity and events it is particularly important that the governor negotiates initiatives and that they are subservient to the therapeutic imperative—a new skill to learn!

Motivating/Supporting

This involves sustaining and developing staff (including managers) to help them to deliver. It involves steering and coaching and personal supervision.

Motivating/supporting are sensitive issues in an environment of professional senior staff with the expertise to help staff develop their skills in delivering therapy. However, there are clear needs for the governor and other generalist managers to support staff in the interface between the two elements of the regime and to help professional therapy staff to understand the wider environment of prisons in which the prison operates. The delivery of prison-type work should continue to a high standard and arguably ought to be of a higher standard than elsewhere in order to demonstrate the effectiveness of the TC way of working.

Monitoring/Auditing

This involves establishing and developing systems to make sure that what is planned to happen does actually happen on the ground in the way it is intended to and to the required standard. The learning and dynamic organization feeds this back into the next round of planning and resourcing.

Monitoring/auditing are functions relatively easily achieved for measurable activity and can work well with quantitative aspects of prison work but it is notoriously difficult to capture the qualitative nature of the work of a TC apart from the observed change in people over time. In order to achieve that process of change there may well be difficult and disruptive behaviour which has to be accounted for in the order of prison things.

Traditional strengths of governors were in the middle two areas of work with a strong emphasis on 'management by presence' for which they were often criticized. The shift of emphasis over the past five years particularly has been towards the first and last functions in order to deliver the accountability for work within the line structure of the Service. However, unless governors maintain all four functions in some balance and ensure that their senior staff also contribute to the process there is unlikely to be improved performance by the prison.

Specialized Functions

Responsibility for a Society in Miniature

This includes all the human and organizational pressures involved. A particular managerial feature is the range of activity and responsibility, including staff, prisoners, buildings, relations with the local community, with the media, with the criminal justice organizations locally and all this within the setting of the prison service at national and area level.

Within Grendon there are five *societies (communities) in miniature* for which the governor has a responsibility, all of which exhibit the cyclical movement of ups and downs in the way they are experienced by members, including staff. There is little that the governor can do to influence these changes apart from being supportive, exploring options with those concerned and ensuring resourcing and training issues are dealt with as sympathetically as possible. The overall society of the whole prison is more clearly an area which can be worked with in order to enable those staff not directly concerned with

Staff Issues: Aptitude, Antipathy and Training

therapy to support that work as effectively and sympathetically as possible. This is particularly important with the group of staff with a special responsibility for security matters in the prison.

Diplomacy

The coercive nature of the custodial experience brings an intensity to the functions of management which are not present elsewhere. The environment is a highly charged one in which the management of feelings is a key requirement and probably the element which creates the greatest pressure and stress. What is unique about managing prisons is managing the staff/prisoner interface. This is complicated by the generally low self-esteem in which prison staff across the world hold themselves and the painful psychological deprivations which prisoners experience whilst in prison. This results in pressure on governors to take sides. A question often asked of an incoming governor is, 'are you for the prisoners or the staff?'

Coercive experience is different in Grendon to which prisoners come voluntarily, although that motivation is within an overall context of having to complete a sentence of custody. The pains of imprisonment are still experienced intensely by most in a TC prison because they often feel the potential of a better future and yet still have to complete their time in prison. The interface between staff and prisoners is not a highly charged one of distrust, as is often the case in other settings but generally is dominated by a more personal and individual series of relationships of openness and mutual support. The stresses on staff can be intense through the demands of such relationships within a dialogue about serious behaviour. The governor has a responsibility to be aware of these stresses and to make support systems available to staff in order to help them manage their work and the pressures on them.

There are thus more dimensions to governing in Grendon, specifically, and in TCs generally, than in many other prisons. There are many advantages present in the prison that make it a delight to be part of, including the environment of openness and friendship at all levels, the great dedication of staff and prisoners to engage in the painful process of dialogue and enquiry, the presence of a rich variety of skills within the multidisciplinary teams, and the knowledge that there is real benefit to many disturbed, damaged and potentially dangerous men through their experience within the prison, leading to fewer victims in the future.

The governor and senior staff continue to represent the qualitative aspects of the healing regime with other prisons. The symbolic nature of Grendon within the UK Prison Service provides a stimulus to others to respect the potential for change within prisoners and to work hard to provide for opportunities for it to take place.

PROGRAMME INTEGRITY

It appears that programmes that describe themselves as TCs have no agreed criteria by which to do so. It is perhaps time that this was changed in order that everyone who enters the arena of TCs either as worker or resident is able to acknowledge common features of a TC and therefore to have the opportunity to have reasonable expectations of what they are going to experience. At least they should have some sort of framework with a definable rationale based on a supportable philosophy. It is likely that at the moment those in the TC movement would debate long and hard about this issue, but for those of us in the prison system we are already experiencing the accreditation of offence-related behaviour courses and interventions. It is only a matter of time before we are asked to enter into a dialogue regarding our therapeutic credibility and hence our accredibility. This is a serious issue because the implication is that in the future finance will not be available for non-accredited therapeutic activities.

At this time there appears to be no active forum to take this forward. Perhaps the newly formed prison section of the Association of Therapeutic Communities needs to deal with this issue urgently *within the British setting*. It is an issue that needs to be considered not only in the context of British prisons but in the wider international perspective. Now would be a good time for the British Prison Service to host an international conference on this issue. In doing so it would be following in the footsteps of those English hospitals that did so much to pioneer the work of TCs in the early days of the concept. The question seems to be 'What boundaries, where?'

With the issue of integrity comes the question of who should be responsible for this. Here the debate is between those who think 'professionals' or 'consultants' should have the responsibility as opposed to entrusting it to multidisciplinary staff teams. How best are the boundaries of TCs maintained in order to provide the therapeutic efficacy of the TC? What is clear is that within the prison system there is a demand for an identifiable management structure that can be held accountable for the therapeutic integrity of the TC and also the way in which the TC balances and fulfils its obligations as part of the general prison system. What is clear is that a TC in a prison that cannot balance the needs of the community with the real and reasonable constraints of the prison will have checks and restrictions placed on it. The message is that TCs must be managed by people who can perform both these functions, the therapeutic integrity and the penal role. This is clearly not the province of a single profession. The debate here is who selects such people and how such selection takes place.

An extension of the safeguard principle for TCs is that there should be a recognized organizational structure which is applied when a TC is spawned in a host establishment. An example of this would be an independent steering committee that could act in such a way as to monitor the functioning of the TC and to help the management of the host organization to be supportive and balanced in its approach to the TC issues that arise.

A suggested innovation that would draw some of the above issues together would be the forming of an overseeing and co-ordinating body to take responsibility for encouraging and supporting the TC network in the prison system. It could promote good practice, broker finance, commission research and co-ordinate a positive network with a view to sharing experience and learning. This could range from an identified group within the current prison service to setting up a separate agency to take responsibility for TCs in the prison setting.

There needs to be a concerted effort to initiate a co-ordinated research programme across the TCs in prisons. There is still much work to be done on what kind of TC structure is most appropriate for which kinds of offenders. The need to be able to find ways of structuring the organization's response to the rehabilitative needs of the individual is an important future objective that must be dealt with. As the pressure continues to mount on TCs to include more discrete therapy programmes such as the behavioural/cognitive approaches relating to thinking skills there arises a pressing need for practitioners to know what elements of the adapted TC structure effect what changes in the resident. There is an assumption that some of the discrete interventions carry with them the same effects within the TC environment as when they are applied out of the TC environment. The evidence for this needs to be produced. There is an urgent need to know how the mixing and matching of interventions interact, if they do, in order to ensure that the residents of communities are enabled as opposed to overloaded.

In the same way that the therapeutic factors of group psychotherapy were educed, a critical examination is needed of what factors the TC environment brings with it. There appears to the assumption that a TC can be treated as one big group experience in which the therapeutic factors work. The question remains 'what are the therapeutic factors of the TC experience?'. It seems to the authors that this question requires an answer before it is going to be possible to know what the interactions are between community therapeutic factors and group therapeutic factors.

There appears to be a drift towards an accepted status quo of what a TC should be in the prison setting. TCs by their nature challenge boundaries and innovate according to the needs of their residents and staff teams. It would be helpful if a re-examination of the current structure could take place and new approaches be suggested. For example, a TC might be founded on a Jungian framework, or on an Adlerian one in which power was the focus of the structure. At present the perceived wisdom of TCs is rooted in the group therapy research and there is increasing demand to objectify the therapy base of TCs. It would perhaps be healthy to balance this with ideas that start from the point of view that not all prisoners see the universe working in the same way and that they require a TC in which they could explore a way forward for themselves more in tune with their view of the universe. For example, many long-term prisoners find great sense and inspiration in Buddhism. Is there a place in our prisons for a TC which is Buddhist in nature and places emphasis on rehabilitation through spiritual development and living a 'right life'?

Another key issue for progress integrity is that of the ethics of therapy in custody. Chapter 2 provided a critical analysis of some of the questions that should be raised and answered, concerning the imposition of interventions which programme managers and therapists presume to be empowered to conduct. Although the European tradition is that participants in TC regimes have given consent to treatment for *both* their current interpersonal and prior offending behaviour, the same cannot be said for either alternative UK programmes or for American TC regimes. Centrally organized and specific treatment modalities such as the Sex Offender Treatment Programme (SOTP) and the Cognitive Skills, or R & R Programme have a strong element of imposition about them. Increasingly, completion of these programmes are prescribed by the Parole Unit and the Lifer Sections of the Prison Service Agency as *conditions* for progressing through sentences to release. Offenders are in the invidious position of being obliged to both complete their sentences and to complete programmes advocated to be effective at reducing the risk of reoffending. For those serving indeterminate sentences, this has introduced an additional factor. The alternative ethical question is, of course, whether it would be 'right' to release criminals back into society knowing that a risk remained and that a treatment programme existed to possibly reduce that risk but which they were not obliged to attend. The Phoenix House TC regimes are clearly, in that sense, compulsory and hold the public interest to be of greater ethical concern than the rights of the individual imprisoned.

TRAINING

What are the minimum requirements for a person to work in a TC staff team in the prison setting? At present there is no minimum standard beyond basic prison officer training in the British Prison Service. Neither is there any obligation to provide training in the TCs for staff who volunteer to work in them or who are transferred into them. The training that staff obtain is at the behest of their host establishment or due to their own interest and motivation. This is a state of affairs that needs to cease as quickly as possible. There needs to be a central group who produce an analysis of core competencies relevant to working in a TC. Once this has been achieved a training programme needs to be devised that leads to an accredited qualification.

The stage that follows the initial qualification would then be a method of continuing professional development based on a series of further accredited training events. Part of the training require of post-qualified TC staff would be to undertake enough of the professional development courses so as to earn sufficient points in a given period to satisfy a development criterion. It would be possible to couple this process with the issuing of practising certificates that would be renewed each year on the production of evidence that enough professional development credits have been gained. A scheme such as this would demand commitment from staff and their organizations but the pay-off would be that over time the expertise of the teams would grow and impinge on the rest of the organization through the sharing of skills.

FINANCE

One crucial issue is whether or not TCs within the prison setting are cost-effective. At the moment all the TCs in the English Prison Service are funded by public money, therefore the issue of cost-effectiveness is one that is in the public domain. Current expenditure by central government is contracting and there is emphasis on building a lean and efficient service based on what are perceived to be the benefits of a mixed public and private sector prison service. The outcome of this is that TCs in future will have to be cost-effective within a competitive market, not just within the monopolistic Prison Service.

This situation appears to be paralleled in the European arena as the overall economic trend is forcing central governments to reduce public sector borrowing requirements in order to align economies prior to a common currency. Faced with rising unemployment levels which will affect prison populations the cost-effectiveness of all prison systems face the same problems. The way in which TCs in a number of economies tackle the problems of funding and cost-effectiveness will provide useful cross-fertilization, not only for TCs but also for fiscal policy makers.

Currently the one prison in England, Grendon Underwood, that is devoted to therapy through a TC model is demonstrably cheaper to run than comparably sized prisons of the same security category, referring agencies such as some Special Hospitals and, on average, those prisons that refer to Grendon. The issue of scale is important here, as it is likely to be internationally. Grendon is a total prison that is able to structure its management, resources and endeavours to the single purpose of therapy. Being able to do this allows it to make economies of scale which small units embedded in host establishments are unable to do. The small TCs housed in small residential areas are faced with the fact that the staff/prisoner ratio is always going to be difficult to adjust to compete economically. If a unit only holds a small number it is not possible to reduce the staff team beyond a certain size because of the security requirements and the safety elements of prison work that requires minimum staffing levels. What is required is a study of comparable size units that have other functions. The authors believe that dedicated small staff teams in small TC units offer the most cost-effective way of using the accommodation that would otherwise still have to be staffed for a non co-operative population of prisoners. Once again international comparisons would be useful.

Other ways of tackling the problems of cost-effectiveness include looking at the savings made to the organization by the elimination of delinquent institutional behaviour. The cost of dealing with this is large in most establishments but Grendon has demonstrated that this can be reduced drastically. A small TC, the Gartree Therapeutic Community, in its first two years is beginning to collect data that suggests this may be true for its population as well (Hodkin & Woodward 1996). Genders & Player (1995) also found that prisoners returning to the prison system were less likely to commit delinquent institutional acts. These benefits are difficult to quantify and to explore but it is an area that needs investigation and inspection over a longer period of time especially, where long-term and life-sentence prisoners are concerned.

The basic financing of TCs in prison settings needs to be thought through and a clear policy based on the cost required for an effective TC put into operation. It is becoming clear that the effectiveness of TCs depends on their ability to provide a therapy that is relevant to their individual target populations. It might be, for example, that TCs that specialize in working with prisoners at the start of a long sentence require a different investment base than one whose target population is one that is to be discharged into the public community. Here the finance base might require the extension of the TC experience by transfer to community-based TCs whose function would be supportive reintegrative therapy. Having acknowledged that such models are required, the costings relating to function need to be made and then provided. Below a certain level of funding the situation may become more harmful to the residents than therapeutic.

With the setting up of new TCs both in England and abroad the comments above need to be addressed with some urgency. When the British Prison Service is currently acknowledging the efficacy of its only fully therapeutic prison and is now planning to ask the private sector to build and run a new one, it needs to have a detailed knowledge of the financial profiles of TCs in order to monitor and develop its policy regarding the offering of 'therapeutic imprisonment' balanced against a humane but austere alternative. With Germany and America offering an increasing number of alternatives in their correctional systems, the British Prison Service would appear to need to consider what it is going to offer the estimated 2000 prisoners who are in need of such intervention (Maden et al., 1994).

It is perhaps time to consider funding from a variety of sources for TCs in prison. A user-based charging scheme could be considered. Where establishments or agencies make referrals then perhaps fees should be charged. It might be possible to consider sponsorship and partnerships. It would help enormously if the funding for a TC unit could be joint between the prison service and a humanitarian foundation with an interest in the rehabilitation of prisoners. As users of many different branches of therapy it might be possible to encourage the Arts Council to provide a stable pool of workers to provide for the TC network.

RESEARCH

Research must remain the lynch pin of TC development. However TCs of the future develop, it must be on the basis of sound knowledge. TCs evolve and need to make rational choices based on information that is relevant to their functions—research provides this.

Outcome research in recent years on an international basis has been increasingly encouraging. It is important that this impetus is maintained and that co-operation between communities extends into the international arena.

Some of the areas that remain to be explored to the full include the differential effects of elements of therapeutic programmes. Many TCs have developed programmes that include different elements—art therapy, psychodrama, drama therapy, cognitive/behavioural programmes and specific issues courses, e.g. alcohol abuse. It needs to be clarified what each of these elements contributes to the TC process and with what population. If multimodal programmes are more effective than psychotherapy alone, then practitioners should be asking what each of the elements contributes.

For those TCs using the group experience as the focus of the therapy work it is valid to ask once again whether the therapeutic factors of group psychotherapy as espoused by Yalom (1985) and Bloch & Crouch (1985) continue to be prominent and effective. We know that different factors are important at different stages with different populations (Whiteley & Collis 1987); a complete picture of these combinations needs to be built up in order to compare the effectiveness of TCs.

Within the prison setting there must to be a consideration of whether or not such factors as type of sentence and sentence length have a bearing on the effectiveness of a TC. There is also the issue of at what point in a sentence and under what conditions a TC experience is beneficial. This relates to what kind of TC structure is best suited for the various prison populations. In the prison setting TCs must investigate how they can respond to the individual re-habilitation needs of prisoners and the requirements of throughcare.

The opportunity to produce cross-cultural research would greatly enhance researchers' abilities to look at specific groups of prisoners as defined by different criminal justice systems, in the differing prison structures which are generated as a result. Any consistent results generated by such research could be seen as being robust in their definition of underlying processes.

A neglected field is the staff groups of TCs in prison. Work needs to be done on the characteristics of a successful staff team and how they apply themselves to the task. The way in which the staff team operates as a group and how this contributes to the process of the community is especially important in the prison setting because of the role conflicts that their position produces.

Becoming more relevant to the prison situation is the use of programmes such as the Phoenix House programme. There appear to be no studies using control groups using alternative substance abuse treatments. When working with offenders the coupling of TC experience with the community-based resources would suggest that the effectiveness of all options needs to be known to make best use of what is available.

COMMUNITY LINKS

At present there are difficult interface problems between TCs and the prison environment and TCs and the outside world. Throughcare appears not to be geared to the needs of those leaving a TC in prison to return to the normal community. We know that there are adjustment problems for people who leave TCs and those people who leave prison. How much must this be compounded when someone leaves both a TC and the prison environment at the same time? The ability to move from a TC in prison to a TC in the public community would provide a continuity of experience that would provide the opportunity for sustained and progressive growth in an integrated way. At the moment we ask much of the people on whom we have lavished attention when we push them out into the world and expect them to deal with reintegration and separation at the same time.

It is perhaps time that TCs became part of a planned process of rehabilitation and reintegration as opposed to islands of support with few if any bridges to the wider world. This is particularly true of those TCs in prison where a person can go from a highly accepting situation into one that is rejecting and alienating.

SUMMARY

Therapeutic communities are far more than programmes, detailed procedures or structures for change. They are defined by the qualitative aspects more than the quantitative, with a sense of tradition and a spirit of communality writ large. They are sustained by cultivating relationships and by reducing the barriers to friendships. Formal hierarchies and relatively rigid procedures for dealing with the minutiae of daily living cannot be allowed to usurp these traditions. Equally, narrow professional perspectives must be subordinated to the larger principles of therapeutic communities which hold individual dignity, respect and humanity as paramount.

The theme that runs through all of the above is that 'TC should talk unto TC' and that this should happen internationally. It is an area where the widest dialogue gives the greatest advantage. The more internationally public the TCs for offenders are, the more likely they are to produce accredited standards of therapeutic delivery, accredited training of staff, accredited development of the managers of them and finally the sharing of knowledge and research which we all need in order to continue developing TCs and ourselves effectively.

REFERENCES

Bloch, S. & Crouch, E. (1985). *Therapeutic factors in Group Psychotherapy.* Oxford: Oxford University Press.

Genders, E. & Player, E. (1995). *Grendon: A Study of Therapeutic Prison.* Oxford: The Clarendon Press.

Maden, T., Swinton, M. & Gunn, J. (1994). therapeutic community treatment: a survey of unmet need among sentenced prisoners. *J. Assoc. Ther. Coms.*, **15**(4), 229–236.

Whiteley, J. S. & Collis, M. (1987). The therapeutic factors in group psychotherapy applied to the therapeutic community. *International Journal of therapeutic Communities*, **8**(1), 21–31.

Hodkin, G. & Woodward, R. (1996). Another British first: Gartree's therapeutic community for lifers, *Prison Service Journal*, **103**, 47–50.

Yalom, I. D. (1985). *The Theory and Practice of Group. 3rd edn.* New York: Basic Books.

Index

Related titles of interest from Wiley...

Addicted to Crime?

Edited by JOHN HODGE, MARY MCMURRAN and CLIVE HOLLIN

Criminal behaviour that is highly repetitive appears to bring "internal rewards" for some offenders. In this book, expert researchers and practitioners attempt to explore the potential link between addiction and crime.

Wiley Series in Offender Rehabilitation
0-471-95079-3   1997   232pp   Hardback
0-471-95777-1   1997   232pp   Paperback

Clinical Approaches to Working with Young Offenders

Edited by **Clive R. Hollin** and **Kevin Howells**

Examines clinical approaches used with specific groups of offenders, including adolescent sex offenders, firesetters, and alcohol and drug related crime, and reviews successful prevention programmes.

0-471-95348-2   300pp   1996   Hardback

What Works: Reducing Re-Offending

Guidelines from Research and Practice

Edited by **James McGuire**

Offers a critical review of research and practice with the focus on identifying interventions and models of offender treatment that really do work and are practical, and ways of evaluating treatment and offender services.

0-471-95053-X   264pp   1995   Hardback
0-471-95686-4   264pp   1995   Paperback

Handbook of Psychology in Legal Contexts

Edited by **Ray H.C. Bull** and **David Carson**

Highlights and emphasises both the extent to which psychologists are already assisting and informing the legal system and the potential that exists for collaboration between lawyers and psychologists.

0-471-94182-4   694pp   1995   Hardback

Visit the Wiley Home Page at http://www.wiley.co.uk